Image Patterns in the
Novels of F. Scott Fitzgerald

Studies in Modern Literature, No. 53

A. Walton Litz, General Series Editor

Professor of English
Princeton University

Jackson R. Bryer

Consulting Editor for Titles on F. Scott Fitzgerald
Professor of English
University of Maryland

Linda Wagner

Consulting Editor for Titles on Ernest Hemingway
Professor of English
Michigan State University

Other Titles in This Series

No. 44 *Ernest Hemingway: Journalist and Artist*   J.F. Kobler

No. 45 *The Indestructible Woman in the
Works of Faulkner, Hemingway,
and Steinbeck*   Mimi R. Gladstein

No. 50 *The Religious Design of Hemingway's
Early Fiction*   Larry E. Grimes

No. 51 *Hemingway and the Hispanic World*   Angel Capellan

No. 54 *The Cinematic Vision of
F. Scott Fitzgerald*   Wheeler W. Dixon

Image Patterns in the Novels of F. Scott Fitzgerald

by
Dan Seiters

UMI RESEARCH PRESS
Ann Arbor, Michigan

PS 3511
.I9
Z845
1986

08357/6953

Produced and distributed by
UMI Research Press
an imprint of
University Microfilms International
A Xerox Information Resources Company
Ann Arbor, Michigan 48106

Library of Congress Cataloging in Publication Data

Seiters, Dan, 1939-
Image patterns in the novels of F. Scott Fitzgerald.

(Studies in modern literature ; 53)
Revision of author's D. thesis (doctoral)—Southern
Illinois University, 1976.
Bibliography: p.
Includes index.
1. Fitzgerald, F. Scott (Francis Scott), 1896-1940—
Style. I. Title. II. Series.
PS3511.I9Z845 1986 813'.52 85-24593
ISBN 0-8357-1695-3 (alk. paper)

To my wife Judy, my son Damon, my mother Maxine

Contents

Acknowledgments   *ix*

Introduction   *1*

1   *This Side of Paradise* and *The Beautiful and Damned*   *15*

2   *The Great Gatsby*   *57*

3   *Tender Is the Night*   *89*

4   *The Last Tycoon*   *119*

Conclusion   *135*

Notes   *143*

Selected Bibliography   *157*

Index   *163*

Acknowledgments

Special thanks to Henry Dan Piper, John M. Howell, and Jackson R. Bryer, three men who have read my work with greater care and more intelligence than anyone has a right to expect.

Introduction

My approach to the novels of F. Scott Fitzgerald is that of a curious mechanic who would take apart a complex machine and learn how it works, what it means, how to build another like it. I am convinced that the essence of Fitzgerald's fiction is patterned imagery, and further, that a study of imagery best shows what each novel is made of and what the various parts mean in relation to the whole. My investigation first yielded the uncontroversial notion that experience made Fitzgerald a better novelist; the bulk of this study will be devoted to showing how and why Fitzgerald developed as an artist. I contend that much of his technical advancement stems from his deepening understanding of the possibilities inherent in image patterns and, of course, his greater facility in establishing these patterns.

Basically I plan to demonstrate that in spite of Fitzgerald's skill with dialogue and his early ability to turn the epigrammatic phrase, *This Side of Paradise* remains a diffuse novel without impact because Fitzgerald established no patterns. Imagistically, *The Beautiful and Damned* marks an artistic advance over the first novel in that many patterns exist. But because Fitzgerald assigns only the most traditional of meanings to those images, the patterns fall dimly into the background and the reader ignores them. Because the images fail to surprise, they fail to delight. But with *The Great Gatsby* and *Tender Is the Night,* images constantly surprise and delight. Irony is the added ingredient.

Specifically, Fitzgerald lulls the reader by making him believe that traditionally positive images are indeed positive. (Water, for example, is a traditional symbol of fertility, the moon a traditional symbol of romance). Long before midpoint in *The Great Gatsby* and *Tender Is the Night,* however, positive images begin to acquire negative shades; as each novel closes, images of vitality and life obviously have been transformed into symbols of death. In *The Last Tycoon,* however, Fitzgerald chose to trade this ironic tension for dramatic irony. From the beginning of *The Last Tycoon,* death imagery strangles those images traditionally associated with life. Just as the audience knows the fate of Oedipus Rex before the great man steps on stage, the reader comprehends Monroe Stahr's doom almost from page one. Image patterns point to these conclusions, as later chapters will demonstrate.

In his discussion of Shakespeare, G. Wilson Knight points out that the atmosphere of a play remains static (except that it becomes clearer as it grows more pervasive), while the plot marches on in time.[1] This observation helps explain how irony develops, and it partially defines the function of image patterns in works that qualify as art. The world of the play, of the novel, never changes, although in Fitzgerald's fiction, the reader might later note that his first impression of that world was 180 degrees awry. Irony, like rust, lurks ready to corrode the glittering surface world in a Fitzgerald work; the seeds of destruction are always planted in the early paragraphs, but the reader, fooled by the gilded landscape he takes to be the real world, misses these early signs. Fitzgerald's world pits romance against reality. Characters react within that world, suffer defeat, celebrate within that frame. In the end they are changed utterly by time and the reality that buffets them. But the world of the novel does not change at all; it merely becomes more clear as images, brush stroke by brush stroke, fill in the outline.

In the world of *The Great Gatsby,* for example, it appears at first glance that Fitzgerald has balanced the gaudy Gatsby of West Egg against the tastefully-ordered establishment of East Egg. So obvious is the difference that only a "gull" soaring overhead would fail to note it, and yet the gull certainly has the best perspective. Nick, in fact, is gulled because apparent differences mask important similarities, as image patterns will show. The Eggs seem as different from one another as both do from the ash heap that mocks their apparent prosperity. But the differences are superficial. The Eggs, the valley of ashes, and Myrtle's apartment share one striking similarity; all represent a dream tarnished. Only the fresh green breast, defiled in the moment of discovery, offers any real foil to these three settings.

The pattern to emerge from the sum of images in a Fitzgerald novel will prove the single image—especially the positive image—to have been used ironically. What appears to be ideal weather for life and love will prove to be the rain of death. What appears to be substance will prove shadow. What appears a tale of life will prove a story of death, just as *The Great Gatsby,* ostensibly a fable of the East, proves finally to deal essentially with the West.

In any case, Fitzgerald knew too well Omar Khayyam's pronouncement in *The Rubaiyat:* "How little while we have to stay, and once departed may return no more." He knew that the very sperm of life nurtures the seed of death. Perhaps deeply within Fitzgerald lodged the conflict expressed earlier by Keats. The first halves of *The Beautiful and Damned, The Great Gatsby,* and *Tender Is the Night* show a Fitzgerald who apparently believes what Keats wrote in a letter to Benjamin Bailey:

> I am certain of nothing but the holiness of the heart's affections and the truth of Imagination— what the imagination seizes on as Beauty must be truth—whether it existed before or not.[2]

In the latter half of each novel, Fitzgerald proves his kinship with the darker Keatsian sentiment expressed at the end of the imaginative flight in "Ode to a Nightingale": "The fancy cannot cheat so well as she is famed to do."

Of the protagonists in Fitzgerald's novels, only Anthony Patch, passively awaiting wealth, remains earthbound because he lacks a vision of beauty. Gatsby, whose eyes remain fixed in a limited way, nevertheless makes his dream come true. Dick Diver, with a more profound vision, duplicates on earth the heaven in his head; Monroe Stahr, the most imaginative of Fitzgerald's protagonists, uses his art to make his own ideals, his illusions become the illusions of a nation. Every Fitzgerald protagonist soars on fancy's wings—for a while. But time, as it ushers in fatigue, corruption, and death, brings all of them back to earth. Time, reality, clips the wings of fancy.

Milton Hindus sums up metaphorically what most critics find in Fitzgerald's work: "Fitzgerald's formula is to mix in a dash of romance with a liberal portion of the most brutal realism and to drench the whole thing in irony."[3] A clear example of this irony occurs often in his use of color imagery. Anna R. Gere notes that

> because he believes that man is born good and becomes corrupted by forces of life, Fitzgerald sees this corruption as a distortion of nature and his use of color emphasizes distortion by employing individual colors in a context opposite from their usual associations.[4]

Gere, noting that Fitzgerald uses colors in a "context opposite from their usual associations," provides the key to reading most Fitzgerald symbols. Again, a traditionally positive image remains so until the latter half of the novel when the opposite, negative association begins to dominate. Images traditionally negative remain so throughout.

Imagery carries most of the burden of the irony. Having finished a Fitzgerald novel, readers must reconsider the early pages, this time in light of the irony that emerges as the world of the novel becomes clearer and more significant. Viewed alone, any image may lead to false conclusions. Fitzgerald wants this. He wants to seduce the reader, wants to sell him the romantic world created by the imagination. He wants the reader to share with Anthony Patch, Jay Gatsby, Dick Diver, and Monroe Stahr the romantic view of the world as a palace of infinite possibility, a place where the best the human race has to offer are artist-gods who fashion from chaos an order and perfection. Thus the reader participates, experiences the fall, the disillusionment, exactly when the protagonist does. Critical readers realize that the fall is inevitable, that even in the beginning, images hint at disaster. While the reader may misconstrue the single image, the pattern soon becomes unmistakable. As Wolfgang H. Clemen suggests,

> An isolated image, an image viewed outside its context, is only half the image. Every image, every metaphor gains full life and significance only from its context. In Shakespeare, an image often points beyond the scene in which it stands to preceding or following acts; it almost always has reference to the whole of the play.[5]

Similarly in Fitzgerald's fiction, an image, metaphor, or at times just a simple reference to something can be understood solely as it functions within the novel as a whole.

The method I use to draw the above conclusions from image patterns in Fitzgerald's fiction is neither new nor of my own devising. For guidance I have turned not to Fitzgerald scholars,[6] but to twentieth-century critics of Shakespeare[7] and the tradition started by Caroline Spurgeon's *Shakespeare's Imagery and What It Tells Us*.[8] Five years prior to *Shakespeare's Imagery,* Spurgeon took an initial step toward validating the study of imagery when she stated, however conservatively, that image patterns "play a part in raising, developing, sustaining and repeating emotion in the tragedies which is somewhat analogous to the action of a recurrent theme or 'motif' in a musical fugue or sonata."[9] It is this very point that Robert B. Heilman rejects when he accuses Spurgeon of regarding imagery "merely as a kind of soft music background, helping to catalyze and amplify feelings which are to be understood as created by other means."[10] Spurgeon, in other words, stops short, actually undervaluing her discoveries. Heilman would give this much importance to imagery: "Image groups are not merely theme supporters, but theme carriers."[11] That image groups both support and *carry* theme is a central tenet in my investigation of Fitzgerald.

Heilman's extension of Spurgeon focuses directly on the work, and whatever light the study sheds on the psyche of the author is incidental, however valuable. This runs counter to Spurgeon, whose essential concern was why Shakespeare conjured certain recurring images. She was more interested in what kind of man would use specific sets of images than in what they meant and how they functioned in a given play. Robert L. Gale, who tabulated images much in the manner of Spurgeon, says this about his study of Henry James:

> My study of imagery in the fiction of Henry James . . . will throw varied lights upon his personality and on the modes of this thought; say much about what in reality especially engages his attention; and finally, help explicate his texts by showing that his imagery habitually paints setting, characterizes, foreshadows, implements plot, and reinforces theme.[12]

This categorically reverses the order of importance.[13] Like Spurgeon, Gale wonders what these images say about the author, not how they function organically within a work.

Because Fitzgerald's life and mind have been explored so thoroughly that I have nothing new to add,[14] I plan to make only incidental comments concerning the man. I will not speculate as to what kind of man would use water imagery as extensively as he did, nor why his attitude toward drinking was so ambivalent that, while he lusted after the glamor of the mad drunken gesture, *The Beautiful and Damned* and to a lesser degree *Tender is the Night* might serve as propaganda tracts for the WCTU. While I find the life fascinating, it is not my concern here. I plan to concentrate in detail only on the way images function within each novel.

A central function of imagery, of course, is to create what Moody E. Prior calls "wholeness." Arguing the superiority of verse drama over prose drama, Prior states that "one of the distinctive qualities of great tragedy is its wholeness—the impression it leaves of being undivided and fused, of being the product of genius under the directing impulse of one impressive dramatic idea.''[15] This is the essence of any work capable of producing great emotional impact. Few deny wholeness to the better novels of Henry James, James Joyce, William Faulkner, even Ernest Hemingway. To the extent that image patterns contribute to the creation of a unified whole, I submit wholeness as a major defining trait of both *The Great Gatsby* and *Tender Is the Night*.

Prior stresses that in verse drama no single image can be properly considered unless the critic takes into account the larger pattern of which the image is a part.[16] Fitzgerald, of course, wrote no verse tragedy; yet his use of image patterns resembles that of all great poets of tragedy. Fitzgerald follows a tradition that began with Greek tragedy[17] and continued into the twentieth century. Wherever he stands on the scale of the world's writers, Fitzgerald shares with the best his use of imagery to carry theme, to unite structure, to create the feeling of wholeness. The differences between a novel and a dramatic tragedy may be legion, but dramatic intent—to create a feeling of inevitability about every line, every action—and the use of imagery to facilitate that intent can never be counted among those differences. As Clemen points out:

> The image is rooted in the totality of the play. It has grown in the air of the play; how does it share its atmosphere or contribute to the tenor? To what degree is the total effect of the play enhanced and coloured by images?[18]

These are the essential questions. Viewed in context, a simple reference may grow, may attain the value of a functioning symbol. Una Ellis-Fermor, discussing imagery in drama, says most commentators see imagery as

> co-existent with metaphor or at most with the figures closely allied with metaphor. This is . . . advisable, even though in the special case of drama [and fiction] there are sometimes reasons for extending it to include the frontiers of symbolism, description, or even . . . the setting itself.[19]

Fitzgerald's first reference to what will become an image symbolic of something larger, more encompassing than itself, may appear to have nothing in common with metaphor, may seem a mere reference to light or water or color or any number of objects or qualities. But as further references to that object or quality appear, image patterns develop. What was once a simple reference becomes a symbol that grows in complexity with each iteration.

Thus an image must be viewed as a integral part of the whole; but before it can make sense in the larger framework, it must be seen in its immediate context. My first question, therefore, is what exactly is happening—what is the context when Fitzgerald plants an image, when he refers to any specific object, such as an automobile, or any quality, such as light?

As to the term *imagery* itself, my definition is common enough. The Thrall, Hibbard, and Holman description of an image as having a "concrete referent in the objective world''[20] is neither too broad nor too limiting for my purposes. The function of the image is to evoke that referent. Any single instance of an image would do no more than evoke the referent, however powerfully. As images recur in various contexts, however, they acquire a meaning beyond themselves, a meaning that deepens with each repetition, a meaning frequently more important than the literal meaning. Thus are connotations born, and in actual speech, connotations—formed as the word lives, interacts in a varied environment—usually overshadow the more static denotations.

Summarizing a portion of Kenneth Burke's concept of the value of image patterns, Hazel Greenberg says, ''Every work has its own inner logic, and the works by one author will have the same kind of inner logic because he has a grammar of logic of his own.''[21] In Fitzgerald's case, the ''inner logic'' becomes quite consistent as he writes *The Great Gatsby* and *Tender Is the Night*. It is less consistently developed, less logical in *This Side of Paradise*, *The Beautiful and Damned*, and the fragment, *The Last Tycoon*. While inner logic is at least partially a product of the subconscious, Fitzgerald, through extensive revision, made art from the raw material of his subconscious mind. He died too soon to complete, let along revise *The Last Tycoon*, so in that work the image patterns, although sometimes carefully set up, are not fully developed. Yet it seems no far-fetched speculation to assume that, had Fitzgerald lived to revise it, *The Last Tycoon*, too, would contain the rich image patterns characteristic of *The Great Gatsby* and *Tender Is the Night*.[22]

In a limited sense, to isolate patterns is to try to define another man's inner logic, the grammar of his life. More to the point, it is to seek the very steps of the creative process. Never would I presume to speculate upon what these steps are, but I would venture that when one writes ''intricately patterned''[23] fiction, he sets up these patterns more or less subconsciously. Not accidentally, though. Patterns emerge because an emotional and intellectual climate—in part the original inspiration—controls the work. Of this process, Fitzgerald says

> Whether it's something that happened twenty years ago or only yesterday, I must start out with an emotion—one that's close to me and that I can understand.[24]

In Fitzgerald's work, images make the emotion clear; the emotion dictates which images will shape the novel. When patterns emerge—as of necessity they must when a single artistic intelligence *controls* the work—the author revises and makes these patterns significant. Two incidents from the writing of *The Great Gatsby* illustrate the point.

Documenting the kind of revision Fitzgerald did, Kenneth E. Eble offers a hint as to how patterning actually occurs. Eble points out that in an early draft of *The Great Gatsby*,

> . . . the green light (there were originally two) came into the novel at the time of Daisy's meeting with Gatsby. ''If it wasn't for the mist,'' he tells her, ''we could see your house across the

bay. You always have two green lights that burn all night at the end of your dock.'' Fitzgerald not only made the green light a central image of the final paragraph, but he went back to the end of the first chapter and added it there.[25]

Originally Fitzgerald had ended the first chapter with the passage containing the "fresh-green-breast-of-the-new-world" image, the passage that in the final draft concludes the novel. Because Fitzgerald wrote this section early in the novel's composition, he apparently had a clear idea what some of the major themes would be. Significantly, he already had in mind many major image patterns.[26] Another change, seemingly minor, but in keeping with the intention of an author deeply concerned with establishing patterns, is the change in Wilson's hair color "from 'yellow' to the more deathly hue of 'pale.'"[27]

Anyone who believes that a dust cover featuring a pair of eyes peering out over New York inspired T. J. Eckleburg's eyes might conclude that a major and most effective symbol evolved through lucky accident. Whatever engendered Eckleburg, Fitzgerald did write to his editor, Maxwell Perkins, "For Christ's sake, don't give anyone that jacket you're saving for me. I've written it into the book."[28] The origin of this image, however, is beside the point. What matters is that in concentrating his energies on *The Great Gatsby*, Fitzgerald created in himself an emotional and intellectual climate in which he could recognize that such an image fit into, actually enhanced the pattern. Eckleburg, a symbol consciously planted, fits perfectly with those that may have emerged subconsciously.

Fitzgerald's conscious mind imposed order on the unconscious. Extensive revision made the final product intricately patterned indeed. Fitzgerald sorted out and used what would work within his original impulse, and he assimilated whatever might come from the outside. Saying essentially the same thing, C. Day Lewis discusses the interdependency of images within a work. Images shape theme; theme controls images. The process is one of "images lighting the way for theme and helping reveal it, step by step, to the writer, the theme as it thus grows up controlling more and more the development of images."[29]

Discussing psychological implications of bird and insect imagery in Shakespeare, Edward A. Armstrong says that thematic imagery occurs because of a "thought exciting frequent appearance of images all connected to one another under a specific interest."[30] This causes consistency. Viewing it from the opposite direction—looking at the result of an imagery study—one discovers the ideas distilled from the conglomeration of images.

However formed, image patterns create nerve networks within a novel. These networks, scarcely noted at first, form the essential texture and structure of a work. These sinews and nerves stretch through the novel, ultimately define it, show what it is, what it means. Much of the *art* in writing is focused on the creation of image patterns. A writer's art gives life to ideas; the theme might be a platitude, a dead thing, but art breathes life into dead things.

Studying the novels of Fitzgerald, I want to show that patterns exist, and in so doing, I support James E. Miller's conclusion that in writing *This Side of Paradise* and *The Beautiful and Damned*, Fitzgerald's mentors, Wells and Mackenzie, were not primarily concerned with art. *The Great Gatsby* is such a great artistic leap beyond these two apprentice novels because Fitzgerald switched allegiance to Conrad and James.[31] Early in his career, however, Fitzgerald saw the emptiness of patternless art. Criticizing Stephen Vincent Bénet's *The Beginning of Wisdom*, Fitzgerald wrote to Perkins, "Beautifully written, but too disjointed and patternless."[32] He wrote that letter in 1921, a time when despite his concern for them, complex patterns were sufficiently rare in his own work.

Of his method of composition in *The Great Gatsby*, Fitzgerald wrote to Perkins,

> So in my new novel I'm thrown directly on purely creative work—not trashy imaginings as in my stories, but sustained imagination of a sincere yet radiant world. So I tread slowly and carefully and at all times in considerable distress. This book will be a consciously artistic achievement and must depend on that as the others did not.[33]

Part of the function of this study is to see how well Fitzgerald succeeded in making *The Great Gatsby* an intricately-patterned work. But *Tender Is the Night*, too, is intricately patterned. Not as tightly structured, and in some ways not as successful as *The Great Gatsby*, *Tender Is the Night* contains nonetheless the major elements that make the story of Jay Gatsby a work of rare beauty—blankets of fine prose and complex image patterns highlighting emotion and theme. *The Great Gatsby* is a *tour de force*, a work that triumphs partly because of the singleness of purpose, the limited scope made possible by Fitzgerald's remaining within the relatively narrow confines of myth. *Tender Is the Night* is a larger work, one that pushes its dimensions beyond the shadowy, mythic Gatsby to the equally universal, but more human and complex Dick Diver. In *The Great Gatsby*, Fitzgerald so thoroughly explored the single-minded dreamer at war with reality that later novelists who try to cover the same ground probably err. That he did not exhaust his theme in *Tender Is the Night* does not diminish that work; it does suggest the theme is larger, the artistic risk more perilous, the failure more pronounced, and finally, the work greater. Not as neat as *The Great Gatsby*, *Tender Is the Night* remains a tightly structured novel because of consistent image patterns. Considering the turbulence in the author's life, the many plans he tried and rejected, and the length of time he spent in composition, this sound structure is amazing.

Once attained, however, the habit of careful composition never deserted him. Reminiscing about her role as Fitzgerald's secretary, Frances Kroll Ring makes a comment that reveals both Fitzgerald's writing habits and his continual obsession with art:

> His concern with minor corrections, once a story had gone out to a publication, indicates a certain unsureness of acceptance. Sometimes, the revisions were hardly more than a word or

two on a given page which in no way affected the story, but seemed to relieve some desperate, perfectionist standard of his own.[34]

In spite of Ms. Ring's conjecture that "unsureness of acceptance" motivated these constant revisions, Fitzgerald's conduct seems entirely natural for one acutely aware of the possible vast difference caused by a "word or two on a given page." The point is, however, that Fitzgerald maintained his obvious concern with art even during the days of his Hollywood disintegration. No matter how sick he was, the artistic temperament never deserted him, as *The Last Tycoon* clearly shows. Even in this unfinished novel, images create "symbolic commentary,"[35] lend a special Fitzgeraldian timbre to the "melody of the prose."[36] Thus I conclude that there is much to learn from the exploration of Fitzgerald's imagery.

The present study explores transportation imagery, communication imagery, light-dark imagery, dirt-disease-decay imagery, and finally, water imagery in each of the five novels. Choosing what categories to explore—and then labeling them—is always perilous and, to an extent, arbitrary. Because selecting these image patterns may seem to force exclusions, or equally important, the patterns themselves may seem to overlap, cogent reasons exist for refocusing almost any study. Transportation imagery and communication imagery, for example, are obviously related in that both deal with a major motif in American literature, the intrusion of the machine.[37] The concentration here is on the automobile (a dynamic machine) and the telephone (a static machine), with other incidental machine imagery for support and illustration. The natural connection between light-dark imagery and water imagery is weather. And with the passage of time, water, at first a restorative, loses that power and becomes an agent of corruption, thus linking dirt-disease-decay imagery with water imagery. Time, of course, is that part of the iceberg just below the surface of light and dark, dirt, disease, and decay, and water imagery.

Through the patterns that emerge, I plan to find what the novels do say, not what they should say. I will not burden the reader by mentioning every iteration of the images considered, and because I used no computer in seeking these images, I have undoubtedly missed some. The interpretations, of course, will be somewhat subjective, but will always be based on one principle—*guilt by association*. Whatever is happening, whatever predominates in the immediate milieu when the image appears, is what gives that image its meaning. Snow, for example, traditionally functions as an image of death, of paralysis, as in Joyce's *Dubliners*. If the characters in a novel erect a totem and do a fertility dance around it each time the snow flies, however, snow symbolically takes on quite another meaning. But to better explain what I mean by "guilt by association" and to illustrate the method I plan to use throughout this study, I will discuss here a specific transportation image from *The Last Tycoon*.

Fitzgerald's use of the airplane at the beginning of *The Last Tycoon* typifies his way of planting an image and investing it with significance. The novel opens with the narrator, Celia Brady, flying west to Hollywood from her eastern college. Through Celia's early reminiscence, Fitzgerald sets up the association between death and the airplane:

> The world from an airplane I know. Father always had us travel back and forth that way from school and college. After my sister died . . . , I traveled to and fro alone, and the journey always made me somewhat solemn and subdued. . . . I seldom really fell asleep during the trip, what with thoughts of Eleanor and the sense of that sharp rip between coast and coast.[38]

The dead sister plays no role in the novel. Never mentioned again, either in the pages of the completed draft or in the outline, she serves merely to create the connection between flying and death.

A few paragraphs later, Fitzgerald reinforces the association between death and flying. Celia and the stewardess discuss a young actress who during the Great Depression "kept staring out the window in such an intent way that the stewardess was afraid she was contemplating a leap" (p. 5). Thus death and despair become associated with the Hollywood scene; through the eyes of Celia, Fitzgerald proffers the view that most of Hollywood contemplated at least metaphoric leaps during the economic crash. The actress feared revolution, as did the lawyer and director who acquainted the Bradys with their plots for survival. Both lawyer and actress plotted returns to Hollywood at the end of chaos, but the more pessimistic director knew he had to disappear forever into the crowd. Death, fear of a vaguely-defined revolution, hope for escape from forces about to effect change—these motifs dominate Celia's mind as she flies westward toward home. Hollywood and flight engender gloom.

Having linked the airplane with death, Fitzgerald ties his protagonist, Monroe Stahr, conclusively to the airplane. He does this through the mind of his narrator, whose thoughts dwell even more on Monroe Stahr than on death and flying. Through Celia, Fitzgerald points up a central incongruity: Stahr, a genuine revolutionary in the business world, actually prospered in this climate of timidity, of fear of violent change, of widespread conservatism.[39] But he climbed too high, scorched his wings in the sun.[40]

In this frightened community, no wonder Celia likens Stahr to Icarus, the mortal whose ambition lured him too near the sun, plunged him from the sky to his death. Like his prototype, Stahr has an intense interest in and apparent aptitude for flying, as the pilot explains to Celia. For a while, no height is too great for Stahr. No fat, docile business man, Stahr possesses the vast energy of myth; he is the defiant Prometheus, the heedless Icarus soaring too near the source of light, of knowledge. In defiance of the Icarian legend,

> He had flown up very high to see . . . when he was young. And while he was up there he had looked on all kingdoms, with the kind of eyes that stare straight into the sun. . . . He had stayed up there longer than most of us, and then, remembering all that he had seen . . . , he had settled gradually to earth. (p. 20)

After likening Stahr to Icarus, Celia compares his descent into Hollywood to that of a ''plane coming down into the Glendale airport, into the warm darkness'' (p. 20). This however, is only an omen, not the final Icarian plunge. For the present, Stahr is still using his knowledge; only later must he pay the price for flying too high, for learning how major decisions are reached and why they are adhered to,[41] and for knowing that the universe he inhabits is absurd.[42] Even in this first chapter, the warning rings clear. The reader knows that Stahr must fall, and that his fall, because he has reached heights penetrated only by tragic heroes, must be from the sky. He must plunge from the sky in an airplane, or Fitzgerald has wasted much symbolic material.

If the Icarian legend and Celia's contemplation of her dead sister fail to link flying with death, Fitzgerald includes as part of his death imagery the real death of Manny Schwartz. Stahr and Schwartz, his foil, have more in common than their Jewish heritage. Although never of the same caliber, both share tough ghetto backgrounds, and Schwartz has had, as Stahr now has, a leadership role in Hollywood. What happened to Schwartz can and will happen to Stahr, just as the warning note from the pathetic suicide suggests. By the time Stahr dies, he, who might have ranked as a genuine tragic hero, has deteriorated nearly to the level of Schwartz. At the end he has descended to the same tricks as his adversary, Brady; the two men hatch plots to kill each other.

Later in the novel Fitzgerald reinforces the airplane as a death symbol and strengthens Stahr's solid link with flight. He refers to Stahr's unfinished house, the house he will never occupy, as a fuselage. At this fuselage of a house, the doomed love between Stahr and Kathleen Moore is born, just as the affair between Wylie White and Celia flourished briefly in the actual fuselage of the airplane. But Celia loves Stahr, Stahr loves Kathleen, Kathleen will marry the American, her fiancé. No one gets what he wants, indeed, what he must have. The airplane becomes an image of brief promise before death and should be read as such throughout. Love will founder and Icarus must fall, as the images make abundantly clear from the opening paragraph of *The Last Tycoon*.

I have attacked this problem of imagery in Fitzgerald as a student of writing who would learn from a master. I have learned that an image appearing only once seldom takes on any meaning outside itself; if it functions as a symbol at all, it does so only in that it acquires just the most traditional of meanings. Thus Gertrude Stein is right: seen but once, ''a rose is a rose is a rose,'' or at best, a combined symbol of spring and reminder of the brevity of youth. Fitzgerald, however, has shown that the writer can make the rose symbolize anything. The rose heralds spring, youth, hope, but if death occurs each time the rose appears, youth and hope become ironic. Both spring and the rose gradually begin to symbolize death, thus creating an ironic tension, the quintessence of Fitzgerald's work.

We, as readers, are treated like Pavlov's dog. In that famous experiment, the bell has no intrinsic meaning to the dog until Pavlov invests it with meaning by ringing it each time he feeds the dog. Gradually the bell becomes an omen of food.

The dog salivates at the ringing of the bell, now a full-fledged symbol of food. The difference between what the psychologist and the writer did is that Pavlov gave meaning to something that previously had no meaning. Fitzgerald's task was just a bit different. In simpler instances, he expanded a meaning that already existed. For example, I hope to show later that in *The Great Gatsby*, cars function not only in their normal capacity—utilitarian servants to humanity—but as symbols of death. This creates a minor tension, but as accident after accident occurs, the car gradually comes to symbolize destruction and potential death. The car, like Pavlov's bell, becomes an omen.

In more complex instances, Fitzgerald inverts the meaning of a familiar image. Water, for example, traditionally symbolizes rebirth, baptism, renewal. One point I hope to make later is that Fitzgerald at first seems to use water in its traditionally positive sense; the promise is there, but as water fails time after time to provide rejuvenation, an ironic tension arises. Water begins to symbolize not life, but death. The repetition and rhythm of failure proves that no eternal life springs from water. Time renders the promise absurd.

I have undertaken this study of imagery and irony because techique and style— the essence of image patterns and irony as shapers of theme—remain as areas of fertile investigation in Fitzgerald's fiction. Much previous scholarship focused on Fitzgerald's criticism of the American experience, his universal themes and appeal, literary influences on him, each of his characters but especially Nick, studies of single patterns of imagery in *The Great Gatsby*, and several views of Fitzgerald as bard of the jazz age. Recent studies have explored Fitzgerald's style and language,[43] a movement I would like to align myself with.

Fitzgerald possessed a great intuitive feeling for what motivated human beings and what was wrong with society. That intuition, coupled with a splendid sense of language and the ability to sustain long passages of fine prose featuring frequent unforgettable bright epigrammatic phrases (''as if we were in ecstatic cahoots''), enabled Fitzgerald to give extraordinary emotional depth to ideas that had been stated perhaps more clearly—but not more profoundly—by social critics and lesser artists such as Mencken. The question I propose to address in all of the novels— not just *Gatsby* as has been the pattern—is exactly what stylistic and technical facility enabled Fitzgerald to make the reader *feel* his theme without resorting to the essayist's technique of stating it. Why do we know, for example, that Gatsby's dream is not only tawdry but is the product of a third-rate artist, that by extension the American dream is an adolescent creation in *The Great Gatsby*, the novel that has been called a ''meditation on American history.''[44] The answer can be found in the image patterns that create microcosms of the novel as a whole, that carry and deepen a theme as iterations occur throughout the novel. My concern is technical. How does Fitzgerald do it? How does his technique illuminate and carry his themes?[45]

In closing this introduction, I must remind everyone—myself more than anyone—of the dangers of stressing one element of a work at the expense of all others. Clemen sums up the problem of isolating one element when in reality a work should be seen only as a whole: "It is only by means of the individual study of such isolated aspects that the total development can become tangible and clear. . . . But it is just this method of isolating and cutting out that may easily destroy the living organism of the work of poetry."[46]

Looking closely at any given aspect of a work is much like looking through a microscope. Of necessity, this distorts; the aspect viewed and intensely magnified may come to seem not only the major element of the work, but indeed, the sole element. Focusing closely on image patterns invites distortion, but so does the use of *any* critical magnifying glass.

1

This Side of Paradise and *The Beautiful and Damned*

Considering Fitzgerald's youth and inexperience as a writer, his generally acknowledged anxiety to get his novel published so that fame and fortune would win him the desirable, elusive Zelda Sayre, and above all, his method of composition, it is scarcely surprising that few recognizable patterns exist in his first novel. *This Side of Paradise* evolved from the twice-rejected "The Romantic Egotist," one version a hastily written first draft, the second apparently carefully revised.[1] Examining the manuscript of *This Side of Paradise*, James L. West III discovered "numerous pages from 'The Romantic Egotist' typescript along with pages from a play, a short story, and several poems."[2]

Transportation Imagery

The first major image cluster to be discussed for each of the novels is transportation imagery. Unlike the other novels, *This Side of Paradise* fails to develop firm symbolic image patterns from transportation imagery. Perhaps this is true because uniquely among Fitzgerald's novels, this first novel does not move inexorably toward tragedy. Although it drifts roughly in chronological order as it follows the education of protagonist Amory Blaine, this episodic novel has no real structural movement. This does not mean, however, that modes of transportation do not take on meanings outside themselves, or that they do not function symbolically.

The automobile, for example, plays various roles in the education of Amory Blaine. From ages four to ten, Amory tours the country in a private limousine belonging to the father of Beatrice, his eccentric mother. This tour comprises his early adventure and education. More than anything else, he learns about Beatrice, the magnificent hypochondriac. Much of the rest of the novel deals with Amory's struggle to escape the eccentricity taught him by his mother.

At Princeton, the automobile provides a learning lab more viable than the classroom. For Amory and friends, the car makes possible a leap from the static campus of dull classes into adventure, a kind of escape and learning experience combined. One such trip occurs when they return to Deal Beach a stolen car abandoned at Princeton. Without money or sleeping quarters, they spend three days on the beach where they live by their considerable wits. It is a course in survival. They have cut classes, brazenly outfaced a waiter who presents them a bill for food they have eaten but cannot pay for, picked up and treated as a queen the ugliest girl on the beach. On the third day, they hitchhike back to Princeton, now closer friends than ever.

Not all automobile adventure cements friendship, however. On one such trip, Dick Humbird dies in an accident. Like all episodes in *This Side of Paradise,* this provides a learning experience, but one that casts the car in a somber light. No longer a vehicle for romance alone, the car becomes for the first time an instrument of death. The accident reduced Humbird, once Amory's idol and mentor,[3] to a "heavy white mass . . . Amory stepped outside the door and shivered slightly at the late night wind—a wind that stirred a broken fender on the mass of bent metal to a plaintive, tinny sound."[4]

But Fitzgerald fails to establish a pattern of death and tragedy here, as he would have had he written *This Side of Paradise* after he learned to control his craft. He does not plant a succession of death images following the accident, but rather has Amory and Isabelle drive through the countryside in search of romance: "For a delicious hour . . . they glided the roads . . . and talked from the surface of their hearts in shy excitement. Amory felt strangely ingenuous and made no attempt to kiss her" (p. 88). In later novels, the juxtaposition of the death of a friend with a romantic joyride would bode a tragic end for that romance, with the automobile acting as instrument of disaster. This romance ends, but without a flicker of tragedy; it is merely one more chapter in the education of Amory Blaine.

Like the many other artifacts of imagery in Fitzgerald's fiction,[5] the car provides one more mark for measuring the distance between man and nature. The car is a product of civilization, its presence a constant reminder that civilization still exists. Fitzgerald stresses this when he has Burne Holiday tell Amory that to kill his fear of the dark, he actually walked through the forest at night. Amory is impressed: "I couldn't have done that. . . . The first time an automobile passed and made the dark thicker when its lamps disappeared, I'd have come in" (p. 31). In its absence the automobile thickens the dark, places humanity closer to and more at odds with the natural environment, perhaps with itself.[6] When the accouterments of civilization drop away, men and women stand alone. But Fitzgerald does not follow up the possibility of the human being meeting its own heart of darkness, either. Amory's education never, not even for a brief moment, places him on equal footing with his natural surroundings; always he remains a city boy learning to cope with his urban environment.[7]

Fitzgerald so frequently uses the automobile as a characterizing device that the kind of car one drives and the way one drives it is always important. Beatrice, for example, shows such extreme caution in driving a car that she becomes a dangerous pest on the highway:

She looked left and right, she slipped cautiously into a speed of two miles per hour, beseeching Amory to act as sentinel; and at one busy crossing she made him get out and run ahead and signal her forward like a traffic policeman. (pp. 19–20)[8]

This is interesting because Beatrice cherishes a romantic vision of herself, believes herself to be a bold, adventuring lady confronting life. Perhaps she more clearly resembles the anachronistic electric car she drives. On the road she is as dangerous and out of place as are the careless drivers of Fitzgerald's later novels. Careless drivers are careless people and not to be respected. But Beatrice carries caution to an extreme as distant and as mad as the carelessness of drivers like Jordan Baker and Tom and Daisy Buchanan.

Cars also characterize Isabelle and her trail of suitors. When Amory first becomes interested in Isabelle, he finds his competition pretty fast. They are "terrible speeds" who have flunked out of a university or two and almost to a man drive red Stutzes (p. 67). Fitzgerald allows the car to do all the work of characterizing these young men: they are their cars, just as Beatrice is her ancient electric.

Both the electric and the Stutz Bearcat are emblematic of solid social position. Psychologically, however, they stand years apart, with the essential difference, in fact, being youth vs. age. The ancient electric, coupled with the sedate driving habits of Beatrice, project an eccentric dignity that belies the image Beatrice entertains of herself as the wild vivant about whose style the narrator can comment, "If it was not life, it was magnificent" (p. 8).

The Stutz Bearcat, on the other hand, connotes carefree youth who will dare anything. But the red Stutz too perfectly conveys this impression. The Stutz has been so carefully chosen as to deny the image of impetuous youth among the choosers. Too clearly, this red car is part of a plan sufficiently inflexible to exclude even the hint of spontaneity. Because it is time to sow wild oats, these young men and their women—the Isabelles by their sides—will drive red Stutzes. When it is time to drive another car, they will do so. In the meantime, however, the car serves as social and sexual arena for Isabelle and her ilk:

The future vista of her life seemed an unending succession of scenes like this: under moonlight and pale starlight in the backs of warm limousines and in low, cosy roadsters stopped under sheltering trees—only the boy might change. . . . (pp. 69–70)

Although he never owns one, the automobile characterizes Amory, too. To exemplify the conduct of an impractical man, Amory cites his own practice of driving without knowing how to change a tire. He takes pride in this impracticality, this sign of aristocracy, this indication that his mind travels through spheres higher than that of a mundane, practical man. He will outgrow that stage.

Fortunately Fitzgerald has established Amory's character and has gained reader identification before he places his protagonist in the limousine of the wealthy Ferrenby near the end of the novel. Here Fitzgerald performs unintentional character assassination simply by placing Amory in the car and letting him talk. Called the "magnificent Locomobile," this car serves as soap box for Amory's immature Fabianism. Luxuriating in a limousine, Amory explains—with much supercilious weariness—why he has jumped from the economic treadmill to become a radical socialist. Ironically, this socialist riding in a luxury car consents to discuss issues with Ferrenby, the capitalist who picked him up as he hitchhiked, but tells the little man, the proletarian chauffeur, to shut up. He even boasts about it in a chapter entitled "The Little Man Gets His" (p. 275). Neither narrator nor author seem to note the irony implicit in Amory's position. Instead, both writer and protagonist—who are too close to one and the same to allow for artistic perspective—piously ride in the limousine and deplore the lack of intellectual honesty.

Finally, Fitzgerald's uses of the automobile in *This Side of Paradise* are too varied to form an image pattern. He uses the car most consistently as a tool of characterization, but even here no symbolic pattern emerges; no set of references run through the novel with sufficient consistency to create in the reader an expectation every time the image appears.

Much less diffuse, but occurring too infequently to set up patterns, are references to trains. In all Fitzgerald novels, trains signify major moves, long journeys emblematic of a change in life, or of an attempt at change. The motive for the journey might be the return to somewhere that cannot be reached, as in *Tender Is the Night* where Dick Diver tries by car, boat, and train to return to his roots when his father dies. Sometimes the trip may involve the preparation of attitudes to face a new adventure. Amory always prepares his attitudes carefully, as he does on his various train trips to prep school, to New York, to Princeton. The reader may safely assume that a train ride in *This Side of Paradise* signifies the death of one way of life, the start of another. At the end of each trip, Amory has changed significantly. Using trains this way, Fitzgerald simply falls in line with a host of his fellow novelists; a major move, in life as in literature, usually signifies significant change.

In *The Beautiful and Damned,* modes of transportation often function as vehicles of escape that later become traps. Or, they serve as characterizing devices. Fitzgerald might characterize an entire city, for example, with one extended transportation image. This is Anthony Patch's New York at night, and to him it is grotesque. Highlighting this monster city is a cacophonous blare:

> The soft rush of taxis by him, and laughter, laughter hoarse as a crow's, incessant and loud, with the rumble of subways underneath—and over all, the revolutions of light, the growings and recedings of light—light divided like pearls—forming and reforming in glittering bars and circles and monstrous grotesque figures cut amazingly on the sky.[9]

A confused image, certainly, and perhaps too diffuse to have much impact, but it serves two purposes: it shows that for Anthony New York is a baffling monster of many parts; and in its very confusion, the image mirrors Anthony's mind, indicates the quality of intellectual contribution one might expect from him.

Associated with Gloria, the car becomes a symbol of amoral romance, which exactly characterizes Gloria herself. Gloria enters in her diary that Stuart Holcome "had run away with her in his automobile and tried to make her marry him by force" (p. 145). Her diary fails to speculate on the morality of abducting young ladies. To her, this ranks as high adventure. As it does for Isabelle in *This Side of Paradise,* the automobile for Gloria provides excitement, but never real danger. She even admires Larry Fenwick, who demands that she kiss him, or get out of the car and walk (p. 145).

Romantic to Gloria, the automobile causes Anthony acute embarrassment. Anthony's flaws, his incompetence, surface because of the car. Riding in a taxi, for example, Anthony first exposes to Gloria his physical cowardice: his cowardice "first showed itself in a dozen incidents of little more than nervousness—his warning to a taxi driver against driving too fast . . . ." (p. 157).

Because Gloria's driving thoroughly terrifies Anthony, the car naturally becomes an initial source of friction during their early married years. Gloria's handling of the car supports the theory that as people drive, so do they order their lives, and as they drive, so do they live:[10] "With a horrible grinding noise the car was put into gear, Gloria adding an accompaniment of laughter" (p. 175). Gloria is reckless, Anthony terrified:

> Their heads snapped back like marionettes on a single wire as the car leaped ahead and curved retchingly about a standing milk wagon. . . . Anthony turned to Gloria with the growing conviction that he had made a grave mistake in relinquishing control and that Gloria was a driver of many eccentricities and infinite carelessness. (p. 175)

Anthony's observation captures Gloria exactly. She would destroy the machine as she would destroy everything she touched.

Her recklessness castrates Anthony, paralyzes him, reduces him to the role of a fussing old man: "'Remember now!' he warned her nervously, 'the man said we oughtn't to go over twenty miles an hour for the first five thousand miles'" (p. 175). Gloria replies that the car is old in spirit; she means that Anthony is old in spirit.

Nor is this the last role the car will play in what might be called a castration scene involving Anthony. When Joseph Bloekman, movie tycoon and her former lover, visits Gloria to try to persuade her to attempt a movie career, that visit creates just such a scene. Gloria still has sufficient beauty for a movie career, and in spite of their troubles, she is still precious to Anthony. When Bloekman leaves, his car looks like "a wraith of dust down the road" (p. 214). His manhood threatened, Anthony rages, furious that Gloria would consider a career, any career. Strangely, Gloria heeds this absurd fury, and the single chance she had to accomplish something vanishes with Bloekman's car in that "wraith of dust." When Bloekman returns later to take Gloria away in his car, Anthony again fumes. Unable to find them, his fear converts his anger to hysteria. When Gloria returns, excited at having driven Bloekman's car, Anthony cannot remonstrate. The man is impotent.

The car becomes a source of humiliation once more when Anthony must taxi to his broker to cash a bond. Physically weary, exhausted from a constant round of parties, Anthony and Gloria face financial disaster. With just two dollars in his pocket, Anthony must get out and walk when the meter reaches that amount. A Walter Mitty distraught, Anthony fantasizes the scene he wants to play. He dreams that the meter spins too fast, and at his destination, he pays only what he owes. The driver complains and, selfrighteous, Anthony knocks him down with a single blow. But the dream melts into base reality:

> Anthony leaned forward hurriedly and tapped the glass. The taxi was only at the Brooklyn Bridge, but the meter showed a dollar and eighty cents, and Anthony would never have omitted the ten per cent tip. (p. 226)

The conventional, cautious Anthony has married a lady who has cemented a new philosophy: she will live without care, without regret. She has chosen to "seek the moment's happiness as fervently and persistently as possible" (p. 226). Temperamentally, the man unable to omit the tip is not suited for that philosophy. Nor, finally, is Gloria.

But the greatest damage the automobile inflicts on Anthony and Gloria occurs when a taxi delivers an old classmate, Fred E. Paramore, to their door. A second taxi deposits Maury Noble and sets the scene for a wild, disastrous party. At the moment least opportune, Adam Patch, Anthony's puritanical, parsimonious grandfather, arrives with his equally puritanical secretary, Edward Shuttleworth. Of course these two men who hold the purse strings to Anthony's future also arrive by taxi. Those still sober enough to recognize Adam as Anthony's grandfather stand aghast. And this confluence of taxis causes Anthony and Gloria to be disinherited. Because the money represents the one possibility for meaning in their lives, the blow falls doubly hard on them—loss of fortune, loss of selves.

Both symbolically and realistically, Anthony's deterioration nears fulfillment when he meets Parker Allison, whose "notion of distinction consisted in driving a noisy red-and-yellow racing car up Broadway with two glittering, hard-eyed girls beside him. He was the sort who dined with two girls rather than one . . . ." (p. 415). This arrested adolescent is one of the few who will associate with Anthony. An older version of the Stutz drivers who courted Isabelle in *This Side of Paradise*, Allison stands far below Maury Noble, who snubs an Anthony so derelict that he is now reduced to seeking funds from old friends. Protesting great need for haste, Maury escapes with his girl in a cab. Anthony waits alone, contemplates his fate in darkness. Indeed, for Anthony, the night is very late. He has spent too many nights "sprawled across the back seat of a taxi . . ." (p. 423).

The pattern develops. The automobile, especially the taxi, is so closely associated with humiliation that its very appearance becomes ominous. The first rip in the Patchs' marital bliss occurs when, in view of every yokel in Marietta, they battle about whether Gloria will take a train to New York, or ride home with

Anthony by cab. Anthony physically forces her to enter the taxi, and doing so, breaks her spirit, kills part of her love for him. Her spirit, vivacious and wild, flourishes only when unencumbered by life's conflicts. This episode with the taxi precipitates humiliation; neither Gloria nor Anthony recover. It fits the pattern, the association between taxis and humiliation.

While it helps characterize Anthony as a weak man who could never hope to avoid humiliation, the automobile makes clear Gloria's carelessness and, surprisingly in one whose strong will is apparent, her indecisiveness. Gloria's carelessness on the road is so important that it even determines their residence in the grey house in Marietta.[11] They could go no further because "Gloria, hesitating between two approaches, and making her choice too late, drove over a fire-hydrant and ripped the transmission violently from the car" (p. 177). If ever a scene provided a key to character, this one does. Gloria always decides too late, tumbles violently between choices, as her abortive movie career suggests. Not only is it consistent with her general style that she decides too late, but also, like Tom and Daisy, she perennially causes things to be broken, breaks them. Anthony is timid, Gloria rash, insensitive—that is the moral of the automobile.

Communication Imagery

Although transportation imagery can scarcely be said to form patterns in *This Side of Paradise* and *The Beautiful and Damned*, the automobile at least tells the reader a great deal about the characters in those two novels. Communication imagery, however, does not assume its full importance until *The Great Gatsby*. In *This Side of Paradise*, for example, the many letters that pass to and fro form no apparent pattern. Mostly, they serve as machinery for exposition. One flaw in the novel is that letters do not communicate to the character receiving the epistles; instead, they merely provide information for the reader, much in the manner of a messenger, or a maid who answers the telephone at the opening curtain of a play.

Telephones are more integrated into the novel, but they are seldom used and form no patterns. Fitzgerald approaches his later feelings concerning the telephone, however, when he uses it not as a device to help get something done, but as an instrument to postpone responsibility. Amory, who should be making up the *Daily Princetonian*, is on a three-day excursion to Deal Beach. A brief inner struggle subdues his conscience, and he telephones back to Princeton to postpone work on the newspaper. This is doubly interesting, because, in theory at least, newspapers serve as organs of communication. Here the telephone not only helps Amory evade responsibility, but also delays communication by postponing the newspaper.

A common and major form of mass communication, the newspaper may either inform or misinform. Pretending objectivity, a paper may obscure truth, may inflate or puncture reputation. Amory points out to Tom D'Invilliers the irony that even one of the best periodicals fails to communicate truth:

What's your business? [he asks Tom]. Why to be as clever, as interesting, and as brilliantly cynical as possible about every man, doctrine, book or policy. . . . The more strong lights, the more spiritual scandal you can throw on the matter, the more money they pay you, the more people buy the issue. You, Tom D'Invilliers, a blighted Shelley, changing, shifting, clever, unscrupulous, represent the critical consciousness of the race. (pp. 214-15)

Amory admits to having been equally cavalier when he wrote book reviews in college: "I considered it rare sport to refer to the latest honest, conscientious effort to propound a theory or a remedy as a 'welcome addition to our light summer reading'" (p. 215). This theme disappears until Amory resurrects it near the end of the novel. Carping at the lack of honesty in journalism, he defines the problem in these terms: papers rest in the hands of "spiritually married" men, men who can be bought, bribed. Those without price, the "spiritually unmarried," lack power. The spiritually married man

has garnered in the great newspaper, the popular magazine, the influential weekly—so that Mrs. Newspaper, Mrs. Magazine, Mrs. Weekly can have a better limousine than those oil people across the street or those cement people "round the corner." (pp. 271-72)

Staunch supporters of the status quo, newspapers make no real attempt to communicate. In Amory's view, wealthy hands cradle the intellectual conscience of the nation. Again, this criticism occurs too seldom to form a pattern. Beyond question, though, the theme of communication devices that neither inform nor tell a truth graces every Fitzgerald novel.

Communication devices in *The Beautiful and Damned* function in two ways: they carry bad news with alacrity and clarity; if the news is good, or if it absolutely must reach the proper destination, the device fails to communicate. Sometimes much can be learned from that failure. After going to the army, Anthony writes letters to Gloria, but they communicate nothing. Reading between the lines, however, Gloria readily sees that Anthony's love has cooled. Because the news is bad, the letter speaks more than the writer intends.

Efficient though letters may be, the telephone reigns in *The Beautiful and Damned* as champion bearer of ill tidings. The pattern begins early. After his return from Rome, for example, Anthony fervently hopes to find his grandfather deep and harmless in the ground, but the old man's voice on the other end of the telephone explodes that prayer. In practical terms, this means Anthony must wait so long for his inheritance that he will never enjoy it. For a man like Anthony, nothing is good if he has to wait and struggle for it. When he finally gets the money, he is barely a shell of a man. He still dreams, yet he has little more substance than a fleshed skeleton, a mere scarecrow like his grandfather, Adam Patch.

Near the beginning of the novel, Dick Caramel and Anthony announce themselves by telephone when they want to meet Gloria Gilbert. Consistent with Fitzgerald's idea that telephones foul up as instruments of communication, the two find Gloria absent when they enter her apartment. They attempt dialogue with Mrs.

Gilbert, who speaks the "conventional lady-lady language" (p. 38), a language, of course, that does not facilitate communication; lady-lady language blocks it.

Maury Noble, too, uses the telephone not to communicate, but to isolate himself, to sever communication with those outside his tiny island of intimates: "The telephone girl received the most positive instructions that no one should ever have his ear without first giving a name to be passed upon" (p. 44). But Maury, intellectual though he is, seldom communicates much. Either he indulges in trivial conversations like the discussion between himself and Gloria concerning legs and tans, or he couches himself in sophisticated cynicism that saves him from having to reveal himself. Often he is actually inarticulate. Note his inability to describe Gloria:[12] "Well, I can't describe her exactly—except to say that she was beautiful. She was—tremendously alive. She was eating gum drops" (p. 48). Except for the detail of Gloria's eating gum drops, which certainly captures the child-woman, Maury's description could fit a million women. He says nothing about Gloria, but much about himself. The sane one in the novel, the one who represents reason, Maury articulates well enough when discussing abstract theory. Like Enobarbus, that Shakespearean symbol of limited reason in *Antony and Cleopatra,* Maury cannot, probably does not even want to, deal with human beings. Just as Enobarbus plays reason to Antony's towering, destructive passion, Maury plays a comparable role to Anthony's considerably less towering, but equally destructive, love. Like Maury expounding a pet theory, Enobarbus really waxes warm in the description of the glory, the luxury, the pomp that is Cleopatra:

> The barge she sat in, like a burnished throne,
> Burned on the water; the poop was beaten gold;
> Purple the sails, and so perfumed that
> The winds were lovesick with them; the oars were
>   silver,
> Which to the tune of flutes kept stroke, and made
>   the water which they beat to follow faster
> As amorous of their strokes. *(Antony and Cleopatra,* II, ii, 196–202)

These are the words of a man who can make vivid anything that excites him. Yet of Cleopatra the human being he can only say: "For her own person,/ It beggar'd all description" (II, ii, 202–3).

Marking the similarity between Maury and Enobarbus tempts one to ask Shakespearean questions: who would be Enobarbus when he might be Antony? Who would be Iago when he might be Othello? Who would be Horatio when he might be Hamlet? But the question in Fitzgerald's least intriguing novel, *The Beautiful and Damned,* must be who would be either Anthony or Maury if he could be anyone else?

Lack of interest in humanity may cause characters to be inarticulate in certain situations, but compared to the device that fails to function, this is a minor bar to communication. The most perverse of all communication devices is the telephone.

Before grandfather Adam Patch arrives to discover Anthony and Gloria at the pinnacle of their debauched party career, for example, the pious secretary, Edward Shuttleworth, calls to announce their arrival. But Fred E. Paramore answers the telephone, thinks the man called himself Butterworth, does not understand the message, forgets the call entirely. Comic, absurd, disastrous in its consequences, this is a scene worthy of Hardy and fairly typical of Fitzgerald. This communication failure causes Anthony and Gloria to lose old man Patch's money, the single thing that might have lent a glimmer of meaning to their lives.

Anthony derives accidental benefit from the telephone—once. After the armistice, Anthony, who either could not, or did not want to, call Gloria to tell of his arrival in New York, combs the house seeking her. Only when a Mr. Crawford telephones—wanting to talk to Gloria, but getting Anthony instead—does he learn that Gloria may be dancing at the Armistice Ball at the Astor. This single coincidence apparently works well for all. In that it is hardly good news for Anthony to discover a Crawford in his wife's life, though, this coincidence follows the Fitzgerald pattern. As surely as if it were carried through sleet and hail by the legendary postman, bad news will arrive.

Even when the telephone works and seems to enrich life, the blessing of communication proves a bane in disguise. Nearly broke, inhabiting progressively cheaper dwellings, Anthony and Gloria determine to economize, which means drastically trimming their entertainment fund. Yet their fascination with one another has waned to the point where an evening alone together is as attractive as pain. Gloria "would stand in the doorway, chewing furiously at her fingers. . . . Then the telephone rings, and her nerves would relax" (p. 376). Another party, more wine, less money.

While Gloria, when she was still young and beautiful, never waited for anything or anyone, later on she sits for hours by the telephone. The girl who dismissed movie tycoon, Bloekman, as a "Blockhead," who deserted him for Anthony, nervously awaits his call when he schedules her screen test. The telephone rings, and—shatters her last illusion. Youth and beauty have fled; the telephone dashes her final hope. For Gloria, the telephone functions less as an instrument of communication than as a creator of mischief. Some may benefit immensely from a confrontation with reality, but not Gloria. The strong may build from the rubble of defeat, but Gloria, youth gone, stripped of beauty, robbed of illusion, has nothing left. As T. S. Eliot said in both "Burnt Norton" and *Murder in the Cathedral,* "Mankind cannot stand very much reality." Gloria and Anthony can stand less than most.

Communication imagery is practically nonexistent in *This Side of Paradise.* In *The Beautiful and Damned* the pattern is consistent: communication devices fail to communicate, disrupt lives, misinform, or bring bad news. This becomes a minor theme in the novel and a thread that runs throughout not only this novel but Fitzgerald's fiction. The image patterns reveal Fitzgerald's attitude toward communication devices and toward attempts to communicate. These patterns also reveal something of the nature of the world of the novel, but finally communication imagery does little but comment on communication devices themselves; its contribution is not major in either *This Side of Paradise* or *The Beautiful and Damned.*

Light-Dark Imagery

Much more important is light-dark imagery in both novels. In *This Side of Paradise,* for example, Fitzgerald relies mainly on three qualities of light—natural sunlight, moonlight, artificial light—and darkness. He has not yet concluded that the natural light of day must kill the dream. Quite the contrary; when Beatrice suffers an attack of nerves, she and Amory must ''leave this terrifying place and go searching for sunshine'' (p. 5).[13] In a later scene, daylight stimulates creativity. Before composing his acceptance to Myra's party, Amory retrieves his invitation, which had nestled in his dark pocket juxtaposed with a ''dusty piece of peanut brittle. During the afternoon, he brought it to light'' (p. 9). Ironically, nothing can make Beatrice well, and the inspiration Amory gains by exposing Myra's invitation to the sun is meagre enough. His reply is stiff, childishly insincere. When he turns off the lights to write love letters to Isabelle, his prose improves.

Fitzgerald never decides whether light should represent reason or romance. Inspired by ''L'Allegro'' to seek the joys of Arcady, Amory moves ''his bed so that the sun would wake him at dawn . . . .'' (p. 33). Romance, obviously. Further in the romantic vein, an enthralled Amory first views Princeton in full light of day. Seeing Princeton as light personified, he notes the ''wealth of sunshine creeping across the long, green swards, dancing on the leaded window-panes, and swimming around the tops of spires and battlemented walls'' (p. 37).

Sunlight also blesses the episode where Amory and several merry Princetonians head for Deal Beach without money, without itinerary. But Amory, who hates to consider such things, notes that ''night will descend'' (p. 76). Night never falls during this trip, but it does during a later excursion when Dick Humbird dies. Even before this, Amory fears darkness. Burne Holiday explains that not reality, but the imagination persists in ''sticking horrors in the dark'' (p. 130). Knowing Burne to be correct does not, however, purge dread from Amory's night.

Although Fitzgerald toys with the notion of making night a time of horror, this pattern unravels, also. Amory's nocturnal introspection is harmless; when he breaks up with Isabelle, he wonders in darkness how much he cares. Morning light answers: ''What an ironic mockery the morning seemed!—bright and sunny and full of the smell of the garden'' (p. 94). The only irony stems from Amory's melodramatic moaning that Isabelle has spoiled his year even while he realizes he is just as happy without her.

The introduction of Clara, ''a daughter of light alone,''[14] makes sunlight even more diffuse, with idealism the added element (p. 145). Light seemingly cuts through the sham, yet the image pattern is muddled, even at the end of the novel: ''It was a day easily associated with those abstract truths and purities that dissolve in the sunshine or fade out in mocking laughter by the light of the moon" (p. 267). The day is grey, the "least fleshly of all weathers"; such a climate fosters ideals totally divorced from life (p. 266). Thus Amory's brand of socialism.

Unlike natural sunlight, artificial light usually represents escape. The shining lights of Broadway seduce Amory. The "bright star in February," the neon signs, the "women's eyes at the Astro," and the actress "whose hair [is] drenched with golden moonlight" all spell wonderment, New York, theater (pp. 29–30). On this holiday from St. Regis, Broadway lights provide an escape from what Amory considers a purgatory. The theatrical light of romance makes him forget the reality of St. Regis, where he is miserable and vastly unpopular.

When Amory finally makes a friend of Rahill, president of the sixth form at St. Regis, the two talk elementary philosophy "late at night with their cigarettes glowing in the dark" (p. 33). In a communion atmosphere of high seriousness, they discuss school problems. With Amory, who has a penchant for classifying, Rahill discusses trifles—the difference between a "slicker" and a "big man." An older Amory will learn that people cannot be classified, that the once useful category, "slicker," must be so heavily qualified as to be rendered useless. It was a category evolved in the artificial light of cigarette heads. By such light, the two friends can disguise as profound the trivia of their lives, the shallowness of their intellectual pursuits.

Artificial or man-made light creates illusion for the Amory who early grew fascinated with theater. *Capable* of distinguishing reality from tricks of light— either sun or moon, or sometimes theatrical neons and spots—Amory seldom *chooses* to differentiate between the two. Always he is drawn to illusion. But one form of artificial light, the naked bulb, destroys romance. Amory's affair with Isabelle gains intensity only when Amory turns "out the electric light, so that they were in the dark except for the red glow that fell through the door from the reading room lamps" (p. 68). The setting is perfect for romance. Amory becomes sententious, a trifle absurd, and suggests that this may be their last and finest meeting. What would prove embarrassing by daylight, by night leads to love.

Isabelle plays Cinderella in this story-book romance. She weeps at the plight of the people in a problem play as she and Amory hold hands in the darkened theater. And Amory, changing clothes after the play, experiences what will become a recurring motif in Fitzgerald's fiction: "As he put in his studs he realized that he was enjoying life as he would probably never enjoy it again. Everything was hallowed by the haze of his own youth" (p. 88). Amory suffers the intellectual's worst flaw; instead of enjoying the moment, he regrets that it must pass. That slays joy. Nursing that same mood, however, Amory does what few Fitzgerald characters can do. He celebrates himself in the light, turns on "all the lights [and] looked at himself in the mirror. . . . There was little in his life now that he would have changed" (p. 89).

The romantic escape offered by artificial light suffers a severe turnabout in the devil scene. When he sees Dick Humbird as the devil, Amory perhaps is repenting his role as one who "continued into the dimmer hours and gathered strange dust from strange places" (p. 110). Fitzgerald never makes clear why the "devil's feet came into view in the sickly electric light . . . " (p. 114). At any rate, fright forces Amory from the party and into the streets outside. "Down the long street came the moon and Amory turned his back on it and walked" (p. 115). Feeling something behind him in the moonlight, he fears even his own shadow. At dawn, when the moon surrenders to morning, the devil disappears. Back home, Amory and his roommate leave all lights burning. In moonlight, a youthful imagination is dangerous.

When Amory falls in love with Rosalind, he becomes propriatory toward the night:

> the pageantry and carnival of rich dusk and dim streets . . . it seemed that he had closed the book of fading harmonies at last and stepped into the sensuous vibrant walks of life. Everywhere these countless lights, this promise of a night of streets and singing. . . . How the unforgettable faces of dusk would blend to [Rosalind]. . . . (pp. 186–87)

This theater light illumines the section set up as a play. In the play, Amory takes the role of lover beneath the magic lights of the theater, the gaudy carnival lamps.

Those same lights, however, lose their magic after Rosalind's marriage and the death of Monsignor Darcy, friend and spiritual mentor who replaced his mother as life's guide. No life, no health beats in this November rain, no romance streams from the lights of Broadway:

> The air became gray and opalescent; a solitary light suddenly outlined a window over the way, then another light; then a hundred more danced and glimmered into vision. Under his feet a thick, iron-studded skylight turned yellow. (p. 254)

Obviously this New York is no more real than the New York hidden beneath layers of romantic light. Amory survives this mood, too.

More artificial than any man-made light in a Fitzgerald novel, however, is the moon. Amory fancies himself in love with Myra, the first love of his early teens. Enchanted by moonlight, Myra admits to Amory that she likes him "the first twenty-five. . . . And Froggy Parker twenty-sixth" (p. 14). Fitzgerald often undercuts romantic scenes when they veer too close to stickiness: "Froggie had fallen twenty-five places in one hour. As yet he had not even noticed it" (p. 14). Fitzgerald's sense of irony functioned even in this first book, but at times it served him badly. Often his editorial comments were sufficiently clever and cute to halt the narrative.

The scene involving Amory, Myra, and the moon is natural, but during one bright evening meeting between Amory and Beatrice, Fitzgerald mixes moon and motherhood into a dangerous Oedipal concoction: "It was on one of the shadowy paths that Beatrice at last captured Amory . . . " and "took him for a long tête-à-tête in the moonlight" (p. 20). Amory reacts: "He could not reconcile himself to her beauty, that was mother to his own, the exquisite neck and shoulders, the grace of a fortunate woman of thirty" (p. 20). A perilous situation, obviously, but perhaps the danger lessens when Beatrice bores Amory with her vision of beauty—borrowed fiftieth-hand from tired literature.

At Princeton the moon is glorious once more as it transforms the campus into a place of light, even at night:

> The great tapestries of trees had darkened to ghosts back at the last edge of twilight. The early moon had drenched the arches with pale blue, and, weaving over the night, in and out of the gossamer rifts of moon, swept a song, a song with more than a hint of sadness, infinitely transient, infinitely regretful. (p. 41)

Mingled with luxuriant and melancholy music, light plays across the campus by day and night, an almost whimsical light, elusive, defying definition. It makes mysterious these halls of lore and represents the possibilities from what Amory views as an immemorial campus.

The more sensual side of love appeals to Amory, too. An Olympic petter, inventor of the term *petting,* he works amorous wiles "in the moonlight, or the firelight, or in the outer darkness" (p. 58). He loves in every light, even the "winter twilight hovering outside" (p. 59). In fading dusk Amory declares his love for Clara and learns that she will never marry again. When she couches her refusal in kindly terms that do not consume Amory's ego, they race, like children, through "pale-blue twilight," and when they stop, Clara stands "safe beyond the flare of the corner lamp-post" (p. 146).

A "cold moon," an "evil moon" bathes Amory's affair with Eleanor Savage (p. 222). Fitzgerald acknowledges his debt to Poe; Eleanor discovers Amory roving the fields chanting "Ulalume." This establishes the feeling of decadence, of planned destruction that shadows their love. Love blooms in storms and flashes of lightning, a lightning that splashes through the dark to make everything "vivid and grotesque" (p. 224). Without the lightning, darkness is total. The lightning is violent and the moon that follows is eerie:

> One night they walked while the moon rose and poured a great burden of glory over the garden until it seemed a fairyland with Amory and Eleanor, dim phantasmal shapes, expressing eternal beauty and curious elfin love moods. Then they turned out of the moonlight into the trellised darkness. . . . (p. 233)

They strike a match, and once more theatrical light prevails: "The night and scarred trees were like scenery in a play" (p. 234). And in the symbolic sex scene that follows, "moonlight twisted in through the vines and listened . . . the fireflies hung upon their whispers as if to win his glance from the glory of his eyes'' (p. 234). In a cold moonlight plunged into darkness, they realize they are both acting. The affair dies a natural death, the only thing natural about their love. Finished with Eleanor, he "turned homeward and let new lights come in with the sun" (p. 240). Yet for a while the night reduced them to romantic voices and the moon made them more lovely than they were.

In *This Side of Paradise*, the one light image that remains constant enough to form a symbolic pattern is moonlight. This pattern, however, strengthens the novel very little. Fitzgerald uses the moon so conventionally that it does not clarify a theme; nor is moon imagery strong enough to unite sections of this virtually unstructured novel.

In every Fitzgerald novel, the moon, a magnificent artist, paints the world as the world is not; the sun sets the picture straight, but few characters like the work of the realistic artist. In *The Beautiful and Damned*, darkness holds all the terrors of Anthony's imagination; artificial light allays those terrors, often through a distortion as great as the moon's, sometimes by holding at bay the forces of life.

The moon is the great symbol of romance, and in *The Beautiful and Damned*, Fitzgerald employs little irony in its use. To show how little store Anthony sets by reality, for example, Fitzgerald has his protagonist, often accompanied by the sophisticated Maury Noble, view ancient Rome by moonlight. Both Anthony and Maury seek to mask even the grandeur of Rome in the light of the moon. No man for the light of day, this beautiful, delicate Anthony might parch in the sun.

Naturally, such a man would build love firmly in moonlight. The moon spills silver liquor when he and Gloria desert the Bloekman party to be alone. Up until this point, movie tycoon Bloekman seems to be winning Gloria, but now Anthony makes his decisive move. They leave together and in the taxi her face looks

> pale under the wisps and patches of light that trailed in like moonshine through a foliage. Her eyes were gleaming ripples in the white lake of her face; the shadows of her hair bordered the brow with a persuasive unintimate dusk. (p. 102)

For Fitzgerald, this is the classic atmosphere of love.

Anthony and Gloria patch their first quarrel on a sunlit day, but life grows even more lovely by night when Anthony,

> with the lights out and the cool room swimming with moonlight, . . . lay awake and played with every minute of the day like a child playing in turn with a pile of long-wanted Christmas toys. (p. 127)

Anthony is a child whose natural element is romantic moonlight. So is gum-drop eating Gloria; this becomes clear when the moon metaphor expands to include her:

> After a fortnight Anthony and Gloria began to indulge in "practical discussion," as they called those sessions when under the guise of severe realism they walked in an eternal moonlight. (p. 131)

Love blossoms for these moon children during the first autumn of their marriage, and the gray house in Marietta is quintessentially romantic:

> Close together they would wait for the moon to stream across the silver acres of farmland, jump a thick wood and tumble waves of radiance at their feet. In such a moonlight Gloria's face was of a pervading, reminiscent white. . . . (p. 179)

Moonlight love wanes, however; life becomes so dull for the Patches that Gloria finally decides she must escape the prison of the gray house and her life with Anthony. She rushes out into a storm, plays an obvious rebirth scene entirely in flashes of lightning and later in the light of the moon.[15] Gloria should discover herself in this scene, but neither lightning nor moon paint true pictures. A light that drips silver on the most commonplace object is not the light of self-discovery. Gloria's grand adventure leaves her the same girl who labors to avoid life. She sleeps as morning breaks. Only the cynical Maury Noble sees it, and he feels no joy at facing a new dawn: "He was wondering at the unreality of ideas, at the fading radiance of existence, and at the little absorptions that were creeping avidly into his life, like rats into a ruined house" (p. 259). Thus ends the chapter that contains at center the promise of rebirth in rain.

Fitzgerald shows specifically what moonlight can do during Anthony's affair with Dorothy: "The moon came slanting suddenly through the vines and turned the girl's face the color of white roses" (p. 329). In moonlight, this commonplace girl resembles Gloria, and perhaps the difference *is* slight. Dorothy shatters the spell when she asks Anthony if he loves her, however: "The spell was broken—the drifted fragments of the stars became only light" (p. 329). The magic gone, Anthony tries repeatedly to break up with her, then relents and invites her back into his arms: "With a sob she wound her arms around him and let him support her . . . while the moon, at its perennial labor of covering the bad complexion of the world showered its illicit honey over the drowsy street" (pp. 242–43). No author ever described more explicitly the function of the moon. It was too explicit, of course.

Fitzgerald becomes equally explicit after the passage where Anthony and Gloria seal a pact of love in moonlight:

> The stark and unexpected miracle of the night fades out with the lingering death of the last stars and the premature birth of the first newsboys. The flame retreats to some remote and platonic fire; the white heat has gone from the iron and the glow from the coal. (p. 103)

After the magic of the night, "a chill and insolent pencil of sunlight . . . " interrupts Anthony (p. 103). Reality banishes fantasy. No man for the sun, Anthony Patch.

Fitzgerald heroes never escape the sun, however, although Anthony, because of the meaning he unconsciously assigns to it, tries harder than most. Even in his romantic fantasy of Chevalier O'Keefe, light symbolism runs contrary to what might be expected. When the Chevalier renounces life, gives up sex to reside in a monastery, he sees "a golden shower of sun" (p. 91). The life symbol becomes symbolic of the renunciation of life. The Chevalier soon dies because he meant no such renunciation. Anthony's creation has more life than his creator, as should soon be apparent.

Anthony fails to thrive in the palest of natural lights. In the gray light at five o'clock on the morning of his wedding, he sees many flaws in himself. At the wedding a flood of sunlight illuminates the ceremony; Anthony and Gloria do not look at one another, but the sun's rays reflect crassly on the clergyman's gold teeth. Lovers still, Anthony and Gloria can ignore this bizarre bit of reality.

Gloria, in fact, is never bothered when the light of reality shines on something else. The light at General Lee's monument of a home is "harsh, repellent" (p. 165). Here Gloria sees well. She opts for life, for letting natural processes carry through, for letting relics decay. Daylight shows her the folly of Lee's monument, but she never turns that light upon herself. She can not maintain her resolve to let time take its course. She fears life and the natural processes of decay as much as Anthony does.

To this point, the flood of reality from the light of day has been restricted to other people. Not until Anthony and Gloria quarrel on the station platform at Marietta does the "dusty yellow sun" force them to a realization about themselves. Except for unusually traumatic experiences, however, they avoid light. One such experience occurs when Gloria, a night person, feels the "inevitable callousness of the bright morning" when she first awakens to find Anthony gone to war (p. 362).

By the end of the novel, Anthony is incapable of sensation. Destroyed by drink and misfortune, he has reached the point where he can look "blindly down the sunny street" (p. 443). Blind, he stares into light, sees no reality. He returns, broken, to the safety of childhood when his sole problem was his stamp collection. When Gloria and Dick Caramel return bearing news that the Patches have won their suit for the money, they find Anthony "sitting in a patch of sun on the floor of his bedroom" (p. 446). Anthony fails to see what has happened to him, but everyone else can, even Gloria. He sits in the sun with his stamp books, the child he always was.

Like a child, Anthony finds horrors in the dark. Yet he hides there, too. One cold, crackling dusk, Anthony insults his novelist friend, Richard Caramel, for taking himself too seriously, for considering his function too divine. Beneath the cover of darkness, the cowardly Anthony wears a mask of courage and says what he wants to say. The dark also hides the defects of the gray house when the Marietta realtor shows it to them. Morning eventually comes, however; the house becomes symbolic of all that is wrong with their lives. The house is dull, gray, as are *The Beautiful and Damned*.

Generally, though, Anthony sees darkness as an omen of evil. In pitch dark, he peoples his universe with thieves and devils. Noises in darkness terrify him, lead to his public humiliation, to proof of his fear. He calls the police to protect him from phantoms of his imagination. Gloria, trying to blot the memory of his cowardice, clamps her eyes so tightly that "blue moons formed," but even these fail to outshine reality (p. 160).

Before his marriage, Anthony hears, or imagines he hears, sounds of lovers in the dark, but the sound of a woman's laughter blots out these romantic sounds. This laughter, raucous, a sound from life, disturbs Anthony: "Life was that sound out there, that ghastly reiterated female sound" (p. 150). Laughter in the dark, possibly a coarse joke. Even on the night before his wedding, Anthony fears life.

The cold February of the Patch's love and expectation soon blasts their spring love, and winter dusk is absolutely black. Anthony and Gloria talk in darkness, hurling scorn back and forth until Anthony, unable to tolerate the dark, rises to switch on the light. For Anthony, neither light nor dark offer refuge. Both hold so many terrors that he might say with Milton's Satan, "I myself am hell." Gloria resides there with him, but in another compartment. Life together has grown so dull that despite acute financial distress, Anthony and Gloria never resist an expensive party when night falls. Both day and night are hell for the damned.

For Anthony, only man-made light—electric or fire—promises protection from life. Long before his collapse, he "often read until he was tired and . . . fell asleep with the lights on" (p. 7). A hypochondriac and physical coward, Anthony would like to sleep forever with the lights on. His major problem is fear of life. The sights, sounds, smells of New York, the teeming life of the city cause wilting depression. Anthony retreats to his own apartment to contemplate in the dark. Night sounds and the luminous clock remind him not of life, not of experiences in the real world, but of "a fantastic romance he had lately read in which cities had been bombed from aerial trains . . . ." (p. 27). The following paragraph sums up his entire existence and attitude as anti-life:

> There were the bells and the continued low blur of auto horns from Fifth Avenue, but his own street was silent and *he was safe in here from all the threat of life.* . . . The arc-light shining into his window seemed for this hour like the moon, only brighter and more beautiful. (p. 27; italics mine)

Anthony *would* find artificial light "brighter and more beautiful" than the moon. He fears the natural, the real. He seeks sanctuary in his well-appointed bathroom. Its major feature, according to Anthony, is the absence of outside exposure. He has made it a citadel lighted by a single electric bulb of his choice.

The fireplace, as romantic a light as the moon, frequently illumines Anthony's apartment. He and Maury spend hours discussing themselves by firelight, and once they discuss Gloria's tan. When Richard Caramel and Gloria visit Anthony, the illumination, appropriately, is firelight and electric bulb. Anthony studies Gloria in the glow of the lamp: "On a photograph she must have been completely classical, almost cold—but now the glow of her hair and cheeks, at once flushed and fragile, made her the most living person he had ever seen" (pp. 57–58). She is lovely, of course, but not living. She fears life as much as Anthony does. This cold, classical face can look at Anthony only for a short period before life overwhelms her: "Her glance rested on him a moment and then flitted past him—to the Italian bracketed-lamps clinging like luminous turtles at intervals along the walls . . . ." (p. 58). Gloria, too, prefers artificial light to the sun, chooses artifact over life.

Safe in his apartment fortress, Anthony forgets life outside:

> It was black dark without now and Anthony wondered that his apartment had ever seemed gray—so warm and friendly were the books and pictures on the walls and the good Bounds offering tea from a respectful shadow and the three nice people giving out waves of interest and laughter back and forth across the happy fire. (p. 61)

As anti-life as Anthony, Gloria experiences a blend of misery and terror when she fears she might have a child. Frightened in twilight, she pleads for light—not to examine her life, but to prolong the day, which, she perceives, is shorter than those of June:

> The lights snapped on and it was as though blue drapes of softest silk had been dropped behind the windows and the door. Her pallor, her immobility, without grief now, or joy, awoke his sympathy. (p. 204)

In this light, Gloria decides to be true to herself, to abort the child.

Because Anthony and Gloria opt for romance, not life, the war seems to offer them a chance to view each other again in a romantic light. Fitzgerald hints possible reconciliation, then undercuts it with this light image: "Through the dark light of enclosed train-sheds their glances stretched across a hysterical area, foul with yellow sobbing and the smells of poor women" (p. 309). No romance here, no possibility. And the wartime romance with Dot proves as barren as his marriage with Gloria.

Back in New York after the war, Anthony sees Broadway as a "riot of light" (p. 355). Jaded, he notices only bright, chaotic light. And at Gloria's screen test, lights blare in her eyes, reducing director Debris to a disembodied voice uttering commands behind the glare (p. 400). The stage-lights show Gloria as she is, prove conclusively that she is no longer a romantic lead; her last illusion sears in the lights.

Anthony's last illusion also dries up in light. Maury snubs him as the pitiful beggar he has become, leaves him standing in a light circle cast by the street lamp. Perhaps Anthony sees himself clearly for a moment. At any rate, he reacts desperately, goes to Boul' Mich' and engages Bloekman in a disastrous fight.

Generally, though, man-made light either distorts reality or creates a haze over it. Fitzgerald uses an interesting light image to describe this effect of Gloria upon Anthony:

> Gloria had lulled Anthony's mind to sleep. She . . . hung like a brilliant curtain across his door-ways, shutting out the light of the sun. In those first years what he believed bore invariably the stamp of Gloria; he saw the sun always through the pattern of the curtain. (p. 191)

Anthony finds Gloria's voice "full of laughter undefined as the varying shadows playing between fire and lamp upon her hair" (p. 60). To him she is a

> sun, radiant, growing, gathering light and storing it—then after an eternity pouring it forth in a glance, the fragment of a sentence, to that part of him that cherished all beauty and all illusion. (p. 73)

Illusion is the central word. Anthony creates the light he sees in Gloria. Only Anthony sees this light, yet the reader sees all there is to see.

That light fades. In the bleak November of their love, they find "a lusterless sun peering bleakly in at the windows" (p. 292). As the sun tries vainly to break through, they learn that Adam Patch has cut them from his will. Their love can brook no reality as momentous as impending poverty, even though they do not yet know what "poverty" means.

The image of light trying to penetrate recurs. After an orgy, Gloria awakens, heavily hung over, to find an anemic February sun trying to pass through leaded window panes. But the Patches let no sun into their lives, even though Gloria finds morning without it "rusty and chaotic" (p. 221). And the image of an external, man-made force obscuring light occurs once more in the novel. The major image of the trip from New York to Camp Hooker is one of smoke, which obscures light. This is in keeping with the general confusion of a troop train; more particularly, though, it symbolizes Anthony's state of mind, now and in general. He sees nothing clearly. He even reads by a "dim yellow light" (p. 316). During the day, the sun that penetrates the train windows is a "tired and ancient sun, yellow as parchment and stretched out of shape in transit" (p. 317). Such light alters spiritual and physical vision. Neither Anthony nor Gloria ever see by better light, however.

Dirt-Disease-Decay Imagery

If light-dark imagery accentuated an anti-life attitude on the part of the characters in *The Beautiful and Damned,* the dirt-disease-decay imagery adds even greater emphasis to that theme. In fact dirt-disease-decay imagery forms the very essence of *The Beautiful and Damned,* as is proper in a book about the disintegration of two beautiful people. And for a novel about youth, *This Side of Paradise,* too, features a wide array of dirt-disease-decay imagery.

In *This Side of Paradise* Amory begins his life acutely conscious of disease because of his mother, Beatrice, a world-class hypochondriac. Proud of her delicacy, fretful of body and soul, Beatrice entertains corps of doctors and priests waiting to serve as she gains and loses health, gains and loses faith. When her breakdown finally occurs, it bears a "suspicious resemblance to delirium tremens" (p. 8). Constantly with his mother, Amory experiences early both illness and alcohol. Because his mother's apricot cordial pleases him, he samples enough for intoxication, after which he "succumbed to a vulgar, plebeian reaction" (p. 5).

Egotism often emerges as hypochondria, and Amory, "The Romantic Egotist," mirrors his mother in this regard. He revels in the role of magnificent dissolute courting destruction. Seeking sympathy as his mother does, he boasts to young Myra St. Clare that "I been smoking too much. I've got a t'bacca heart" (p. 12). One real illness during adolescence—a burst appendix—terminates his constant travels with his mother and quite probably enables him to become a genuine human being, not just a poseur with a head full of imaginary ills. At the bursting of the appendix, Beatrice wields sufficient frantic power to turn the ocean liner back toward America. As the narrator says, "if it was not life, it was magnificent" (p. 8).

Appendicitis frees Amory from his eccentric mother, but she still sees him occasionally. After one prolonged absence, she wants to detail for him how he has neglected his heart. She also mentions her latest breakdown, a "sturdy, gallant feat" (p. 21). At Princeton Amory receives a loving letter from Beatrice, the bulk of which admonishes him not to wear his summer underwear in winter: "It not only inclines a young man to pneumonia and infantile paralysis, but to all forms of lung trouble" (p. 101). But by this time Beatrice wields scant influence. Without her, Amory has fewer phantoms to fight, and as Burne Holiday proves when he survives diphtheria, real disease can be conquered. Burne loses the prize he sought—first place on the *Princetonian*—but returns to win it another year. Holiday, however, is made of sterner stuff than is Amory, who flunks out of school partially because of illness. The kind of hypochondria instilled in Amory can be treated, never cured.

The hypochondria motif manifests itself most blatantly in the shock Amory suffers when Dick Humbird appears as the devil.[16] Thinking Amory drunk, his companions accuse him of fearing a "purple zebra" (p. 113). This scene, which equates sin with filth, weakens Amory, makes him sick, though perhaps not as sick as the reader before the scene ends.[17] At any rate, Amory stands absolutely and self-righteously convinced of the filthiness of Broadway. Supposedly changed, he heads back to the purity of Princeton in such a state that the "presence of a painted woman across the aisle filled him with a fresh burst of sickness and he changed to another car" (p. 118). Far more disgusting than a simple hypochondriac, Amory surrenders to monstrous self-indulgence, to morbid histrionics. Amory's diseases all reside in his head, but fortunately this one lasts only for one chapter. Fitzgerald must have had this scene in mind when he wrote to Perkins eighteen years after the publication of *This Side of Paradise:* "Looking it over, I think it is now one of the funniest books since *Dorian Gray* in its utter spuriousness."[18] He completed that sentence with these words: "And then, here and there, I find a page that is very real and living."[19] Most critics would concede that, too.

Fitzgerald never thoroughly delves into the problem of corruption in *This Side of Paradise*. Amory, for example, gets totally fed up with the advertising business, quits, embarks on a four-day spree that culminates in his being beaten up. This is not real decay, not genuine squalor, however. Next to the prolonged debauchery of Anthony Patch in *The Beautiful and Damned,* Amory's drunken spree ranks as a simple prank. And Amory feels none of the pain, the humiliation that Dick Diver experiences after a beating at the hands of taxi drivers in *Tender Is the Night.* Just another learning experience, this is part of his education, his initiation.

Near the end of the novel, a corruption conceit functions as a fairly effective mirror of Amory's mind. Depressed, down and out after the death of Darcy and the marriage of Rosalind, Amory conjures images of filth. No great lover of mankind at this point, Amory contemplates "dirty restaurants where careless, tired people helped themselves to sugar with their own used coffee-spoons, leaving hard brown deposits in the bowl" (p. 256). He continues with this speculation concerning humanity:

> It was not so bad where there were only men or else only women; it was when they were vilely herded together that it all seemed so rotten. It was some shame that women gave off at having men see them tired and poor—it was some disgust that men had for women who were tired and poor. It was dirtier than any battle-field he had ever seen, harder to contemplate than any actual hardship moulded in mire and sweat and danger, it was an atmosphere wherein birth and marriage and death were loathsome, secret things. (p. 256)

This attitude is squeamish, anti-life, especially in one about to embrace socialism. Amory admits that he sees only "coarseness, physical filth and stupidity" (p. 256).

Except that Amory does not view himself as a saint, his state of mind here resembles that of the devil scene. Here, however, images of filth and decay actually convey Amory's mental condition. Humbird, hoofed and horned, a one-dimensional allegory of evil, elicits no response from the reader. Compare the impact of this comic refugee from a morality play with that of the image of "dirty restaurants where careless, tired people helped themselves to sugar with their own used coffee-spoons . . . ." One image, obviously from the experience and imagination of the author, shows Amory's state of mind; the other image shows nothing, gets in the way.

In this desolate frame of mind, Amory resurrects Beatrice, whom he has forgotten for 150 pages. He wonders if she went to heaven, concludes she missed that goal. It is appropriate that he remember her in this morbid hour, just as it is appropriate that he recall Froggie Parker's mother's warning that "sitting on a wet substance gave appendicitis" (p. 259). His recalling Beatrice, hypochondriac of the western world, and the absurd advice concerning disease from Froggie Parker's mother, places in perspective the validity of his present attitude. Here Fitzgerald gains distance from the protagonist, and the images work. The absurdity of both Beatrice and of Mrs. Parker's edict casts ironic light on the corruption images. The reader takes less seriously Amory's contemplation of the filthy state of French rivers, or his grotesque curiosity concerning the present state of Humbird's body. Present and past swamp him, and in his depression he fails to fend them off; yet when Fitzgerald skillfully undercuts images of genuine decay with the reminder of hypochondria and absurdity, he intimates that Amory's state of desolation will not hold constant until the end of the novel.

In light of these images of decay, Amory's conversion to socialism appears as temporary as his deep depression. While the reintroduction of Beatrice and Mrs. Parker modifies the images of filth and decay, these images *still* exist, *still* provide the single graphic view of Amory's state of mind and his concept of humanity. Reviewing his past, Amory *still* looks " futilely back at the stream of his life, at its glitterings and dirty shallows" (p. 260). Finding no meaning, he decides he would like to "deteriorate pleasantly," that he would like to leap into the "long chute of indulgence which led, after all, only to the artificial lake of death" (p. 262). In this state of unexamined pessimism, "his instinct perceived the fetidness of poverty, but no longer ferreted out the deeper evils of pride and sensuality" (p. 262). Combined, this confused moral state and self and human condemnation lead Amory to a blurred concept of socialism. Nowhere does he show evidence that he could even define socialism; this, however, never slows his conversion, never impedes his discussion of his new politics.

As the novel ends, Amory ostensibly is still searching, still hopeful, even though he sees "nature as a rather coarse phenomenon composed largely of flowers that, when closely inspected, appeared moth-eaten . . . ." (p. 279). Anti-life, he nevertheless emerges a moderately cheerful man after observing the "rusty vaults" in the cemetery; the education provided by life leaves him disillusioned, but hardly defeated by all that his generation has lost, by values decayed. He continues the search; the only ominous note as the novel ends comes from his willingness to accept simplistic answers, from his habit of reducing life to aphorism: "The problem of evil had solidified into the problem of sex" (p. 280). One trouble with a talent as potent as Fitzgerald's is that he can make utter nonsense sound plausible, even probable.

From dirt-disease-decay imagery, the suggestion emerges that Amory, by temperament and early training, inclines toward hypochondria. Given the emphasis on the education-of-a-young-man theme in this novel, Fitzgerald probably wanted the imagery to move Amory from an egotistical hypochondriac to a human being aware of something outside himself.[20] The images are too muddled to show this or any other definite movement, however. But the images show clearly enough a man of melancholic temperament. Fitzgerald implies that the introspective, exploring Amory can overcome his tendency toward self-righteous morbidity. Amory's admission that "I know myself . . . but that is all" suggests that he has earned the requisite humility for a man who would search and not be bound by preconceptions, who would continue to learn and discover. Unlike later Fitzgerald protagonists, Amory, at the novel's close, retains the strength to struggle.

A major theme in *The Beautiful and Damned* is that life is meaningless. Dirt-disease-decay imagery certainly supports that theme. For the beautiful, life holds infinite promise; but these beautiful people, born into a corrupt world, suffering Adam's curse of mortality are damned long before they know it, indeed from birth, and the fulfillment of the curse comes when they learn of their damnation. Or so Fitzgerald would seem to be saying—if the novel worked. Unfortunately this novel projects no universal condition, convinces no one that *all* of the beautiful are damned, that if these people must suffer hell, the rest of us languish with no shred of hope. Who does not feel superior to Anthony and Gloria? The declines of Dick Diver, Jay Gatsby, Monroe Stahr, the fall of Michael Henchard, the damnation of Faustus, the blinding of Oedipus, the utter defeat of Macbeth—these tragedies send waves of warning to every man. Each tragic protagonist, if not very good, stands at least very strong. If these men fall, all men face danger.

I would be amazed, though, if any reader felt his own position precarious because Anthony and Gloria failed to survive corruption. Both enjoy physical beauty, but nothing else. Heirs to every flaw of flesh, they stand defenseless against time. They fall, as they must, but not necessarily because of universal corruption. Corruption ravages the world, as *The Beautiful and Damned* shows, but Anthony and Gloria would succumb no matter how much or how little corruption threatened them. The story of two beautiful people fighting and losing against incredible odds would have produced a powerful novel; it always does. *The Beautiful and Damned,* however, is not an angry shout protesting the dirt, disease, and decay that plague men and women on the road to the grave; it is a whimper. The weakness of the characters saps the irony. The novel documents individual corruption and decline, not the inevitable fall of proud strength.

Even so, the pattern of corruption imagery exists so clearly as to mark this novel a technical advancement over *This Side of Paradise.* References to corruption appear early in this long novel and continue until the end. In the first reference, Anthony wonders if he himself might be "oil on a clean pond" (p. 3). Oddly, as the novel progresses, this metaphor attains a certain aptness. But the figure is not totally appropriate. Life is not a clean pond, and by the end, Anthony is more sluggish and corrupt than oil. Regardless of Anthony's worries, however, Anthony and Gloria at first seem safe from corruption, or anything approaching it, including mortality. When Anthony asks Gloria why she plans to marry him, she answers,

> Because you're so clean. You're sort of blowy clean like I am. There's two sorts, you know. One's like Dick; he's clean like polished pans. You and I are clean like streams and winds. I can tell whenever I see a person whether he is clean, and if so, which kind of clean he is. (p. 131)

Balanced against later deterioration and corruption, this statement becomes a bitterly amusing irony.

This very cleanliness is symptomatic of a problem Anthony and Gloria share: both are squeamish to the point of being anti-life. Anthony, for example, "was very clean, in appearance and in reality, with that especial cleanness borrowed from beauty" (p. 9). Anthony, who considers himself and his life a work of art, never gets close enough to real life to get dirty. Reality disgusts him, and he fears that ultimate reality—time. One victim of time, a woman on the street, strikes him as a "piece of wind-worried old orange peel" (p. 25). When he meets Mr. Gilbert, the theme continues: "The young man and the old touched flesh; Mr. Gilbert's hand was soft, worn away to the pulpy semblance of squeezed grapefruit" (p. 41). Anthony perceives the ravages of life as too vile to contemplate. In fact, one reason Anthony cannot find anything to do is that everything seems vulgar in his eyes. He thinks of "himself in Congress rooting around in the litter of that incredible pigsty . . . ." (p. 56). Even Congress contains too much real life for Anthony. In this sedate legislative body, men grow old.

Gloria is a greater fanatic about cleanliness than Anthony, especially as their lives grow more deeply disoriented. Women especially must be clean. Judging women, she is

> concerned with the question of whether women were or were not clean. By uncleanliness she meant a variety of things, a lack of pride, a slackness in fibre and most of all, the unmistakable aura of promiscuity. (pp. 234–35)

When the decline begins in earnest, this description fits Gloria.

A woman conducting a desperate search for cleanliness should not meet Joe Hull, a refugee from the real world, a world neither Anthony nor Gloria have ever seen. Gloria reacts badly to Joe, views him as a "personality filthy under its varnish, like smallpox spots under a layer of powder" (p. 243). Anthony reacts the same way to filth of any kind. Heading toward his army base, Anthony might lodge a thousand legitimate complaints; what really disgusts him, though, is that the straw seats on the train need cleaning (p. 313). At Camp Hooker, he smells garbage (p. 317).

Like Anthony, Gloria takes no stimulation from real-life situations. When she decides to become a rich, famous actress, she visits a motion picture employment agency, but

> her sense of smell worked against her good intentions. The employment agency smelt as though it had been dead a very long time. . . . She walked briskly out into the farthest recesses of Central Park and remained so long that she caught a cold . . . trying to air the employment agency out of her walking suit. (p. 370)

Anthony feels similar disgust when he tries to become a salesman. Appalled by squalor, he plummets directly toward the most squalid of lives (p. 377). His foray into the world of work causes him to get raving drunk and then to pass out when he gets home. Gloria finds him with "his breath filling the air with an unpleasant pungency, his hand still clutching his open brief case" (p. 388). Thus ends Anthony's career as salesman.

At the slightest confrontation with reality, Anthony and Gloria either get drunk or sick. Illness, in fact, dictates much in the lives of the Patches. An attack of sclerosis led old Adam Patch to a greater sickness, the illness of the reformer (p. 4). Adam started a chain of illness when he married an "anaemic lady of thirty, Alecia Withers," who had borne Anthony's father, Adam Ulysses Patch (p. 5). Anthony's mother died when he was only five, and on the single trip Anthony took with him, "his father died with much sweating and grunting and crying aloud for air" (p. 6). From his devitalized family, Anthony inherits little of value except the promise of money and a "hypochondriacal imagination" (p. 7).

Disease plays curious games in the lives of Anthony and Gloria. It is part of Anthony's luck that his blood pressure keeps him from being an officer, but does not spare him the lot of an enlisted man. Perhaps no one is temperamentally suited to be an enlisted man, but Anthony is less so than most. He becomes ill, depressed in the state-side army. At the peak of his military depression—shortly after his confinement for being drunk and AWOL—he suffers an attack of influenza. His mind runs too much on reality, and the disease relieved him, perhaps maintained his sanity. But disease brings no sustained luck. When his company goes to Camp Mills, Anthony gets no leave because that installation lies under quarantine because of influenza. He is stuck in a "dreary muddle, cold, windswept, and filthy, with the accumulated dirt incident to the passage through of many divisions" (p. 353).

As influenza spared Anthony a mental breakdown, it does the same for Gloria. When she decides to see Bloekman about a job in the movies, she is spared any direct action by an attack of influenza that flowers into double pneumonia. Under the protection of this illness, she hunts in her mind for her mother:

All she wanted was to be a little girl, to be efficiently taken care of by some yielding yet superior power, stupider and steadier than herself. It seemed that the only lover she had ever wanted was a lover in a dream. (p. 394)

No lover of real life, Gloria, and even disease helps her avoid reality.

But time, that most uncompromising aspect of reality, frightens Anthony and Gloria more than anything else. They see in old Adam Patch a living example of the ravages of time. Time has treated the old man barbarously; he has decayed even before he dons sack cloth and returns to dust. Time "sucked in the cheeks and the chest and the girth of an arm and leg. It had tyrannously demanded his teeth, one by one, suspended his small eyes in dark-bluish sacks, tweeked out his hair . . . ." (p. 14). Time renders him a "feeble, unintelligent old man" (p. 14). It appears that his next step is the grave, that he can deteriorate no further, but he does. Through the chief agent of decay, time, Adam grows a "little more wizened and grizzly as time played its ultimate chuckling tricks" (p. 138).

Time is subtle at first, and Anthony and Gloria barely perceive its tricks. Its first theft after a deliciously joyous honeymoon is romance: "The breathless idyl [sic] left them, fled on to other lovers; they looked around one day and it was gone, how they scarcely knew" (p. 156). Time here works with the subtlety of an undefined nostalgic ache. It is not always so.

The most explicit alliance between time and decay occurs at Arlington, the preserved home of General Robert E. Lee. Buses bring tourists who leave trails of peanut shells. Gloria, who knows instinctively about *other people* and *places* what Gatsby never learns—that the past can neither be repeated nor preserved—experiences disgust at the spectacle. Explaining to Anthony that beautiful old things cannot be preserved, she says,

> Beautiful things grow to a certain height and then they fail and fade off, breathing out memories as they decay. And just as any period decays, the things of that period should decay too, and in that way they're preserved in the few hearts like mine that react to them.

Gloria asks the crucial question, certainly rhetorical, as she damns all monuments: "Do you think they've left a breath of 1860 here?" (p. 166). However much one disagrees with Gloria, her attitude is healthier than Anthony's. Anthony never understands that time passes, wreaks irreparable damage. To Gloria, intellectually at least, the passage of time gives meaning to life: "There's no beauty without poignancy and there's no poignancy without the feeling that it's going, men, names, books, houses—bound for dust—mortal" (p. 167). Philosophically, Gloria celebrates the natural cycle of life, while Anthony shies from birth as quickly as from decay; yet her understanding of life helps not at all when her own beauty starts to fade, when age dims the luster of her hair. Philosophy? Good for judging, for advising others, but Gloria finds it worthless when applied to daily life.

If time decays people and objects, it wreaks more serious damage on the dream. Time steals from Anthony and Gloria the illusion that they are the first, the only lovers the world ever knew. Time takes away and, in the case of Anthony and Gloria, gives nothing in return. No inner reserve prepares them for a gray world without romance (p. 192). When they no longer view their love as unique, they alter that love. As Shakespeare says, in "the marriage of true minds . . . Love is not love/ which alters when it alteration finds . . . ." The lovers made in heaven now quarrel so fiercely in a public place that Anthony forces Gloria into a cab. Force was not part of the original agreement until time altered the contract. And this fight proves Gloria, erstwhile free spirit, remarkably fragile: "She seemed such a pathetic little thing now, broken and dispirited, humiliated beyond the measure of her lot to bear" (p. 201).

Inevitably, time and life take their toll, perhaps sooner than necessary because of the continual circle of parties that make up the existence of the Patches:

> Gloria noticed that she lacked complete muscular control; when she moved it was not a sinuous motion. . . . It was a tremendous effort of her nervous system as though each time she were hypnotizing herself into performing an impossible action. (p. 219)

Time renders Anthony a hopeless drunk; Gloria ages. When Gloria turns twenty-nine, dirty snow covers the ground. Seeing herself as desperately near old age, she takes a screen test. The set impresses her because it is clean. She does not have to smell the grease paint or see the "soiled and tawdry costumes" she saw on stage (p. 398). Nothing from real life intrudes, nothing revolts her. Yet time steals her golden girlhood, leaves her nothing.

In essence, *The Beautiful and Damned* is about decay, the ravages of time, but more specifically, personal deterioration. For Anthony, that decay starts the day of their marriage. Early on his wedding day, he awakens, examines himself in the mirror, finds himself unusually

> white—half a dozen small imperfections stood out against the morning pallor of his complexion and overnight he had grown the faint stubble of a beard—the general effect, he fancied, was unprepossessing, haggard, half unwell. (p. 150)

Anthony's mirror reflects present, foretells future decay.

Anthony and Gloria base their love on physical perfection and the expectation of vast amounts of money. Physical familiarity begets boredom, and they tire of the gray house in Marietta, their first home after the honeymoon. The seat of ennui rests not within the house, of course, but within themselves. They blame their troubles on the house, though, and resolve to leave it. But by drunken accident, they renew the lease. The car, too, deteriorates with the marriage. It becomes a "rattling mass of hypochondriacal metal" (p. 232). Mistake follows mistake, and they lose luxury after luxury.

Wherever they go, they find boredom and poverty. Like Satan hurled from heaven, they carry hell within themselves:

> Before they had been two months in the little apartment of Fifty-seventh Street, it had assumed for both of them the . . . almost material taint that had impregnated the gray house. . . . There was the odor of tobacco always—both of them smoken incessantly; it was in their clothes, their blankets, the curtains, and the ash-littered carpets. Added . . . was the aura of stale wine, with its inevitable suggestion of beauty gone foul and revelry remembered in disgust. . . . People broke things; people became sick in Gloria's bathroom; people spilled wine; people made unbelievable messes of the kitchenette. (p. 296)

Decay is general. Even Richard Caramel's talent has decayed. His later prose fails to compare with his first novel, a book destined to die before the birth of another generation.

Many found purpose in the war, solace in the army's simple routine, but not Anthony. Rather, army life hastens his decline:

> Anthony's affair with Dorothy Raycroft was the inevitable result of his increasing carelessness about himself. . . . He could say "No!" neither to man nor woman; borrower and temptress alike found him tender-minded and pliable. Indeed he seldom made decisions at all, and when he did they were but half-hysterical resolves formed in the panic at some aghast and irreparable awakening. (p. 324)

Anthony's foil at Camp Hooker is Pop Donnelly, a platoon sergeant with a "complexion shot full of holes" (p. 370). Like Anthony of the future, this man is always drunk, "worn thin by drink" (p. 330).

Even as they fall apart, Anthony and Gloria maintain their respective philosophies. Of course philosophy does them absolutely no good, but they maintain it. Anthony, for example, breaks up with Dot and explains pompously that gratified desires "turn to dust" (p. 341), a reference to Gloria as well as Dot. The irony is that Anthony misses the truth of his platitude when finally he inherits the money. He still carries a baggage of great expectations. And Gloria, aware that her dream of a movie career was only a dream, looks in the mirror, appraises herself:

> "Oh, my pretty face," she whispered, passionately grieving. "Oh, my pretty face! Oh, I don't want to live without my pretty face! Oh, what's *happened?* " (p. 404)

The bold philosophy that bade Lee's relics to crumble to dust breaks up before tiny wrinkles in her face.

Gloria's face shows wear, but Anthony's deterioration is more marked: "His stomach was limp weight against his belt; his flesh had softened. . . . He was thirty-two and his mind was a bleak and disordered wreck" (p. 406). Even Caramel grows fat, but his deterioration is mild next to Anthony's; that paragon of cleanliness now wears dirty shirts with frayed cuffs (p. 418). And Gloria's hair has "changed . . . from a rich gold dusted with red to an unresplendent light brown" (p. 425). Gloria views this as tragic, and Caramel takes scant joy in fat, but the serious falling off occurs all within Anthony. That former paradigm of decorum starts a senseless fight with Bloekman, once his wife's lover, who beats him bloody, knocks out one of his teeth, leaves him alone to spit blood and spew ironic laughter.

Finally, Anthony descends to second childhood—as Gloria wanted to do during her illness—and once more collects stamps. When he inherits the money, he sails to Europe as a "bundled figure seated in a wheel chair . . . ." (p. 447). Anthony and Gloria have shattered their own lives, have destroyed Shuttleworth's life. (He bolted himself in a hotel room and shot himself when the court failed to award him the money.) The motif of dirt, disease, and decay pervades the book, becomes the major theme and source of irony. The final irony is that Gloria, who always sought and admired cleanliness, no longer seems clean herself. To the girl who provides the eyes for the reader's view of Anthony and Gloria on their voyage abroad, Gloria appears "sort of dyed and unclean" (p. 448).

Water Imagery

The last image pattern to be considered in this chapter is water imagery. A great theme carrier and source of irony in *The Great Gatsby, Tender Is the Night,* and

The Last Tycoon, water imagery is too muddled to form a pattern in *This Side of Paradise* and not well enough developed to be effective in *The Beautiful and Damned.*[21] In *The Beautiful and Damned,* in fact, water is far less important than dirt-disease-decay imagery, the pattern that bears the greatest burden of carrying the theme of the futility of life. That water is not as important in Fitzgerald's first two novels as it will be in his mature work, however, does not mean there is nothing to be learned from observing how Fitzgerald uses it. If water imagery is diffuse in *This Side of Paradise,* that shows just how much Fitzgerald had progressed as an artist by the time he wrote *The Great Gatsby.*

Various water images in *This Side of Paradise* fall outside the main pattern—that of the restorative power of water followed by the loss of that power. Snow, for example, is a form of water, but certainly not restorative. Because the affair between Amory and Myra St. Claire, his hostess at the bobsledding party, begins in winter, one might presume that at best the love will be transient. Not symbolism, however, but the prematurity of the emotion dooms this love. The lovers are thirteen years old. The scene is atypical; most affairs in Fitzgerald's fiction flower in a glow of hope, then wilt in bitter spring. No one expects this love to be eternal. Thus there is no irony.

Older lovers make the affair between Amory and Isabelle more plausible, but it is destined to go the way of the earlier infatuation because it, too, is engendered in snow. As Isabelle tries to envision Amory, she watches "the snow glide by in the frosty morning" (p. 62). Winter-born love lacks promise; once more the scene is atypical because without images of hope, no irony exists.[22]

It is also unlike Fitzgerald to use water as a staple in a romantic cliché, but he does so in *This Side of Paradise.* Beatrice fashions a weary water image to describe one of her phony visions during her breakdown. Borrowing the tiredest of images from romantic literature, she says, "I saw bronze rivers lapping marble shores" (p. 21). Amory, of course, is absolutely his mother's son during his early years. For him water conjures romantic heroism as he dreams during a football game at his prep school, St. Regis. A mythic hero, he views himself as "one with the sea-rover on the prow of a Norse galley, one with Roland and Horatius, Sir Nigel and Ted Coy, scraped and stripped into trim and then flung by his own will into the breach, beating back the tide" (pp. 31–32). Born of an identical romantic impulse, the visions of both mother and son are hued in deep irony. This water imagery differs from that in later works because the main thrust of these scenes is humor; water imagery in later works—and in some scenes from this novel—forms a more bitter pattern of irony.

In *This Side of Paradise,* the initial reference to water occurs when Beatrice advises Amory to take a hot bath to relax his nerves. Thus even in the opening pages of his first novel, Fitzgerald refers to water as medicinal, as a restorative. But many pages and water images intervene before he reinforces this image and begins to establish a pattern. In a chapter entitled "A Dark Symbolic Interlude,"

Fitzgerald has Amory reach back to archetypal roots, back to the very roots of the human race. Lying on the damp grass during the rainy April of his first Princeton year, Amory nearly becomes one with the ages. In the rain, he is almost born out of his own ego. His romantic vision in rain and fog shows him "the transience and unimportance of the campus figures except as holders of the apostolic succession" (p. 54). Promising to work harder next year, to become worthy of the tradition he aspires to join, he suddenly comprehends his place in the scheme of the university, and by extension, the universe. With undergraduate naiveté, he describes the heart of Princeton as a "stream where he was to throw a stone whose faint ripple would be vanishing almost as it left his hand. As yet he had given nothing, he had taken nothing" (p. 54).

The dream over, he undercuts his noble sentiments with this awkwardly-phrased observation: "'I'm very damn wet,' he said aloud to the sundial" (p. 55). The scene is flawed because it is too obviously symbolic. It exists because Fitzgerald decided to plant a symbol, not because of its inherent necessity in the narrative. Artistically clumsy and a blatant shout, this scene nevertheless sounds a major Fitzgerald theme. Born of this wet interlude is a dream teeming with possibilities.

Water frequently makes Amory pensive and even more romantic than usual. Awed by the ocean at Deal Beach, where he has gone on a joyous journey with several classmates, "Amory ate little, having seized a chair where he could watch the sea and feel the rock of it" (p. 78). After lunch they sit and smoke, quietly, thoughtfully. The sea, beautiful by day, at night becomes a body of mystery, of infinite possibility: "The evening sea was a new sensation, for all its color and mellow age was gone, and it seemed the bleak waste that made the Norse gods sad" (p. 78). The timeless sea flows back to the Norse gods, washed the beginning, will wash the end. The sea inspires awe, induces a feeling of tragic nostalgia that leads men to seek some indefinable thing irretrievably lost.

In this novel, Fitzgerald also associates water with evil. Closing "The Egoist Considers" chapter, Amory discovers evil inherent in sex and in the life around Broadway. Amory suffers a dark night of the soul, which too closely resembles that of the far superior retreat scene in *Portrait of the Artist as a Young Man*. Out on the town with a friend and two girls, Amory discovers a hoofed devil whose face is that of his old idol, Dick Humbird. On this boozy night rich in possibilities for sexual adventure, the devil links sex and evil. Amory drinks nothing, participates in no active sex, but the mere temptation terrifies him. He condemns his past. His friend, who does not see through the eyes of a recent convert, "seems no longer Sloan of the debonair humor and happy personality, but only one of the evil faces that whirled along the turbid stream" (p. 117). The water conceit, the turbid-stream image, continues when Amory, prodded by the odor of tonics and powders in the barbershop, recalls the seductive smile of the girl he had just left: "In the door way of his room a sudden blackness flowed around him like a divided river" (p. 117).

The devil vision makes Amory a new man. No longer does he admire Sloan; Humbird has appeared as Satan; and if ever man suffered rebirth, Amory did: "It was raining torrents," and that, in all Fitzgerald novels, is the weather for rebirth (p. 118). Far from the filth of Broadway, Amory approaches Princeton with the joy of a man new and clean: he watches "the yellow squares of light filtered through the rain" (p. 118). A new man in May, baptized by spring rain, and next morning, "May birds hailed the sun on last night's rain" (p. 119).

Very neat. Beyond question the water imagery in this devil scene is consistent with that in other Fitzgerald novels. Yet how might one take this scene seriously? The symbolism stands out as if set in boldface type. The author has used many words, said little; the scene stands as a monumental embarrassment to all who admire Fitzgerald. The rebirth and dark night of the soul are at best watered Joyce. Unlike Stephen Dedalus, who struggles fiercely with his redemption before resuming his career as artist, Amory slips back into his dilettantish ways on the first page of the following chapter.

Amory also might become a new man through the thoughtful Clara, with whom he fancies himself in love. Here, too, a water image signifies possibilities: "Sometimes they would go to church together . . . and he would walk beside her and revel in her cheeks moist from the soft water in the new air" (p. 144). Difficult as it may be to revel in someone's cheeks, the promise of love exists. In Fitzgerald, however, love is doomed, even love formed under ideal conditions. No amount of water—signifying promise and hope—can make a love affair last in a Fitzgerald novel.

Except for tears at the death of love, only two water images appear in connection with the Rosalind affair. Amory's salt tears, of course, hold scant symbolic significance compared to Rosalind's dive from the roof of a "rickety, thirty-foot summer house" (p. 189). Howard Gillespie saw that "Rosalind, her arms spread in a beautiful swan dive, had sailed through the air into the clear water" (p. 189). Whatever her motives—seeking rebirth, merely bored—Rosalind turned to water. She forces Gillespie to make the same dive and then, to humiliate him, complains that his stooping over "took the courage out of it" (p. 189). Water imagery here is secondary to the event itself, which characterizes Rosalind perfectly.

A sentimental Amory looks back on this love, sees it as blessed in water. Symbolic of the affair are "February streets, windwashed by night, blown full of strange half-intermittent damps, bearing on wasted walks in shining wet snow splashed into gleams under the lamps" (p. 219). Fine as that sounds, it makes little sense, bears less relationship to the affair, violent and short, between Amory and Rosalind.

By contrast, the shorter, more violent love between Amory and Eleanor Savage begins when he hears her voice "in a weird chant that soared and hung and fell and blended with the rain" (p. 224). As love blooms, "Amory flushed, happily invisible under the curtain of wind and rain" (p. 224). When Amory learns her name and says she looks as if she would be Eleanor, they share a sense of mystery: "There was a silence as they listened to the rain" (p. 227). This weird temptress in the rain enchants Amory:

> The storm was dying down softly and only the wind kept up its ghostly surge. . . . Amory was in a trance. He felt that each moment was precious. He had never met a girl like that before—she would never seem quite the same to him again. (p. 228)

Mutually fascinated, the lovers walk on paths bejewelled by water: "A transcendent delight seemed to sparkle in every pool of water, for the moon had risen and the storm had scurried away into western Maryland" (p. 230). Even as the affair wanes, Amory uses a love-in-water metaphor to describe his predicament. Curious about his life, wondering if he is wasting it with the fascinating Eleanor, Amory sums up his personality this way:

> For months it seemed that he had alternated between being borne along a stream of love or fascination, or left in an eddy, and in the eddies, he had not desired to think, rather to be picked up on a wave's top and swept along again. (p. 223)

This is a rare moment when Amory admits, his efforts notwithstanding, he is not a mover and shaper of events. He is not always in control.

Summer and the affair simultaneously complete their courses. Perhaps a trifle self-conscious for the role, Eleanor from first to last resembles one of Thomas Hardy's mad women of the earth. Like Eustacia Vye, Arabella, or Tess, Eleanor is not the type to cancel love without a grand gesture. To mark the end of the affair, she plans to ride off the edge of a cliff where "a hundred feet below, a black stream made a sharp line, broken by tiny glints in the swift water" (p. 237). At the last second, though, she opts for life and leaps from the horse, which plunges to its death. The gesture would have immortalized their love in black water below. It would have left a flowing monument to romance. But her courage flagged; she ends not as a romantic legend, but as a tearful, pitiful girl. The affair, which Amory would later call "Summer Storm," concludes with a disappointment tinged by hatred on both sides. Another love baptized in the water of spring fails.

Finished with Eleanor, Amory returns to the sea at Atlantic City. In a passage presaging the ending of *The Great Gatsby,* Amory contemplates the sea's mystery. By the Atlantic at dusk, he is

> lulled by the everlasting surge of changing waves, smelling the half-mournful odor of the salt breeze. The sea, he thought, had treasured its memories deeper than the faithless land. It seemed still to whisper to a Norse Galley ploughing the water world under raven-figured flags, of the British dreadnoughts, gray bulwarks of civilization steaming up through the fog of one dark July into the North Sea. (p. 243)

Alec Connage and friends interrupt these October musings. His mind too full of the ocean and of Rosalind to accommodate the riotous Connage party, Amory takes a short drink, a short ride, and excuses himself to return to sea thoughts. Unfortunately, he does not return to the sea before promising to occupy an excess room that Alec had rented. And here, right at the source of life—the sea—Amory enmeshes himself in the sordid affair of saving Connage from prison for violating the Mann Act. Amory's volunteering to take the blame is a grand, empty gesture, totally impersonal, finally unnecessary. Nothing is born of this sacrifice except the certainty that Connage will later subconsciously hate Amory because of it. Amory leaves, amused, detached. Water no longer serves as a source of strength, of life.

By November, Amory finds himself in New York without money. He watches the people and the "unwelcome November rain" (p. 254). The rain "gave Amory a feeling of detachment, and the numerous unpleasant aspects of city life without money occurred to him" (p. 255). Gray skies and thoughts of poverty lead him to conclude that he dislikes people. Catalysts for this conclusion are the marriage of Rosalind and the death of Msgr. Darcy. In the rain, he contemplates loves he has won, all lost now, and he wonders "what Humbird's body looked like" (p. 258). Solemn, grotesque, these musings lead him to the river, where he rests. "Misfortune is liable to make me a bad man," he decides (p. 260).

Not the water of life, of rebirth, this is the water of weariness, death. Water becomes the "waters of disillusion [that] had left a deposit on his soul, responsibility and a love of life, the faint stirring of old ambitions and unrealized dreams" (p. 282). Amory grows pensive in rain, and a musing Amory is a maudlin Amory. Introspection leads to dullness in Amory and in the novel. Water in later works signals and inspires some of the most impressive prose. In *This Side of Paradise*, water often signals Fitzgerald's least effective writing and strangest syntax. The problem is simple: Fitzgerald cannot yet allow water to function as a symbol created from images. The design is consistent, and if Fitzgerald only trusted himself, the symbol would work because of the pattern. He does not accompany each water image with action that will sustain its meaning, however; he writes a short essay detailing what he had in mind.

The initial reference to water in *The Beautiful and Damned* is curious. Anthony, who has a magnificent bathroom, spends much time there. He decides that if he "had a love he would have hung her picture just facing the tub so that, lost in the soothing steamings of the hot water, he might lie and look up at her and muse warmly and sensuously on her beauty" (p. 12). Anthony retreats to the tub to prepare for any social occasion, familiar to unfamiliar. Seeking rejuvenation through tepid tub water, Anthony is considerably less vital than other Fitzgerald heroes, as the rest of the novel will attest.

The second water reference is even less akin to Fitzgerald's common practice with water imagery. Here the audience at a play, *High Jinks,* is described in an extended water conceit:

> There were jewels dripping from arms and throats and ear-tips of white and rose. . . . Most of all there was the ebbing, flowing, chattering, chuckling, foaming, slow-rolling wave effect of this cheerful sea of people as tonight it poured its glittering torrent into the artificial lake of laughter. (p. 24)

Again, hardly the classic portrait of rejuvenation, of vitality.

The meeting of Gloria, too, is symbolically suspect from the first. Both Anthony and Maury Noble meet her not in soft spring rains, but in winter's frozen snow. Similarly, Anthony's intellectual endeavors seem doomed, if water and weather imagery remain constant. The desire to know about himself and about others like him "sent him out through the soft slush of November to a library which had none of the books he most wanted" (p. 54). That the library might have been barren of books was predictable. Symbolically at least, November's soft slush makes less than solid footing for finding oneself.

Snow as an ominous water image touches everyone from Anthony to novelist Richard Caramel. It ends Caramel's journalistic career. Assigned to cover a parade, but hating snow, Caramel stays at home and writes of the parade he assumes had taken place. But the paraders loved snow no more than Caramel; the parade was cancelled and Caramel's job, because he wrote beautifully of a parade that never occurred, was also cancelled. Snow stops life, activity. It is an agent of paralysis.

Images surrounding the night Anthony and Gloria fall in love—the night he wins her from Bloekman—are for the first time in this novel consistent with the way Fitzgerald will use water imagery through the rest of his career. This and other affairs in Fitzgerald's fiction begin with promise and end with that promise unfulfilled. In this particular case, Anthony and Gloria leave the party and venture into a night

> alive with thaw. . . . For a hushed moment the traffic sounds and the murmur of water flowing in the gutters seemed an illusive and rarified prolongation of that music to which they had lately danced. (p. 101)

Traffic noises and running water that sounds like music may be a trifle incongruous, but nevertheless, this is infatuation. The lover studies Gloria, thinks "her beauty was cool as this damp breeze, as the moist softness of her own lips" (p. 102). Whether the water imagery subtly satirizes the blossoming love, or whether it comments, with equal subtlety, on the magic generated by this beautiful pair, the relationship, doomed and damned, has sprung into being—accompanied by a symphony of traffic sounds and water flowing through the gutter. Yet the rhythm of the prose and the feeling it generates matches that of the absolutely traditional romantic scene; nothing in the tone suggests that this will not be a story where lovers live happily ever after. Only later does the reader worry because the water flows to the gutter.

Just as love roots in thawing waters, the first major quarrel occurs on a night so cold that "moisture froze on his lashes and in the corners of his lips. Everywhere dreariness had come down from the north, settling upon the thin and cheerless street" (pp. 116–17). Hardly designed to endure winter, their southern love withers in north winds. They reconcile during a "mellow damp, promising May and world of summer" (p. 126). For a while the winds blow only balm.

Even at courtship's peak, water imagery occasionally hints at disaster. Often the image is not *purely* romantic: "One afternoon they found front seats on the sunny roof of a bus and rode for hours from the fading square along the sullied river" (p. 135). Scarcely does "sullied" describe the rivers of life and promise. Physically and philosophically, this image of reality stands galaxies from the private swimming pools and private rivers watering their dreams for the future. For themselves they see "Halcyon days like boats drifting along slow-moving rivers" (p. 137), not the sullied rivers of New York.

Gutter water and sullied rivers plunge water images into a minor key of irony. Even the images that merely nourish memories, that feed romance, must be balanced against those tinged by irony. Even the rain image in Gloria's diary becomes suspect:

> There in a graying blur was the record of her first kiss, faded as its intimate afternoon, on a rainy veranda, seven years before. She seemed to remember something one of them had said that day, and yet she could scarcely see the page. She was crying, she told herself, because she could remember only the rain and the wet flowers in the yard and the smell of the damp grass. (p. 148)

Rain becomes a near fetish for the romantic moment; when they marry, the short-lived radiant hour frequently is washed by the quiet summer rain.

Rain, however, expands, grows into something greater than a mere image for enhancing romance. Fitzgerald uses a water image, a striking simile, to describe the drift of their lives in California:

> And as the waves met and splashed and glittered in this most placid of bays, so they joined this group and that, and with them shifted stations, murmuring ever of those strange unsubstantial gaieties that wait just over the next green and fruitful valley. (p. 191)

That simile accurately foreshadows their later existence, their later relationships.

In another simile, Fitzgerald uses a curious water image to describe Gloria's tone of voice during one of their frequent arguments: "Her last words were as gentle as fine snow upon hard ground. But for the moment neither was attending to the other—they were each engaged in perfecting his own attitude" (p. 211). Like any snow image, this is ominous, just as portentous as their failure to listen to each other.

During a "damp and uninspiring" March, Anthony prepares to become a salesman, but his complete lack of enthusiasm dooms the venture. When damp spring fails to inspire, their love wilts as surely as Anthony's resolve to be a salesman. Love further deteriorates during the rains of summer. On a "sultry afternoon late in July," Richard Caramel and Maury Noble bring the disreputable bum,

Joe Hull, to the Patch home. During the dinner—punctuated by rain, by thunder, destroyed by the brazen Joe Hull—Gloria suffers disillusionment with their way of life. On this mad night Tanya, the Japanese butler, plays weird melodies on his flute; Joe Hull juggles and drops candles; and rain and thunder and lightning create chaos in the dining room. Desperate, Gloria flees to her own room:

> Upstairs she fumbled for the electric light switch and missed it in the darkness; a roomful of lightning showed her the button plainly on the wall. But when the impenetrable black shut down, it again eluded her fumbling fingers, so she slipped off her dress and petticoat and threw herself weakly on the dry side of the half-drenched bed. (p. 241)

The mad party calms below, and outside the storm abates, becomes one of those pleasant, seemingly-fertile summer showers that often appear in Fitzgerald's fiction. Lying on the dry side of the bed, hearing the rain, Gloria becomes oppressed; an almost physical force presses on her breast. The intangible oppression takes form as she finds herself, without benefit of petticoat, under the gaze of Joe Hull. Here, with chaos rending the civilized life she knows, she seeks change, rebirth in water:

> She knew what she must do—now, now before it was too late. She must go out into this cool damp, out, away, to feel the wet swish of the grass around her feet, to feel the fresh moisture on her forehead. . . . She must go from this house where the thing hovered that pressed upon her bosom. (p. 243)

Baptismal rains drench her as she leaves the house: "A hundred drops, startled by a flare of wind from a dripping tree, scattered on her and she pressed them gladly to her face with hot hands" (p. 244). Soaked and free, Gloria eludes Anthony in the chase through the fields and over puddles gilded in moonlight. Yet intruders spoil the romantic portrait of a beautiful young girl racing through a wet, moonlit forest; the picture is marred by the hobo who looks like a corpse and by the electric train with an intrusive light and whistle and wheels clacking on rails. The train gone, however, "silence crept down again over the wet country; the faint dripping resumed and suddenly a great shower of drops tumbled upon Gloria, stirring her out of the trance-like stupor which the . . . train had wrought" (p. 246).

This wet scene concludes with weary reconciliation among Anthony, Gloria, Dick, and Maury. New life seems possible, yet the train roared through. That train, a snake in the garden, foreshadows ill, a later sterility, even in this scene awash with fertility images. Yet the train is not the major intruder. The ironic elements in this scene are age and experience. For lovers newly come upon the joys of life, water acts as a restorative, but for those of Anthony's and Gloria's experience, it holds no promise. The scene is classically romantic—except that the lovers no longer fill the roles of hero and heroine of romance. More than the train, time and experience form the intrusive reality fatal to love.

This chapter, entitled "Symposium," ends with a cynical discussion of the meaninglessness of life, led by Maury Noble. The intruding train returns again to take Gloria, without Anthony, to New York. Weariness, absolutely tired pessimism ends this chapter; yet the action has been washed in vats of water. Perhaps the greatest irony is that this chapter, for all its ominous signs, actually comprises one of the more fertile moments in the marriage between Anthony and Gloria; for once at least, they overcome their timidity, their repugnance to life, and go out into the night to explore.

This chapter also provides the final hour of promise in the novel. The next chapter, "The Broken Lute," employs little water imagery, or any other image of fertility. The dominant feature of this chapter is the appearance of old Adam Patch at the wildest party ever orchestrated by Anthony and Gloria. The sole source of vitality for either of them is money, and when old Adam disinherits them, meaning slips from the lives of these beautiful people. The single water image of this period occurs when they leave the gray house: "Came a day in September, a day slashed with alternate sun and rain, sun without warmth, rain without freshness" (p. 280).

Until Anthony meets Dorothy in the army town, water imagery virtually disappears. Dorothy and "damp nights and cool, rainy days" offer but temporary solace to Anthony (p. 336). The love cannot be. Dorothy, certainly as complete a human being as either male or female protagonist, ironically seems much inferior to Anthony.

Sullied by illness, by threats of suicide, by a messy parting near the end, this affair endures nearly a year. Dorothy, excellent as a war wench, simply will not suffice following the armistice. Anthony met her during a damp November; he left her to return to Gloria during an equally damp November. Winter symbolizes his future—both with Gloria and with Dorothy.

Winter chills the marriage after the war, and water images take the form of snow: "They sat there until a flurry of snow drew a languid sigh from Gloria" (p. 374). Languid at best, their lives receive no spark even from brisk snows of winter. Time passes and they have only a vague hope of getting the money they assume will pump blood back into their weary lives. By their standards, they grow old; Gloria awaits with distaste her twenty-ninth birthday:

> It was February, seven days before her birthday, and the great snow that had filled up the cross-streets as dirt fills the cracks in a floor had turned to slush and was being escorted to the gutters by the hoses of the street-cleaning department. (p. 395)

Snow compared with dirt, and snow changing to slush destined for gutters, metaphorically states the quality of their lives. Only the gutter beckons as they sink from rent district to rent district, from class to class, from languor to apathy. Strikingly, this image of deterioration—melting snow in the gutter—differs in tone, but not in content, from the snow-melting image that ushered in the love of Anthony and Gloria. Stripped of romantic diction, the scene that heralds their love resembles the scene at the end, even down to the gutters.

Sometimes Anthony and Gloria forsake residence in despair and rise to futile wisps of activity, as when Anthony tries to become a salesman. When that fails, Gloria turns to Hollywood. After her screen test, she experiences flashes of hope, possibly encouraged by the weather: "It was a premature spring. Water was drying on the walks and in the park little girls were gravely wheeling white doll-buggies up and down under the thin trees . . . " (p. 402). But this premature spring, full of promise, signifies nothing. The screen test dashes forever Gloria's vision of herself as a little girl, or even as a young woman. Spring warms the little girls pushing doll prams in the park, not Gloria. Although she will play no romantic leads, she might do a character part, "a very haughty, rich widow" (p. 403).

But spring, even premature spring fated to shiver beneath snows of winter reality, plays little role in the sordid lives of the Patches. All water takes the form of snow, usually filthy:

> One afternoon when the snow was dirty again. . . . Anthony . . . entered the apartment to find Gloria pacing the floor in a state of aggravated nervousness. The feverish eyes he turned on her were traced with tiny pink lines that reminded her of rivers on a map. For a moment she received the impression that he was suddenly and definitely old. (p. 424)

And of course he is. At a very young age, he is an old alcoholic who lies to cadge money for booze. The core of his life is neither moral nor aesthetic, but the vague hope that the money will revitalize his broken body, his shattered spirit. He dreams of the water of life, of what he will do when money once more makes him whole. He envisions "the romance of blue canals in Venice, of the golden green hills of Fiesole after rain, and of women, women who changed, dissolved, melted into other women and receded from his life, but who were always beautiful and always young" (p. 444).

The end of the novel emphasizes the futility of that pleasant vision. The very day Anthony inherits the money, which he hoped would solve every problem, he suffers a breakdown that sends him scurrying back to the safety of childhood and his stamp collection. He never recovers. When he returns to the source of all life, the sea, he does so in a wheelchair; from this wheelchair he will view Italy. Sailing on the sea toward what he naively assumes will be a new life, Anthony is a broken old man muttering to himself. To win the hollowest of victories, he has devastated himself. He has the money, and the irony is complete.

Finally, few image patterns exist in *This Side of Paradise*. *The Beautiful and Damned* marks an artistic advancement in that patterns appear, but do not really function as they will in later novels. They are ineffective, and *The Beautiful and Damned* is actually dull compared with *This Side of Paradise*. And of course "not until *The Great Gatsby* would the stern Jamesian aesthetic prevail over the pleasant indiscipline of the Wellsian journalistic novel."[23] Yet a look at the images in these first two novels does more than provide a contrast to Fitzgerald's greater work. For example, in *This Side of Paradise* the automobile, as in every Fitzgerald novel, establishes social position and serves as a characterizing device. It is also a symbol of freedom and power. For Amory Blaine the automobile provides a means of escape. It remains essentially a means of escape, even though one of Amory's friends, Dick Humbird, dies in an automobile accident. The static devices of communication, on the other hand, form no patterns and are of much less help than the transportation imagery in explicating *This Side of Paradise*. The only hint of the way Fitzgerald will handle communication imagery in future novels comes from his handling of newspapers. Men who can be bought, men who have interests to protect, control even the best newspapers. The major job of the newspaper is not to inform, but to maintain the status quo.

Obviously Fitzgerald was not thinking in terms of making coherent patterns of light-dark imagery when he wrote *This Side of Paradise*. Light sometimes represents romance, sometimes reality. And while Amory fears darkness, Fitzgerald puts no real horrors there. He comes closest to establishing a pattern in his use of man-made light, usually associated with romance, escape. Yet Dick Humbird appears as the devil under artificial light, and during Amory's period of depression, the lights of Broadway fail to lift him above two realities: Rosalind has married and his mentor, D'Arcy, has died. The moon consistently symbolizes romance, but in such a conventional way as to add little to the novel.

Dirt-disease-decay imagery plays little part in Fitzgerald's novel of youth and education, *This Side of Paradise*. In a novel where real disease can be cured, hypochondria stands as the capital threat to Amory. He struggles to free himself from his morbid imagination and partly succeeds in exorcizing imaginary diseases infused into his head by his alcoholic mother, Beatrice. He remains forever melancholy, but strong enough to struggle.

Water imagery is the most perfectly developed of the image patterns in Fitzgerald's fiction. Even in *This Side of Paradise*, Fitzgerald understood how he would use water symbolism in every novel through and including *Tender Is the Night*. Until the rebirth scene at Princeton, water imagery is no better integrated than other image patterns in this first novel. The Princeton scene, however, is the first of many of Fitzgerald's rebirth scenes, all of which are washed in baptismal waters of spring. Although this scene is painfully obvious and Amory's change in character remarkably short-lived, the pattern has begun. Amory will also experience rebirth in rain after he has seen Dick Humbird as the devil. And with the exception of the affair with Rosalind—an important instance where Fitzgerald abandons the pattern—each love affair is blessed in spring rain. Each affair shows tremendous promise, and each love fails. That is the pattern—bright promise followed by the blight of failure.

In *The Beautiful and Damned*, Fitzgerald continues the pattern of having the car function as a vehicle of escape; he soon makes it clear, however, that what appeared to be an escape route is actually a trap. Next to alcohol, the automobile proves to be the greatest source of humiliation for Anthony Patch.

By the time he wrote *The Beautiful and Damned,* Fitzgerald had learned much about establishing image patterns. The major communication pattern emerges from skillfully planted references to the telephone. Fitzgerald quickly establishes the pattern he will use throughout his career with the telephone: good news and essential messages will never arrive; news that is bad or in some way detrimental to the protagonist will come through without interference.

Light-dark imagery in *The Beautiful and Damned* is simple and consistent, perhaps too consistent. Fitzgerald creates a moon for romance and a sun for reality. Anthony's imagination populates the night with horrors, and artificial light, like a benevolent mother, banishes the bogey and makes everything all right again. Both light (reality) and dark (nightmare) hold terrors for Anthony. Only when he has drunk himself into a mindless stamp-collecting child do his nightmares cease. He can also stare into the bright sun because, safe in second childhood, he sees nothing.

Fitzgerald's second novel deals not with the education of a young man, but with corruption and deterioration. Dirt-disease-decay imagery powerfully supports *The Beautiful and Damned's* theme—life is bleak, meaningless. Ironically, the single most important reason the Patches viewed existence as meaningless is that Anthony and Gloria found the natural processes of life dirty and repugnant. Repelled by odors and the decay of the world of work, they cannot earn a living. Time, ravager of romance and the beautiful face, literally makes them sick, drives them to the bourbon bottle that hastens their decline. Their love had been a romantic dream, but physical proximity destroys the hopeful idea that they were the first and best of lovers. The dream was foolish, yet all they had. They thought they could live a story-book romance, assumed they could create a static, clinically hygienic world for themselves merely by refusing to participate in life. Both feared life lest they get dirty. They stood back, squeamish and clean, as life passed them by. Suddenly, without having lived, they were old, mentally and morally destitute, dirty.

In *The Beautiful and Damned* Fitzgerald establishes Anthony's vitality through an effective water image. Other Fitzgerald characters instinctively seek revitalization in the rain and the sea. Anthony soaks in his bathtub. Ominously, too, Anthony meets Gloria in winter, and they fall in love as thawing water rushes to the gutter. Even in their most joyful moments of courtship, they ride past "sullied" rivers. While the young lovers would seem to have everything going for them, the water imagery indicates that spring's promise to them is less glowing than for other Fitzgerald characters. Only when Gloria escapes the stultifying life in the gray house and runs wantonly through a night storm does water seem to promise vitality. Yet after this scene water imagery virtually disappears, except for references to snow. The deterioration begins in earnest then.

2

The Great Gatsby

The image patterns that had been diffuse in *This Side of Paradise* and *The Beautiful and Damned* or that had been too conventional to add anything to the early novels finally began to function in *The Great Gatsby,* the novel in which Fitzgerald conquered his art in a major way. The transportation imagery, the communication imagery, the light-dark imagery, the dirt-disease-decay imagery, and the water imagery in *The Great Gatsby* provide not loose motifs that run through the novel, but microcosms of the themes as a whole. Each of these image patterns carries a theme through the novel. Each provides structural unity, an internal unity that is amazing in one whose second novel in 1922 can at best be called flabby.

It should be noted here that Fitzgerald used a multitude of image patterns to carry his theme, not just the ones encompassed in this study. Le Vot, for example, notes a

> whole connotative system . . . erected in climates and seasons of the spirit. A thorough study could bring out the isomorphism of yellow, the sun, heat, dryness and shrillness, for example, in contrast with their opposites, blue, the moon, coolness, moisture and depth. The qualities of day and night, of dawn and dusk, summer and winter are subject to the attraction of these magnetic poles dissociated from their alternation in time, making their influence felt not only in clock and calendar time but in interior space.[1]

Sport imagery, too, plays an important role in the novel, with Jordan Baker and Tom Buchanan in particular characterized by sport (Jordan with her hard boy's body who cheats at her chosen profession and Tom with his string of polo ponies).[2] And the imagery of music—all varieties of music—is associated with Gatsby.[3] Particularly revealing, too, is the imagery of photography. As Lawrence Jay Dessner notes, "Fitzgerald shows us that photography is not merely a means of entertainment, professional or domestic, and a method of documentation, but a way people who are not self-conscious philosophers reinforce their assumptions about the nature of reality and time."[4] More important, the photograph, capable of freezing time, is anti-history.

As important as these patterns are,[5] however, they do not reveal as much about the novel as do the image patterns featured in this study because they are not as fully developed. They give hints of theme and support other theme carriers, but they do not tell as much, for example, as transportation imagery.

Transportation Imagery

In his third novel, Fitzgerald continues the practice of using the car to characterize. As Malcolm Cowley points out, the

> characters are visibly represented by the cars they drive; Nick has a conservative old Dodge, the Buchanans, too rich for ostentation, have an "easy-going blue coupé," while Gatsby's car is a "rich cream color, bright with triumphant hat-boxes and supper-boxes and tool-boxes, and terraced with a labyrinth of windshields that mirrored a dozen suns"—it is West Egg on wheels.[6]

Gatsby's car is an adolescent's dream, the very vehicle for one who formed his ideals as a teenager and never questioned them again. Gatsby is not sufficiently creative to choose a truly unique machine, so he selects a copy of the gaudy dream car spun from the lowest common denominator of intelligence and imagination. Such a car is exactly what an artist might fashion if he were third-rate specifically because he has plagiarized from the common American dream; because he has seen no need for originality; because he has failed to distinguish between romance and reality. Just as Gatsby—part the shadowy gangster who made millions, part the man who could remain faithful to an ideal love for five years—is an odd mixture of pragmatist and romantic, so his car blends colors representing both traits. It is a rich cream color, a combination of the white of the dream and the yellow of money, of reality in a narrow sense. After Myrtle Wilson's death, a witness to the accident describes the car as just plain yellow, which, as color imagery unfolds, becomes purely and simply corruption. White, the color of the dream, has been removed from the mixture.[7] Only the corruption, the foul dust, remains of Gatsby's dream after that hot day in New York. Thus the car becomes one external symbol of Gatsby, his mind, and what happens to his dream.

Even minor characters absorb traits from the vehicles associated with them. Myrtle, who meets Tom on a train and rides to their trysting place in a cab, must depend on others for transportation. With a single brushstroke—one of these taxi rides—Fitzgerald sketches Myrtle: she "let four taxicabs drive away before she selected a new one, lavender-colored with gray upholstery."[8] This choice, worthy of Gatsby, coincides perfectly with the conduct of a woman who would ask, vulgarly cute, whether the dog is a "boy or a girl" (p. 28), who would display McKee's inept photographs on her walls, and who would have "several old copies of *Town Tattle* . . . on the table together with a copy of *Simon Called Peter,* and some of the small scandal magazines of Broadway" (p. 29).[9]

Jordan Baker, too, is characterized by her association with cars.[10] Through her handling and driving of them, she reveals herself as a careless person. Nick does not recall the story that she cheated during a golf tournament until she leaves a "borrowed car out in the rain with the top down, and then lied about it" (p. 58). As for her driving, "she passed so close to some workmen that our fender flicked a button on one man's coat" (p. 59). As Nick says, she is a "rotten driver" fully capable of causing a fatal accident if ever she meets someone as careless as herself (p. 59). She smashes things, as do most careless people. The pattern is plain; recklessness behind the wheel (at first humorous in the Owl Eyes scene) deepens to near tragic proportions when it claims the lives of the Wilsons and Gatsby. Neither Nick nor the reader can trust a careless driver. Perhaps even Nick is careless. He does not deny it when Jordan accuses him of being a bad driver. The essential point, however, is that Nick has become considerably more human. No longer the man to make an extravagant claim to honesty, he does not try to defend himself against the charge of careless driving.

Always a characterizing device in *The Great Gatsby,* the car soon develops into a symbol of death. Fitzgerald begins to establish this pattern at the end of Gatsby's party. As the mass of cars leave,

> a dozen headlights illuminated a bizarre and tumultuous scene. In the ditch beside the road, right side up, but violently shorn of one wheel, rested a new coupé. . . . The sharp jut of a wall accounted for the detachment of the wheel, which was now getting considerable attention from a half dozen curious chauffeurs. However, as they left their cars blocking the road, a harsh, discordant din from those in the rear had been audible for some time and added to the already violent confusion of the scene. (p. 54)

Carelessness plus cars equal chaos, and although the scene with Owl Eyes—who correctly protests that he knows little about driving and that he was not even trying to drive—is a highlight of humor in the novel, it suggests the possibility of an accident, even a fatality, if a car is placed in the hands of a careless person. This scene is designed to establish the pattern, to prepare the reader for Myrtle's death.

Tom's first experiment with infidelity continues the pattern of careless drivers leading careless lives and reinforces the image of the amputated wheel:

> Tom ran into a wagon on the Ventura road one night, and ripped a front wheel off his car. The girl with him got into the papers, too, because her arm was broken—she was one of the chamber maids in the Santa Barbara hotel. (p. 78)

This second accident adds another element to the symbol. Not only is the possibility of injury or death linked with careless drivers, but infidelity suddenly becomes part of the pattern.

Even here, though, where automobile imagery increasingly symbolizes death, Nick finds taxis a part of the very breath and music of New York:

> When the dark lanes of the Forties were lined five deep with throbbing taxicabs, for the theater district, I felt a sinking in my heart. Forms leaned together in the taxis as they waited, and voices sang, and there was laughter from unheard jokes. . . . Imagining that I, too, was hurrying toward gayety and sharing their intimate excitement, I wished them well. (p. 58)

Cars, in addition to dealing death, have the more normal function of carrying people to excitement, or to other destinations. Only the driver defines the car. Viewing automobile imagery from a different perspective, it is significant that Wilson should deal in cars on the edge of the valley of ashes. Like the automobile, he gradually becomes both symbol and instrument of death. As Nick points out, "the only car visible [in Wilson's lot] was the dust-covered wreck of a Ford which crouched in a dim corner" (p. 25). The valley of ashes is the valley of death where everything is dead or dying.

To make sure the reader catches the symbolic significance of the automobile, Fitzgerald, in one master stroke, associates both cars and water with death. As Nick rides with Gatsby over the Queensboro Bridge, they meet a funeral procession: Nick is glad that "the sight of Gatsby's splendid car was included in [the mourners'] somber holiday" (p. 69). To draw attention to this funeral procession and to its importance in the fabric of the novel, Fitzgerald introduces it with the singular, somewhat bizarre phrase: "A dead man passed us in a hearse heaped with blooms . . . " (p. 69).[11]

With everything set up to create expectations of disaster whenever a car appears, the accident that kills Myrtle seems inevitable, not the very strange coincidence it really is. Image patterns have made it possible for Fitzgerald to use an unlikely series of events and to make them seem natural. He has led us carefully to the moment when Myrtle lies dead, one breast amputated like the amputated front wheels in earlier scenes.

Temporarily shaken by the loss of his mistress—even though he has just regained his wife—Tom soon recovers and reverts to type. Leaving Myrtle dead in ashes, Tom "drove slowly until we were beyond the bend—then his foot came down hard, and the coupé raced along through the night" (p. 142). Where caution is seemly, Tom pretends to practice it, but away from the public eye, he speeds up, becomes again the fast driver who broke a girl's arm and sheared off the wheel of his car in an earlier accident. This violent event fails to alter Tom; the pattern of carelessness will continue, and Tom will drive on, harming but unharmed.

To cap off the automobile symbolism, Fitzgerald makes all cars become the death car to Michaelis, who spends the night watching Wilson. Whenever a car goes "roaring up the road outside it sounded to him like the car that hadn't stopped a few hours before" (p. 157). And it is symbolically right that the car, even though it has served its purpose in killing Myrtle, should continue to be an image of death. With Myrtle dead, two still remain to die: Wilson and Gatsby. Gatsby's car, symbol of death, of a tarnished dream, leads them all to the grave.

Communication Imagery

In Fitzgerald's novels, references constantly link mechanical devices that fail to function and people who do not do their jobs. One irony of *The Great Gatsby,* for example, is that the telephone, the chief instrument of communication, helps people understand each other on only the most superficial levels. The telephone, in fact, breaks off communication.[12] This pattern begins when, to everyone's relief, the telephone interrupts Tom's laborious attempts to explain to Nick, Daisy, and Jordan his theory of the superiority of the Nordic race. This self-righteous diatribe, delivered by a white libertine prig, is stalled by a call from Tom's mistress, Myrtle. Tom has nothing to do, no job except to be Tom. Apparently he was so bored with the perfect order of East Egg that he has not only acquired a mistress, but has started reading books like *The Rise of the Colored Empires.*

The telephone shatters Tom's attempt to communicate a genuine concern. And when he answers the telephone, he gets no privacy. Shamelessly, Jordan eavesdrops. Apparently unaware of the irony in her use of the word *decency,* Jordan complains that Myrtle "might at least have the decency not to telephone him at dinner time" (p. 16). The call strains relationships at dinner, but after arguing about it, Tom and Daisy return to the table. Once more "the telephone rang inside, startlingly" (p. 16). The jangling telephone introduces an element of chaos into the seemingly-ordered world of East Egg. Nick's "instinct was to phone immediately for the police" (p. 16).

As in the other novels, the telephone functions as an instrument of communication only when its failure would wreak no mischief. Myrtle and her sister can use the telephone to assemble a party because no major problems would arise if the telephone failed. No message absolutely must be passed on, no communication is vital. But give someone an important message and the telephone fails.

Obviously the fault lies not in the telephone, but in those who use it. A dumb instrument, it is always misused. Often it rings at the wrong time, at a time when communication might occur. Or more likely, those trying to send the message cannot articulate it, telephone or no telephone. Tom and Daisy, for example, can barely talk, in spite of Daisy's magnificent voice. When they utter that rare line with a spark of vitality or originality, they sap every ounce of life from it with the inevitable tag—"or something like that." Tom tells Myrtle.

> "You'll give McKee a letter of introduction to your husband, so he can do some studies of him." His lips moved silently for a moment as he invented. "George B. Wilson at the Gasoline Pump, or something like that." (p. 33)

No telephone can be blamed for this kind of simple-minded stuttering. Tom simply has nothing to say, nothing to communicate once he departs from his tired theories about the Nordic race.

Typical of the interruptions occasioned by the telephone are those that disrupt attempts at personal communication. Just as Nick and Gatsby meet and try to become acquainted, "a butler hurried toward [Gatsby] with the information that Chicago was calling him. . . . " (p. 49). The telephone even interrupts the first assignation between Gatsby and Daisy. This business call is just one of the many sallies by reality into the dream world of Gatsby. The conflict between the dream and reality lurks always as near as the telephone.[13]

If a communiqué arrives on time, if it has something important to impart, and if it does not shatter an existing dialogue, it will be ignored. Gatsby's letter arrives in time to make Daisy miserable, but not in time to keep her from marrying Tom. The letter dissolves in the bathtub, while Daisy gets drunk and marries Tom. The letter cannot alter the determined chain of events.

Newspapers that fail to print the truth add another source of grief for Gatsby. One reason Gatsby's dream of Daisy can remain pure, can actually grow for five years, is that his sole contact with her comes through newspaper society pages. The society columnist makes myths; he glamorizes both bright and dull, makes spectacular the pompous affair. Intellectually insipid, Daisy becomes a rare jewel when polished constantly by newspaper prose and Gatsby's imagination. Time cannot pale what newspapers keep aglow. To Gatsby, Daisy becomes a goddess worthy of veneration by solemn rites, by the ritual of the green light. Gatsby's imagination is that of a society editor, but without the editor's sobering cynicism. He accepts the verbal picture of Daisy; with love, he might have written it.

If newspapers produce Daisy, meretricious gossip and rumor fashion Gatsby. Unwilling to accept the tiny niche assigned him in the universe, Gatsby fosters these rumors. He says little of substance about himself; he becomes the mysterious and important man he thinks Daisy will love. When the reporter comes to interview him, he has nothing to say; nor does he have anything for the public at large. Seldom, in fact, does he say anything. He resembles Tom and Daisy in that respect. Only Nick can articulate; but until he meets Gatsby, he has no story to tell.

Nick, however, cannot quite communicate what Gatsby is, as no man can communicate himself or any other. Nick comes close to the

> elusive rhythm, a fragment of lost words, that I had heard somewhere long ago. For a moment a phrase tried to take shape in my mouth and my lips parted like a dumb man's, as though there was more struggling upon them than a wisp of startled air. But they made no sound, and what I almost remembered was uncommunicable forever. (p. 112)

Almost captured, Gatsby finally eludes definition.

Of course Gatsby himself works to stymie communication, to elude definition. His flamboyant parties coupled with his natural reticence cause wild, wrongheaded speculation. Because he sprang—an adolescent fully armed—from his own head, only enough truth clings to the stories of his background to cause confusion. And when he lets slip some grain of truth that might enable Nick to begin to form an accurate picture of him, Gatsby reacts in a way designed to cast that truth into a shadow of doubt. Nick, for example, asks Gatsby where he came from. When Gatsby tells the truth that he is from the Midwest, he apparently has told Nick more than he intended; he immediately casts his statement into doubt when he says the part of the Midwest he comes from is San Francisco. Gatsby knows that like himself, Nick is from the Midwest. He hopes Nick will assume that anyone who places San Francisco in the heart of the United States has never seen the Midwest, probably has never been west of New York City.

Jay Gatsby would create a myth. He has plagiarized himself from romantic novels of the pulp variety, and as he talks, Nick notes that "the very phrases were worn so threadbare that they evoked no image except a turbaned character leaking sawdust at every pore. . . . " (p. 66). Finally, Gatsby does not know himself, has not read himself any more than he has read the books in his library. He does not understand much, least of all himself. He is a man contained totally in his dream, a dream he conceived as a teenager. He is, in fact, his own private library of unread books. Owl eyes sees deeply into Gatsby's character when, in that library, he takes the book from Nick and replaces it "hastily on is shelf, muttering that if one brick was removed, the whole library was liable to collapse" (p. 46). During the confrontation scene in New York, Tom figuratively removes that book. The elements that make up this dream form a precarious structure and cannot be disturbed, nor can they be communicated simply because they have no objective reality.

Gatsby further blocks communication—admittedly gossip—when he fires his former staff and takes as servants some of Wolfsheim's people. When the parties stop and Daisy begins to spend afternoons at the Gatsby mansion, Gatsby wants people he can trust not to talk. To protect Daisy's name, he changes from the man who invited the world to his door and becomes one who wants no trespassers. The telephone helps here. None of his staff ever have to go outside his pretentious gates. They can telephone for whatever they need. Once again, he cuts off communication by means of an instrument of communication.

As might be expected, the telephone works and the message comes through clearly when Daisy sets up the fatal party at her house, just as it worked when Myrtle arranged the party at her New York apartment. That party ended in violence, and certainly in this emotionally charged situation, violence is probable.[14] On this hot day at the Buchanans', people actually hallucinate. When the butler answers the phone, it seems to Nick that he says, "The master's body . . . ! I'm sorry, madam, but we can't furnish it—it's far too hot to touch this noon!" (p. 115). What he really said was simply, "Yes . . . Yes . . . I'll see" (p. 115). No communication on this day, none in this scene of comic relief. When communication finally occurs, it follows the pattern established in this and other Fitzgerald novels; it breaks rather than forms bonds.

Even when the right message crosses the wire, listeners misinterpret both communication and motives. When Wilson calls Tom to consummate the deal for the car, Daisy thinks it is Myrtle calling to consummate a different kind of deal. Nick assures Daisy that this is indeed a legitimate transaction, but she probably does not believe him. Earlier calls have made her wary enough to suspect Tom of holding down the receiver when he shouts that he will not be hurried, that he will not be called during meals. After all, Myrtle had earlier called him during dinner.

As part of the pattern of telephones that interrupt moments of possible communication, the telephone book falls from the hook just as Tom and Gatsby prepare for their first confrontation. This, too, provides comic relief, changes the direction of the ensuing argument; but it does not really break the tension, and only for a moment does it stave off the battle. Daisy tries to postpone it further by getting Tom to telephone for ice, but again, this is only a delaying tactic destined not to work for long. If successful communication would benefit a sympathetic character, the telephone severs it. Had the conversation been of any benefit to Gatsby, Daisy's delaying tactic would have worked permanently. Since it will destroy Gatsby, the conversation will occur in spite of the telephone.

The telephone always works against Gatsby, but not always against Nick. After the trauma of Myrtle's death and the equally real death of Gatsby's dream, Nick does not want to talk to anyone. Because the butler calls a cab for him, he avoids communication with those he least wants to contact. Possibly the telephone even works to his advantage when Jordan calls the day after the accident. They suddenly learn, over the telephone, that they have nothing to say. Once more, though, this instrument designed to facilitate communication stops it instead. Cementing no relationship, it breaks a bond.

Finally, the crucial call fails to come; Daisy does not telephone Gatsby. She sends no message while he lives, no flowers when he dies. When she fails to call, it is conceivable that Gatsby learns about himself, that at last he understands the quality of his dream, symbolized by Daisy. If so, Gatsby's recognition—because of a failure of communication—places him on the plane of a tragic hero. But one cannot know whether Gatsby comprehends the shallowness of his dream. Nick hopefully speculates that he does.[15]

Communication breaks down again when newspaper reports of the slaying of Gatsby and the suicide of Wilson generally turn out to be "a nightmare—grotesque, circumstantial, eager, and untrue" (p. 164). An organ of communication once more fails to communicate anything but falsity. Fitzgerald first sounded this theme in *This Side of Paradise*. Also, the many calls Nick makes to alleged friends and associates of Gatsby prove fruitless. Nick cannot communicate his concern to these people, cannot convince anyone that Gatsby was in fact a human being and that someone owes it to the man to attend his funeral. And when Slagle calls to report that young Parke got arrested when he handed bonds across a counter, he talks only until Nick tells him that Gatsby is dead: "There was a long silence on the other end of the wire, followed by an exclamation . . . then a quick squawk as the connection was broken" (p. 167). Enough broken connections exist in *The Great Gatsby* and other Fitzgerald novels to form at least a minor theme. The point is that the telephone, letters, and newspapers fail to convey the humanity of Gatsby. Humanity is the real truth, and no mere instrument of communication can convey that. Only Nick's story, the novel itself, conveys the sole truth worth telling.

Light-Dark Imagery

Moving from communication imagery to light-dark imagery, one first notes that *The Great Gatsby* is built around East Egg, West Egg, and the Valley of Ashes, all of which are characterized in terms of light.[16] A fourth setting, New York, appears less vividly in terms of light, although a harsh sun often gleams there. The preponderance of light imagery establishes *The Great Gatsby* as a "novel about seeing and misseeing."[17] Few characters see clearly. Nick, proclaiming himself honesty's model, sees himself but dimly. Only Owl Eyes dons enormous spectacles to correct his vision:

> Despite his imperfection as a seer (like the other guests, he is drunk), this man is able to look through the facade of Gatsby and all he stands for, and, just as important, he is able to see that there is substance behind the facade.[18]

Owl Eyes views Gatsby *only* from the outside, yet he makes the most telling pronouncement—"The poor son of a bitch" (p. 176). He sees Gatsby as a human being, a man deserving decent burial. Nick sees more, enough to speak a volume, but Owl Eyes cuts quickly to the essence, the humanity.

In a novel where everyone more or less has an opportunity to see, total darkness is rare. Darkness does play one important role, however; when Gatsby returns home after his all-night vigil at Daisy's window, he and Nick spend the black morning in Gatsby's house: "We pushed aside curtains that were like pavilions, and felt over innumerable feet of dark wall for electric light switches" (p. 147). Apparently they find no light switches because Nick says, "throwing open the French windows of the drawing-room, we sat smoking out into the darkness" (p. 147). Clearly, this is ritual; on this dark night, Nick and Gatsby form a human bond, and Gatsby, for the first time, talks unreservedly about himself. In light— sun, moon, artificial—they form no such friendship. Like King Lear, who sees only after enduring the black night of madness, like Gloucester, who understands only after Cornwell pops his eyes to dead jelly, like Oedipus, who comprehends only after he has gouged out his own eyes, Gatsby and Nick can see one another only in darkness. Perhaps their relationship could not survive the light of day; a better conclusion, considering Fitzgerald's penchant for ironically twisting symbols, is that darkness offers a more realistic picture than light does. Gatsby *must* become himself because the dark hides his gorgeous suit, his magnificent house, his fabulous car. Gatsby stands as if naked in the dark, and he comes off pretty well. Without his absurd trappings, he is enough of a human being to force the fanatically cautious Nick into a human commitment, something no one else has done.

Just as Nick and Gatsby wait together in darkness on the night of Myrtle's death, Michaelis and George Wilson maintain a vigil in the "dull light" of the garage. At dawn they snap off the light that all through the night has been bombarded by beetles. Wilson looks out over the valley of ashes, not upon the dew and stirring birds as did Nick and Gatsby, but upon the dead eyes of T. J. Eckleburg. Astonished, Michaelis watches as Wilson reveals that he worships Eckleburg as a god. The contrast between the blue-gray dawn of the wasteland and the gold-turning dawn of West Egg is genuine this time, not just apparent. Both Nick and Wilson make commitments in that dawn—Nick to another human being, to life, and Wilson to a gaudy graven image, to death. His commitment is natural in a place where even dawn is described as twilight (p. 160).

Moonlight, which often pierces the night, is a more prevalent image than total darkness in *The Great Gatsby*.[19] The moon in earlier novels symbolized romance; it shed a light that made palatable the harshest realities. Not here, though. The moon becomes the sinister light of nightmare, although it is innocent enough in the beginning of the novel. On the way home from the Buchanans' in chapter 1, for example, Nick notes the brightness of the summer night and the red gas pumps in pools of light in front of the stations. On this night, which teems with life beneath moonlight, Nick sees Gatsby "standing with his hands in his pockets regarding the silver pepper of the stars" (p. 21).[20] Or so Nick thinks. Gatsby sees no stars—natural if romantic lights—but worships the artificial green light at the end of Daisy's dock.

During Gatsby's first party, the moon enhances the atmosphere of unreality. As evening blurs into morning and the moon rises, Nick finds "floating in the sound . . . a triangle of silver scales, trembling a little to the stiff, tinny drip of the banjoes on the lawn" (p. 47). Here even nature—in the form of the moon—cooperates to stagelight the production which is Gatsby's party.[21] Nick suggests that Gatsby's power is such that he can dispense "starlight to casual moths" (p. 80).

Moonlight at this point still epitomizes romance. The birth of Jay Gatsby and simultaneous departure of James Gatz occurs under a fantastic moon image. A dream is born; Nick describes the labor pains that bring forth romance:

> A universe of ineffable gaudiness spun itself out in his brain while the clock ticked on the washstand and the moon soaked with wet light his tangled clothes upon the floor. (pp. 99–100)

A romantic adolescent gives birth to a dream. That dream never grows, never changes.

Gatsby's dream, however, suffers a blow in the moonlight when Daisy disapproves of the party. The death of Myrtle then sends it reeling, and suddenly the moon is no longer the fabric from which dreams are spun. The moon becomes associated with the grotesque after Myrtle's death: Tom, Nick, and Jordan return from New York, "the Buchanans' house floated suddenly toward us through the rustling trees" (p. 142). Tom becomes callous, decisive in the moonlight: "As we walked across the moonlight gravel to the porch he disposed of the situation in a few brisk phrases" (p. 143). But Gatsby still dreams, stands in moonlight with his pink suit glowing against the dark shrubbery in the background. Whether or not any vestiges of sacrament cling to his vigil, he mans the watch. Moonlight for Gatsby still connotes romance, even intrigue, and Nick leaves him standing in the moonlight, "watching over nothing" (p. 146).

Although he is amazed at Gatsby's belief that he can recapture the moonlit nights with the Daisy of five years past, Nick, too, sets up a romantic image of the West, an image he would recapture. When he leaves the East, which has become an El Greco nightmare under a "lustreless moon," he seeks his Christmas-vacation idealization of the West. He recalls a time when

> we pulled out into the winter night and the real snow, our snow, began to stretch out beside us and tinkle against the windows, and the dim lights of small Wisconsin stations moved by, a sharp wild brace came suddenly into the air. . . . That's my Middle West—not the wheat or the prairies or the lost Swede towns, but the thrilling returning trains of my youth, and the streetlamps and sleigh bells in the frosty dark and the shadows of holly wreaths thrown by lighted windows on the snow. (p. 177)

Nick has learned much about human nature. Oddly, he does not know that this winter Arcady no longer exists for him. His chances of returning to it exactly equal the possibilities of Gatsby finding the pure white Daisy of Louisville. This was the Middle West of youth, not of a man five years too old to lie to himself. It exists momentarily for some people, never again for Nick.

Fitzgerald makes one final comment on what happened to Gatsby's dream. The last time Nick sees the "huge incoherent failure of a house," he finds glowing in the moonlight an obscene word scrawled on the steps with a piece of brick (p. 181). Romantic light on obscenity. With the strength and energy to become anything, Gatsby and America plagiarized an adolescent dream. Fascinating, awesome in execution, the product of that false dream remains forever an obscenity.

Nick would wipe away the obscenity, start over with a new dream. The same moon would shine, but the "inessential houses" would melt (p. 182). Knowing the dream impossible, Nick believes in it. With glowing terms of understanding, he describes Gatsby's belief in

> the green light, the orgiastic future that year by year recedes before us. It eluded us then, but that's no matter—tomorrow we will run faster, stretch out our arms farther. . . . And one fine morning— (p. 182)

The punctuation, the dash comprehends the futility of Nick's hope, as well as the necessity of it. Fitzgerald cannot lie and say the dream might be realized; he dares not proclaim it impossible, and yet he ends the novel with a tone of heavy resignation: "So we beat on, boats against the current, borne back ceaselessly into the past" (p. 182).

The image projected in moonlight, of course, resides in the head of the beholder. Thus moonlight is as man-made as any form of artificial light, and whoever separates the two—artificial light and moonlight—stands on shaky ground. But classifications are always arbitrary, and shaky ground can be profitable. In this case, I think it profitable to discuss artificial light as a separate category.

Man-made light appears first in chapter 1 when Daisy objects to the use of candles. She complains that extra light is superfluous, but that may not be so if one considers light a symbol of knowledge and intelligence. Daisy, with her lovely, fascinating voice, has an exquisite instrument for communication; yet when she opens her mouth, she proves she has nothing to say. As she snuffs the candles, for example, she says, "Do you always watch for the longest day of the year and then miss it: I always watch for the longest day of the year and then miss it" (p. 12). She even misses the summer solstice. All musical tone with a classy style, Daisy has no content. No wonder she feels uncomfortable in the presence of that Promethean symbol of knowledge, fire.

When the telephone jars the serenity of dinner, Nick remembers "the candles being lit again, pointlessly, and I was conscious of wanting to look squarely at everyone, and yet to avoid all eyes" (p. 16). Fitzgerald's placement of "point-lessly" has the same effect as italicizing the word. The telephone throws everyone into confusion, and the candles create no order, little illumination. Nick wants to see without looking into eyes, and when no one will look, the candles shed only random light.

After dinner Daisy explains to Nick her attitudes toward life in terms transparently insincere. When Nick and Daisy rejoin Tom and Jordan, the "crimson room bloomed with light" (p. 18). By lamplight, Jordan reads aloud from the *Saturday Evening Post* in an uninflected, soothing voice, running words together, blurring meanings. Light shines brilliantly through all this—on Tom's boots and dully on his yellow hair. Again, an ironic symbol of intellect.

Another kind of artificial light is the kind of theatrical lighting that distinguishes Gatsby's party in chapter 3. As evening nears, Gatsby's garden grows gaudier, more artificial: "The lights grow brighter as the earth lurches away from the sun. . . . " (p. 40). Theatrical lights outshine the sun. In this carnival atmosphere, Fitzgerald describes the "sea-change of faces and voices and color under the constantly changing light" (p. 40). In surreal twilight, cocktails float through the air, and it all has been arranged by that Belasco of an impresario, Gatsby. His theatrical lighting hides, never exhibits.

References to light are amazingly sparse, considering the reader's impression that every action bathes in artificial light. The accident scene contributes to that impression. After the party, the wreck involving Owl Eyes and the inebriated driver erupts into a chaos of auto horns and headlights. Light washes the whole scene. All of this is transitory, however; as madness grinds on below, "a thin wafer of a moon was shining over Gatsby's house, making the night fine as before, and surviving the laughter and the sound of the still glowing garden" (p. 56). Here the moon is an element of stability, a bit of divinity to contrast with the lighted chaos below.

Gatsby's car itself produces artificial light. This fabulous automobile, Phaeton's car, is "terraced with a labyrinth of windshields that mirrored a dozen suns" (p. 64). The car is practically a universe in itself. On the trip to New York, Gatsby's car "scattered light through half Astoria. . . . " (p. 68). Fitzgerald uses both Promethean and Icarian myths in reference to Gatsby's splendid car, with the emphasis on the Icarian.

As his car scatters light, Gatsby tells Nick his background, makes himself seem a cardboard cliché from a third-rate movie. Nick says ironically, "I saw him opening a chest of rubies to ease, with their crimson-lighted depths, the gnawings of his broken heart" (p. 67). Crimson light, of course, is a feature of the Buchanan home; Fitzgerald hints that the Buchanan's way of life is just as much of a cliché, just as cardboard as this story Gatsby tells. This is one of the things an author can do in an intricately patterned work.

And the pattern expands. After learning from Jordan that Gatsby wants him to set up a rendezvous with Daisy, Nick comes home to find Gatsby preparing his enormous house for Daisy's inspection: "When I came home . . . I was afraid for a moment that my house was on fire. . . . The whole corner of the peninsula was blazing with light. . . . It was Gatsby's house, lit from tower to cellar" (p. 82). Gatsby prepares his house with all his skill and energy, but the lights are artificial, and the wind in the trees lifts and drops the strings of lights, making "the lights go off and on again as if the house had winked into the darkness" (p. 82). Thus can forces of nature destroy artificial light. Gatsby creates much light, but never matches the sun; he cannot really see his creation, cannot judge it. With the energy to create practically anything, Gatsby created a gaudy monster. That he could do so much, that he could imitate his adolescent dream so well is admirable; that he finally failed to create enough light to view it as it is perhaps is tragic, at least pitiable.

One might argue, however, that Gatsby eventually understands the insignificance of his creation. When he sees Daisy in person, for example, the green light loses significance: "Now it was again a green light on a dock. His count of enchanted objects had diminished by one" (p. 94). Still, many enchanted objects exist in Gatsby's world. Until Daisy pierces the dream, everything he owns, all of which he has gathered for her, is enchanted. As creator he can turn on lights, can flip a switch and cause "gray windows to disappear as the house glowed full of light" (p. 96). In a Promethean pun, Nick refers to Gatsby as an "ecstatic patron of recurrent light" (p. 90). Yet in the music room, Gatsby sits in a dark corner with Daisy, as if the fragile dream could not flourish even in artificial light:

> Gatsby turned on a solitary lamp beside the piano. He lit Daisy's cigarette from a trembling match, and sat down with her on a couch far across the room, where there was no light save what the gleaming floor bounced in from the hall. (p. 96)

Gatsby creates whatever light exists; were he a better artist, the creation would have been more substantial. At fourteen, he plagiarized his vision. Never again did he examine it, but set out to make it a reality. Thus the creator, the dispenser of light, last examined his life in his early teens. The adult does perfectly what the child dictated.

When Tom and Daisy finally attend a Gatsby party, they find more shadow than light. Gatsby sees his whole gaudy creation through Daisy's eyes and intuits her negative reaction. Even the moon, once chief agent for Gatsby's illusions, adds no magic this time. At best it spotlights, makes separate the people in a tableau of unreality. The actress and her director, for example, seem frozen just short of love for the duration of the party. Beneath the moon, the director is Keats' bold lover who cannot kiss, "though winning near the goal," and it is this moon, an icy sliver, that keeps them apart: "They were still under the white-plum tree and their faces were touching except for a pale, thin ray of moonlight between" (p. 108). Frozen in this tantalizing position, the lovers cannot touch, although the director does "stoop one ultimate degree and kiss *at* her cheek" (p. 108; italics mine). The moon enhances both the poignancy and loveliness of their situation and, because it is the light only of a dream, keeps them from consummating their affair. Without the moonlight, without the dream, the love between the director and the actress, like the love between Gatsby and Daisy, becomes real and must then perish as living things do. Even artificial light would tarnish this love, but beneath the moon they approach, nearly touch, yet never do. Frozen on a Keatsian urn, their virginal love is art, imagination, never reality.

After the party, Nick waits with Gatsby until all guests leave and the guest rooms are dark. Gatsby knows that Daisy has sat in the dark, has looked up at the windows where "sometimes a shadow moved against a dressing room blind above, gave way to another shadow, an indefinite procession of shadows, that rouged and powdered in an invisible glass" (pp. l08-9). Knowing that Daisy watched as these silhouettes aped and burlesqued human behavior, and knowing that she disapproved, Gatsby essentially turns out the lights forever. He will reject this attempt, try another way to create the white innocence he found in Louisville five years ago. The dream, born, baptized in moonlight, had fashioned the reality of Gatsby's house. On this dark night reality and dream suffer the devastating blow of disapproval from the goddess. The lights in the house fail to go on next Saturday.[22]

A late and effective light image appears inside Wilson's garage where Myrtle lies dead and Wilson teeters near breakdown. The illumination comes from a "yellow light in a swinging wire basket" (p. 139). Wilson's eyes fluctuate from the swinging light to his wife's dead body. Fitzgerald does not say so, but this must be the dim, dirty light found in every garage, a light smeared by grease and the foul dust of the valley of ashes. This pale light certainly is not the light of truth; from such a light can come only misconception. This is true of all artificial light images in *The Great Gatsby.*

In *The Beautiful and Damned,* artificial light symbolized escape; natural sunlight symbolized reason. In *The Great Gatsby,* sunshine *appears* to be a source of energy and life:

> And so with the sunshine and the great bursts of leaves growing on the trees, just as things grow in fast movies, I had that familiar conviction that life was beginning over again with the summer. (p. 4)

The sun provides energy for this rebirth image, and a fantastic image it is. Of course it is ironic; waiting on the threshold stands the end, not the beginning.

The sun shines from many vantage points and has many meanings. Dying sun plays lovingly on Daisy's face, accentuates her beauty:

> The last sunshine fell with romantic affection upon her face. . . . Then the glow faded, each light deserting her with lingering regret, like children leaving a pleasant street at dusk. (p. 14)

Dusk, like autumn, flashes one last romantic glow before darkness. In dusk's glow, a vague sense of impending loss makes everything more valuable, more lovely, more poignant. Dying light lacks the energetic harshness of reality. Daisy can look lovely at dusk, but in full light of day beneath the spotlight of reality, she fares less well.

As Daisy takes Nick on the tour of the estate, the coming of evening casts deep gloom; yet the approaching darkness is a "velvet dusk," not nearly so real as the jangling telephone that had created tension in the group (p. 17). Even as Daisy reviews her disappointments, even as she melodiously avows her cynicism, her life is couched in a "velvet dusk" as lovely and as false as her voice. When sunlight is not direct, it, too, distorts. Crossing the bridge into New York, for example, Nick notes that

> the sunlight through the girders mak[es] a constant flicker upon the moving cars, with the city rising up across the river in white heaps and sugar lumps all built with a wish out of non-olfactory money. (p. 69)

Flickering light creates a distortion that adds to the air of romance and unreality as they enter New York. Yet even in New York, with its "wild promise of all the mystery and beauty in the world," the "roaring noon" comes (p. 69). Nick must blink away the brightness before he can see Gatsby.

In *The Great Gatsby*, direct sunlight always symbolizes reality. One of Fitzgerald's more complex direct sun images closes chapter 3 when Nick contrasts Gatsby's party with the general run of his own life. Going to work each morning, Nick notes that "the sun threw my shadow westward" (p. 56). This creates an interesting balance between the symbol of hope and rebirth (the early-morning sun) and the symbol of death (the west-heading shadow). This is reality. Death is the reality of life. Free from this reality, Nick eats with clerks in dark restaurants and gains affection for New York. Walter Mitty on a busy street, he imagines entering the lives of mysterious women, of getting a smile from them before they fade "into the warm darkness" (p. 57). In that gathering darkness, Nick savors his loneliness, imagines that he, too, will join the eight-o'clock crowd for fun and excitement. He dreams in darkness, in dark places, while Gatsby's dream is bathed in self-created light. Daisy, too, can produce light, or purchase it: "Her porch was bright with the bought luxury of star shine" (p. 149). Daisy's diamonds aglow beneath man-made light, as well as the light at Gatsby's command, make it clear that Fitzgerald considered pretty vast the difference between the natural light of day and artificial light.

Another indication of the power of direct sun occurs when Nick first sees Myrtle: she blocks the light from Wilson's office door. When they get to New York, the taxi drives directly into the sun, but Myrtle quickly turns away, pecks on the glass for the driver to stop so she can buy a dog from a man who bears an "absurd resemblance to John D. Rockefeller" (p. 27). Myrtle, who resembles Gatsby in most ways, shares his dislike for direct light.[23]

During Myrtle's New York party, Nick gets drunk. Alcohol casts everything into a haze in spite of the sun that floods the room until late evening. Haze notwithstanding, Nick sees reality clearly enough to satirize everyone at the party. And when he turns from the party to be alone with himself, the alcoholic haze does not prevent him from making this characteristic judgment: he is "simultaneously enchanted and repelled by the inexhaustible variety of life," as he peers through his single window at all the other windows (p. 36). He exhibits here the double vision mentioned by Malcolm Cowley as being a particular trait and talent of Fitzgerald.[24]

The sun most clearly represents reality, however, in chapter 7 where it creates a withering heat to wilt the hardiest of dreamers. This heat causes irritation and suspicion even among strangers. On this torrid day, "only the hot whistles of the National Biscuit Company broke the simmering hush at noon. The straw seats of the car hovered on the edge of combustion. . . . " (p. 114). Those at the Buchanan estate have retreated into the shadows to escape the heat. Daisy and Jordan, as they were in chapter 1, are paralyzed, although this time it is not the paralysis of happiness, as Daisy had claimed in the first chapter. Such a day forces everyone to take precautions to escape the effects of the sun. And if the sun symbolizes the light of reality, no wonder Tom becomes muddled when he talks about it: "I read somewhere that the sun's getting hotter every year. . . . It seems that pretty soon the earth's going to fall into the sun—or wait a minute—it's just the opposite—the sun's getting colder every year" (p. 118). Tom, of course, considers himself the supreme realist, boasts that he can tolerate heat; but reality's strong light harms him. Yet he fares better in heat than does Gatsby because Tom has not an atom of imagination. A child of neither moon nor sun, Tom can smash up people and dreams and never be aware of what he has done.

After he smashes Gatsby's dream, he can afford to be magnanimous in victory; he allows Gatsby to take Daisy home. And in the heat of the evening even Nick notes that "all human sympathy has its limits, and we were content to let all their tragic arguments fade with the city lights behind" (p. 136). With that attitude, deepened by the knowledge that he has just turned thirty, Nick relaxes against Jordan and rides: "So we drove on toward death through the cooling twilight" (p. 137). The romantic symbol of twilight suddenly becomes a symbol of death. Myrtle dies when she rushes out into the dusk, when the death car "came out of the gathering darkness, wavered tragically for a moment, and then disappeared. . . . '' (p. 138).

After the accident, Nick and Gatsby spend a confessional evening during which Gatsby makes himself known for the first time. With the approach of morning, they open windows to admit the light of dawn, the "gray-turning, gold-turning light" (p. 152). Life begins to stir as usual when Gatsby's last day begins. Generally this would be an ironic comment, except that a rebirth really has occurred—in Nick. Nick has been an observer of human affairs, and generally a not-too-interested observer. Now he becomes a participant. His relationship with Gatsby can tolerate the light of day, can actually flourish in it. It can endure, also, into death and darkness. If Nick's speculation is correct, Gatsby, too, has become a different human being. Nick assumes that when Daisy's call fails to come, Gatsby sees "how raw the sunlight was upon the scarcely created grass" (p. 162). This is the harshest light reality can cast, the ugliest secret she has to reveal.

Dirt-Disease-Decay Imagery

If light-dark imagery in *The Great Gatsby* exposes the dream as the product of a third-rate imagination, a thing a bright teenager might create, the dirt-disease-decay imagery shows the dream as tarnished. Both image patterns examine the American dream, the dream that is the subject of *The Great Gatsby*, *Tender Is the Night*, and *The Last Tycoon*. In one sense *The Great Gatsby* looks forward to *The Last Tycoon;* it is *The Last Tycoon* inverted. *The Last Tycoon* tells the story of the corruption of those who enter Hollywood. Hollywood functions as dream factory, Stahr as plant manager. He tells the writer, Boxley, "We have to take people's favorite folklore and dress it up and give it back to them" (p. 105). Stahr decides what that folklore is, dictates what people dream. Despite Stahr's best efforts as artist, corruption riddles his factory of dreams. And Gatsby, the consumer, takes a dream such as Stahr might weave, thinks it his own. The very purity arising from Gatsby's devotion to the dream paradoxically leads to his own corruption. *The Last Tycoon*, then, deals with the corruption of those who manufacture dreams; *The Great Gatsby* explores the plight of the consumer, the man who buys pot metal, reveres it as gold.

References to decay of various sorts appear often enough in *The Great Gatsby* to form a major motif.[25] Decay images fall under three main headings: the valley of ashes; the ravages of humanity against humanity; and moral rot. Each of these categories appears in Nick's famous line containing the essence of dirt-disease-decay imagery in the novel:

No, Gatsby turned out all right in the end; it is what preyed on Gatsby, what foul dust floated in the wake of his dreams that temporarily closed out my interest in the abortive sorrows and shortwinded elations of men. (p. 2)

The "foul dust" symbolizes the valley of ashes, a vast dead valley that bursts geographical barriers to include both Eggs as well as New York and, by extension, the United States. The valley serves as one huge metaphor symbolic of a land that produces only dust and death. This waste land ranks in sterility with anything in the Eliot poem.[26] While an apparent contrast exists between the waste land and either East or West Egg, the contrast is just that—*apparent.* On West Egg Gatsby produces a "vast meretricious beauty" that serves a purpose for a time, but his empire wilts under the gaze of Daisy. Because his dream was meaningless, hollow, it ends absolutely with Gatsby's death, lies as inert and dead as the valley of ashes. Gatsby leaves no legacy except the story Nick tells.

If the contrast between West Egg and the valley of ashes resembles that of the prairie vs. low, rolling foothills, the contrast between the valley and East Egg should approach that of flatland vs. mountain. Fitzgerald practically forces the comparison by juxtaposing the green light at the end of the first chapter with the waste land images that open chapter 2. Yet East Egg produces nothing that sets it above the dust and death of ashes. The dialogue of East Egg is more sophisticated, but no more original and certainly no nearer any standard of universal truth. Tom's string of polo ponies is of even less practical use than Wilson's aging car. The boredom spawned in each place seems equally intense. And the gray of the ash heaps approaches the dominant color of the Buchanan estate—white.[27]

Foul dust floats from all three places. More clearly than Tom or Gatsby, of course, Wilson sinks into his environment: "A white ashen dust veiled his dark suit and his pale hair as it veiled everything in the vicinity" (p. 26). While Wilson is a part of his environment, he only accepted it, did not create it. Tom and Gatsby are not as guiltless. While both took from others their respective utopian ideas, they at least had a choice over what to plagiarize. Only Wilson, born to exist in the valley of death, had no choice, made no attempt to control.

The waste land pervades both East and West Egg because travelers from either place must cross the valley of death. Nick and Gatsby observe foul dust as they drive into the city:

> We passed Port Roosevelt, where there was a glimpse of red-belted ocean-going ships and sped along a cobbled slum lined with dark, undeserted saloons of the faded-gilt nineteen-hundreds. (p. 68)

Fitzgerald highlights this theme of corruption in two ways: first, Gatsby extricates himself from the clutches of a policeman by showing a Christmas card from the commissioner, thus indicating moral corruption from top to bottom, at least in the police department; second, having solved the problem with the law, Nick and Gatsby encounter a problem no one can handle—death. Crossing the Queensboro Bridge, they meet a corpse, the ultimate corruption.[28] Later they meet Meyer Wolfsheim, corruption personified, and he continues the theme of death with his tale of the murder of Rosy Rosenthal.[29]

Appropriately, Myrtle dies in the valley of ashes. Had she not lived in what becomes a major symbol of death and decay, Myrtle might not have sought outside stimuli. Still, the valley of ashes does not kill her; she dies because she met that interloper into the valley of death, Tom Buchanan. Wilson, a soldier in that great army of living dead, dies for the same reason.

The valley provides the setting for the first death, Gatsby's mansion for the next two. After Myrtle dies, Nick and Gatsby spend the night together at what in tabloid parlance will become the death house. Here they seal a friendship, begin to view one another as human beings. Yet the house resembles a tomb: "There was an inexplicable amount of dust everywhere and the rooms were musty. . . ." (p. 147). Gatsby seems to have given up on his house. Already it resembles the valley of ashes, the smoldering remains of dreams.

Leaving Gatsby, Nick boards the train for work. As he passes the valley of ashes, he crosses to the other side of the car to avoid decay and death. He would spurn reminders of mortality. But no one avoids the ash heap. In *The Great Gatsby,* the foul dust of the valley of ashes functions symbolically as a ubiquitous *memento mori,* the symbolic contradiction of Gatsby's belief that a man might wipe clean the corruption of the past and begin anew as innocent as a virgin child.

Juxtaposed with pervasive dirt and decay imagery are references to the ravages of man. Most destructive of all is Tom, who hurts people, wrecks things. He causes pain, is too insensitive to know he does it. The first proof of this is Daisy's bruised finger; Tom does not recall hurting it. Daisy's injury results from one of many accidents, all of which could have been prevented. Tom causes one of many automobile accidents, Daisy another, a more serious one. Carelessness is universal in this novel, but Tom and Daisy, who care less than most people, cause their hog's share of pain through a series of destructive accidents. Tom, who smashes Gatsby's dream as deliberately as he smashes Myrtle Wilson's nose, sometimes is more calculatingly cruel than careless.

Obviously, others besides the Buchanans dispense destruction and decay. Violence lurks forever just below the surface, remains a constant possibility. Tom, booted athlete whose powerful body strains against his riding clothes, finally threatens no more than Gatsby. Because of the amount of energy—and waste— expended to create these parties, a Gatsby festival always presents the danger of unchanneled force: "Every Friday five crates of oranges and lemons arrived from a fruiterer in New York—every Monday these same oranges and lemons left his back door in a pyramid of pulpless halves" (p. 39). Gatsby's parties, and by extension, his way of life, cause decay, burn things up. Efficiency experts would be appalled at the meagerness of the product compared with the energy expended. And damage must be repaired. When a girl rips her gown, Gatsby, to stave off chaos, replaces it with a more expensive one. As Nick observes, after each party someone must repair the "ravages of the night before" (p. 39). Thus Gatsby establishes a cycle: through the week he creates a haven of perfect order only to loose forces of destructive chaos on Saturday night.

The parties end when Gatsby notes Daisy's distaste for his extravagance. He sees the parties through Daisy's eyes. Disconsolate, he walks with Nick: "He broke off and began to walk up and down a desolate path of fruit rinds and discarded favors and crushed flowers" (p. 111). Here he makes the claim that he can repeat the past. He walks in ruins, the ravages of his party, even as he assures Nick that he *can* repeat the past. As Gatsby states his dream, Fitzgerald repeats once more the familiar motif that just below the surface glitter lies ruin. With remarkable economy, Fitzgerald makes clear the dream and makes a symbolic comment on it.

Daisy and Jordan, too, are entangled in corruption imagery. On the Buchanans' wedding day, for example, the heat matches that of the sweltering day in New York when Daisy again renounces Gatsby and reaffirms Tom. At the wedding a man named Biloxi faints, becomes, like Klipspringer, a freeloading boarder. He sponges for three weeks at the Baker house before Jordan's father kicks him out. Baker dies the next day, but Jordan assures Nick that the eviction and death were not connected. Jordan is correct, but the parallel between Daisy's first rejection of Gatsby and affirmation of Tom and that New York scene is deliberate. The common ingredients are intense heat, rejection of Gatsby, and affirmation of Tom followed by death. True to his common practice in *The Great Gatsby*, Fitzgerald tells the same story twice—once humorously, once tragically.

Corruption surrounds Daisy even before the wedding. After Gatsby leaves for war, Daisy leads a seemingly carefree, innocent life. Yet hints of dirt and decay add ominous hues to the sparkling colors of her social life. At parties feet shuffle the "shining dust" on the dance floor (as Myrtle's feet shuffle "foul dust" of the valley of ashes), and when she falls asleep at dawn, she leaves "the beads and chiffon of an evening dress tangled among dying orchids on the floor beside her bed" (p. 151). Decay images and images of carelessness converge here to indicate that Gatsby's dream is futile from the start. Corruption in Daisy's world is subtle, but definitely present; in Gatsby's world corruption is obvious, but unimportant. Conversely, Daisy's elegance and taste are apparent, but not important; one must search, as Nick does, to ferret out the fine qualities of Gatsby.[30]

This physical evidence of dirt, disease and decay indicates a deep moral corruption, a disease prevalent in humanity, in the environment perverted by man. Myrtle Wilson's fate illustrates the pattern of destruction. Her nose is broken by Tom, her body by Daisy, her aesthetic and moral sense by the ash heap—man's greatest corruption, his monument to the perversion of nature. Corruption is so rampant as to illustrate Tom's correctness when he forecasts rapid deterioration of society. But Tom's fear that the black race will subordinate the white race lacks substance. Corruption permeates the social strata; there the danger lies, not in the black race. No one, in fact, better symbolizes the moral idiocy of his class than Tom. A prig who considers himself a bastion of the *status quo*, Tom never sees himself as a major source of moral decay, a threat to the civilized world. His vast wealth puts him above his fellows, beyond the reach of either tribal or secular law. He suffers the same hubris that has toppled selected despots from Oedipus to Richard Nixon. Hubris causes blindness, and Tom sees nothing.

Moral decay riddles Jordan Baker, too. She is "incurably dishonest," but to Nick this is unimportant: "Dishonesty in a woman is a thing you never blame deeply—I was casually sorry, and then I forgot" (p. 59). A strange reaction from the novel's moral center. Openly, unrepentently, Nick admits he ignores moral corruption in half of humanity. Perhaps he blinds himself to his own corruption, the hubris that allowed him to think himself the only honest man he ever met. If Nick is corrupt—as he may well be before his association with Gatsby humanizes him—the sole moral center of the novel is the story Nick tells,[31] the story he can tell because now he can peer beneath the surface and find the human being. He sees Tom and Daisy for what they are:

> They were careless people, Tom and Daisy—they smashed up things and creatures and then retreated back into their money or their vast carelessness, or whatever it was that kept them together, and let other people clean up the mess they had made. . . . (pp. 180–81)

And he sizes up Gatsby: "They're a rotten crowd," Nick tells him. "You're worth the whole damn bunch put together" (p. 154). Before he could tell the story, Nick had to conclude that "Gatsby turned out all right in the end" (p. 2).

Not a saint, but a believable human being, Nick functions as a "choric character, a *human* moral center through which everything is interpreted."[32] Like other detached observers—Marlow in *Heart of Darkness* and *Lord Jim*, Relling in *The Wild Duck*, Alfieri in *A View from the Bridge*—Nick is a human being with human failings, but people trust him, at least to the extent that he has nothing to gain from any character and is not really involved in the action. He is, however, involved with the characters; he does make moral decisions. To the extent that he sides specifically with Gatsby, he may be untrustworthy. The Greek chorus shared Nick's strength (a powerful desire to tell truth), and his weakness (human sympathy, which is a weakness only in that it gets in the way of objectivity).

Still, corruption is so general that it must touch Nick, even as it touched Hamlet. Hues of corruption range from Meyer Wolfsheim, who played with the faith of a nation and used human molars as cufflinks, to that rather innocuous star boarder, Klipspringer, a "slightly worn young man" (p. 95). One cannot neglect Dan Cody, a "gray, florid man with a hard, empty face—the pioneer debauchee, who during one phase of American life brought back to the Eastern seaboard the savage violence of the frontier brothel and saloon" (p. 101).[33] Corruption is sufficiently widespread to cause physical illness. Wilson, for example, becomes physically ill when he finds himself a cuckold. Wilson is so sick that in bright sunlight his face looks green.

Tom's interference in other people's lives has begun in earnest now. The chain of events will end only when three lie dead. Deranged by Myrtle's death, Wilson kills first Gatsby, then himself. Tom the corrupter plays an important part in these deaths. Yet even Tom suffers momentarily from the general corruption. He is as much of a cuckold as Wilson. Corruption touches all, makes everyone sick. The stench of decay comes from everywhere until finally the dream itself rots. All suffer, but Gatsby pays more, pays the highest

> price for living too long with a single dream. He must have looked up at an unfamiliar sky through frightening leaves and shivered as he found what a grotesque thing a rose is and how raw the sunlight was upon the scarcely created grass. (p. 162)

As Nick sees it, Gatsby gains tragic understanding in this moment of death and rebirth, but a terrible beauty is born. To Nick, learning that a rose is grotesque symbolizes a brutal rape of innocence that causes a deep alienation.[34] Nick sees a cynic being born in this moment of death, a cynic who dies in the next second. Of course no one can know whether Gatsby experienced tragic realization or not. What can be ascertained with some surety is that Nick did. Nick, who projects his own feelings onto Gatsby, knows that the grass suffers harsh sun and that the rose is grotesque, the epitome of the promise about to be denied. Nick has seen the spring and the winter, the whole cycle of seasons, and never again will life look as good to him as it did that fresh green day when he settled in West Egg.

Water Imagery

If consistent use of imagery can infuse a poetic quality into a work of prose, then *The Great Gatsby* resembles a long narrative poem. Image patterns run like threads through this novel, and chief among these threads that bind the novel together are references to water. A careful study of water imagery proves that Fitzgerald saw as a fact of life that the great promises inherent in the rains of spring must go unfulfilled. Through the first half of the novel water promises life, a rebirth every spring; through the second half it symbolizes disaster and death.[35]

As the novel opens, Nick Carraway optimistically goes east in the spring. Rather than live in the city, he chooses as his home an island, one of a ''pair of enormous eggs, identical in contour and separated only by a courtesy bay'' (p. 5). He mistakenly believes this move permanent, thinks himself at home near the sea, close to the sources of life. He actually conceives of his life on the apparently fertile West Egg as a rebirth. Describing his environment and his reaction to it, he says,

> And so with the sunshine and the great bursts of leaves growing on the trees, just as things grow in the fast movies, I had that familiar conviction that life was beginning over again with the summer. (p. 4)

All seems well in this fertile land washed by the sea. Both East and West Egg appear to be identical islands of promise, but the inhabitants of East Egg are neither sustained nor rejuvenated by their idyllic paradise. Tom, a genteel storm trooper, chases women and worries about maintaining the supremacy of the white race.

Daisy and Jordan Baker are witty, sophisticated, but bored. On West Egg, however, the situation differs. Nick is full of hope, and Gatsby is practically a priest of dreams. Gatsby has built his own world, structured his own universe on West Egg, and when Nick first sees him, he stands, like a Druid conducting solemn rites, before the water. Nick says,

> I didn't call to him, for he gave a sudden intimation that he was content to be alone—he stretched out his arms toward the dark water in a curious way, and, far as I was from him, I could have sworn he was trembling. Involuntarily I glanced seaward—and distinguished nothing except a single green light, minute and far away, that might have been the end of a dock. (pp. 21-22)

This immediately plants the suggestion that Gatsby follows a grail, pays homage to a dream. He tries here, as he will through the novel, to go back, to erase the past, to be born again into a spring five years earlier.

Fitzgerald paints the solemn portrait of Gatsby staring at the green light as if he were in the presence of a deity, and he pictures Nick "alone again in the unquiet darkness" (p. 22). Then he moves directly to the valley of ashes, a "fantastic farm where ashes grow like wheat into ridges and hills and grotesque gardens" (p. 23). This valley, populated by "ash-gray" men, lies beneath the scrutiny of Doctor T. J. Eckleburg, who becomes as much of a surrogate god to Wilson as the green light does to Gatsby. Juxtaposing these two scenes, Fitzgerald forces comparison. West Egg at night is a small island bounded by an immense body of water and an even larger sky. Mystery surrounds West Egg, but no sense of romantic wonder touches the domain of Doctor T. J. Eckleburg. The eyes of this man-made god have been "dimmed a little by many paintless days under sun and rain" (p. 23). Unchanging nature will eliminate Eckleburg, a cheap, gaudy foil to Gatsby's simple green light across the Sound. And the water here is not the water of the sea, but a "small foul river" (p. 23). Obviously not the river of life, this is the end of the drain of a dying culture.

Fitzgerald entices the reader into other comparisons, too. Both Eggs, for example, are physically similar, but spiritually antipathetic: East Egg is peopled by the established, the calm, the quiet gentry whose major strength is savoir faire; West Egg is peopled by Gatsby and his crowd. An upstart with a shady background, Gatsby is gauche, gaudy, naive. And if Gatsby looks awkward compared to East Eggers, those at Myrtle's party in New York and the Wilsons from the valley are social clowns. Myrtle Wilson, for example, buys a copy of *Town Tattle* and a movie magazine the moment she arrives in New York. She buys her perfume at the train-station drug store. Her New York apartment is badly and clumsily furnished. McKee, a photographer, claims to be "in the artistic game" and his wife boasts that he has photographed her 127 times. But these apparent contrasts pale before the real similarities among all groups.

Neither the Buchanans nor Jordan Baker are intrinsically better than the Wilsons or the McKees. No one actually does more than McKee, who contributes practically nothing. Nick describes McKee's photograph of Mrs. McKee's mother as an "over-enlarged photograph, apparently [of] a hen sitting on a blurred rock" (p. 29). This oblique reference to an egg comments ironically on McKee's fertility as an artist. Complacency, a willingness to take life exactly as they find it, makes all of these people similar. The only real contrast is between Gatsby and the rest of the world. Because of his love, because of his dream, Gatsby can become whatever he wants to make himself. That Gatsby, like Dr. Faustus, squanders his great gift on adolescent trifles diminishes none of the original luster of the man, pales none of the glow that enticed Nick to tell his story. If the object of his affections was shallow and false, his love was deep and true. His romantic love confronts reality and leads to his destruction. His love is "destructive by reason of its very tenderness."[36]

As the novel proceeds, Fitzgerald aligns the gaudy vitality of Gatsby against the white sterility of the Buchanans.[37] Gatsby's parties reach raucous heights, but Gatsby's inner state, masked by an outer formal placidity that tries to match the calm Buchanans, is perhaps more raucous. As he surveys the world he has created, Gatsby seems as imperturbable as Doctor T. J. Eckleburg. He fails to remain calm in the face of life, however, as his later conduct indicates.[38] At the parties only nature remains unchanged; it acts as a sort of moral index to the follies of man. No amount of celebration can disturb the serenity of the surrounding water: "The moon had risen higher, and floating in the Sound was a triangle of silver scales, trembling a little to the stiff, tinny drip of the banjoes on the lawn" (p. 47). This is Nick's perception. Water does not tremble to the "tinny drip of banjoes"; it is associated with life, with permanence, but before the novel is half finished, Fitzgerald quietly begins to associate water with death, too. As Nick and Gatsby cross the Queensboro Bridge in Gatsby's car, a hearse and a procession of mourners pass them. This serves two purposes: it connects death with both water and Gatsby's car. To stress this point, Nick says, "I was glad that the sight of Gatsby's splendid car was included in [the mourners'] somber holiday" (p. 69).

Because the mention of death is exceedingly casual, water remains primarily associated with life and rebirth. This makes the rain quite effective in the chapter where Daisy and Gatsby meet and presumably renew their love. Rain forms a prominent background here, which would seem to be a blessing. Gatsby, at first awkward, shy, miserable, finally gains the courage to be alone with Daisy. Nick leaves them and points out that

> once more it was pouring, and my irregular lawn . . . abounded in small muddy swamps and *prehistoric* marshes. There was nothing to look at from under the tree except Gatsby's enormous house, so I stared at it, like Kant at his church steeple, for half an hour. (p. 89; italics mine).

The courtship ritual is timeless, has rejuvenated the race through the ages. As rejuvenating rains of spring fall on the roof, Gatsby and Daisy revive a love that has lain dormant for five years. Love is reborn, and Nick notes a "change in Gatsby that was simply confounding. He literally glowed; without a word or a gesture of exultation a new well being radiated from him and filled the little room'' (p. 90).

Reborn, Gatsby recaptures his past. Yet even at this peak when Gatsby has achieved everything he wanted, when his dream has been realized, Fitzgerald sounds several ominous notes. First the green light loses its significance: "Now it was again a green light on a dock. His count of enchanted objects had diminished by one'' (p. 94). The light, of course, had been a symbol of Gatsby's idealized love for Daisy, and Daisy in the flesh can never be as satisfying as the platonic symbol had been. Other hints that this love has been fertilized and reborn only to die occur in the tone of the prose where Fitzgerald describes the rain falling on Daisy and Gatsby. When Nick helps Daisy out of the car, he says

> The exhilarating ripple of her voice was a wild tonic in the rain. I had to follow the sound of it for a moment, up and down, with my ear alone, before any words came through. A damp streak of hair lay like a dash of blue paint across her cheek, and her hand was wet with glistening drops as I took it to help her from the car. (p. 86)

And when Gatsby, having fled the encounter he had dreamed of for five years, returns to the house, Nick says that Daisy

> turned her head as there was a light dignified knocking at the front door. I went out and opened it. Gatsby, pale as death, with his hands plunged like weights in his coat pockets, was standing in a puddle of water glaring tragically into my eyes.
>   With his hands still in his coat pockets, he stalked by me into the hall, turned sharply as if he were on a wire, and disappeared into the livingroom. It wasn't a bit funny. Aware of the loud beating of my own heart I pulled the door to against the increasing rain. (pp. 86–87)

Both of these passages combine the comic, the grotesque, the pathetic. Gatsby's entrance with his hands stuffed in his pockets *must* be hilarious, and yet, as Nick says, "It wasn't a bit funny." It is humorous, also, that before their love can flourish, both must be immersed totally in water. The streak of hair plastered like paint across Daisy's cheek and Gatsby's "turning as if he were on a wire" both border on the grotesque. Something very real pervades both passages, yet there is more that is not real. Wherever Gatsby goes, the hint of fable follows, and the element of the grotesque never quite disappears. It is necessary to ask, finally, whether a love like this can be fruitful.

The chapter following this love scene offers strong proof that Fitzgerald considered water in terms of death and rebirth. Here Nick explicitly describes the death of James Gatz and the simultaneous birth of Jay Gatsby:

> James Gatz—that was really, or at least legally, his name. He had changed it at the age of seventeen and at the specific moment that witnessed the beginning of his career—when he saw Dan Cody's yacht drop anchor over the most insidious flat on Lake Superior. It was James Gatz who had

been loafing along the beach that afternoon in a torn jersey and a pair of canvas pants, but it was already Jay Gatsby who borrowed a rowboat, pulled out to the Toulomee, and informed Cody that a wind might catch him and break him up in half an hour. (pp. 98–99)

On the water, Jay Gatsby "sprang from his Platonic conception of himself. . . . He invented just the sort of Jay Gatsby that a seventeen-year-old boy would be likely to invent, and to his conception he was faithful to the end" (p. 99). James Gatz exists no more. The gestation period sapped him of his vitality, and he ceased to exist when Gatsby sprang fully armed from his head. The idea had a difficult pregnancy. Fitzgerald describes this period when James Gatz's mind swelled with Gatsby, and his central figure is a bizarre water image:

His heart was in a constant, turbulent riot. The most grotesque and fantastic conceits haunted him in his bed at night. A universe of ineffable gaudiness spun itself out in his brain while the clock ticked on the wash-stand and the moon soaked with wet light his tangled clothes on the floor. (pp. 99–100)

Thus Fitzgerald consciously uses water imagery to symbolize death and rebirth. Yet as the novel draws to a close, it becomes increasingly clear that water symbolism makes an ironic comment. The promises of April are false, and Fitzgerald knows it. Almost instinctively, his heroes seek renewal in water. Nick chooses to live on the fertile island of West Egg; Gatsby goes for one last swim. At first water seems to provide the vitality they need, but finally water is rendered powerless against the passage of time. Water cannot return what passing seasons have taken away. Time, after all, killed Gatsby's dream, and thus killed Gatsby.

Fitzgerald's obsession that April promises what it never intends to give robs *The Great Gatsby* of any possibility of being an optimistic summer novel. How could a love spawned in the spring of youth and reborn five years later in the revitalizing rains of another spring possibly fail? How could a man grow old, how could anything die on fertile West Egg? If water were the powerful force of renewal it appears to be in the opening pages of *The Great Gatsby*, none of these things could happen. But they do. Reality is a harsh render of dreams. And the reality is that simply because the rains of one spring engender life, no one can assume that the rains of the following spring will do likewise. What is past cannot be recalled, cannot be repeated even under similar circumstances; a man might grow nostalgic for the very plot of ground where he stands.

Gatsby tries to transplant Louisville to New York, but the actors have changed. In spite of the apparent signs of fertility, Gatsby must watch his love melt on a turgid, brutal day. And Nick believes that before Gatsby dies, he must have learned that his dream was hollow:

He must have looked up at an unfamiliar sky through frightening leaves and shivered as he found what a grotesque thing a rose is and how raw the sunlight was upon the scarcely created grass. A new world, material without being real, where poor ghosts, breathing dreams like air drifted fortuitously about . . . like that ashen, fantastic figure gliding toward him through the amorphous trees. (p. 162)

Nick, too, watches his prospects fade. A new man, but not one revitalized, he enters what he considers middle age. He is thirty and not happy about it: "Thirty—the promise of a decade of loneliness, a thinning list of single men to know, a thinning brief-case of enthusiasm, thinning hair" (p. 136). And because of what he learns through his association with Gatsby, he also must experience a time of thinning hope, if increased humanity.

After Myrtle Wilson's death, water imagery openly foreshadows death. West Egg is no longer a fertile paradise. Fog has moved in, and the fog horn disrupts Nick's sleep. It is autumn, not spring. When the gardener tells Gatsby he is going to drain the pool to keep the leaves from plugging the pipes, Gatsby tells him not to do it. He refuses to admit that spring has gone. The final irony comes, of course, when Gatsby, dead, drifts aimlessly in the pool:[39]

There was a faint, barely perceptive movement of the water as the fresh flow from one end urged its way toward the drain at the other. With little ripples that were hardly the shadows of waves, the laden mattress moved irregularly down the pool. A small gust of wind that scarcely corrugated the surface was enough to disturb its accidental course with its accidental burden. The touch of a cluster of leaves revolved it slowly, tracing, like the leg of transit, a thin red circle in the water. (pp. 162–63)

The key word is "accidental." This is not, after all, a well-structured universe where plans work. Gatsby does not live in a world where "life was something you dominated if you were any good. Life yielded easily to intelligence and effort, or to what proportion could be mustered of both."[40] No, life is not that. Gatsby lives in a universe where dreams, hopes, and merit are equally meaningless.[41] Gatsby died innocently for his dream while Tom and Daisy "smashed up things and creatures and then retreated back into their money or their vast carelessness" (p. 180). The image that closes the novel shows further man's helplessness in an accidental universe: "So we beat on, boats against the current, borne back ceaselessly into the past" (p. 182). This accurately describes man's plight. In such a universe, it is impossible to base hope on the rain that falls during Gatsby's funeral, and the line, "Blessed are the dead that the rain falls on" is an ironic joke (p. 176). Water actually becomes a deterministic symbol of time, the destroyer; it becomes a mindless force beating "boats against the current."

Fitzgerald says in *The Crack-Up* that he "must hold in balance the sense of futility of effort and the necessity of struggle."[42] Charles Weir, Jr., suggests that this theme runs through all of Fitzgerald's work,[43] and I would agree. Certainly water symbolism supports this theme, the idea that man is defeated before he begins, but that the fall starts only when he becomes too weary to struggle. This is exactly what happened to Gatsby. His dream cracked up against the reality posed by Tom, and with the explosion of that dream, he could only welcome death. Time and life had passed him, and he could no longer be enchanted by the "fresh, green breast of the new world" (p. 182). Gone is the time when

> for a transitory enchanted moment man must have held his breath in the presence of this continent, compelled into an aesthetic contemplation he neither understood nor desired, face to face for the last time in history with something commensurate to his capacity to wonder. (p. 182)

Neither Gatsby nor America can return to that Edenic time before they learned their dream was hollow, before they lost their innocence, their purity.

The import of the car deepens in *The Great Gatsby*. At first a flashy and admired symbol of what technological society can produce, the car becomes a despoiler, an image of death. It is the creature that disturbs Eden and creates the valley of ashes, "a product of the technological power that also makes possible Gatsby's wealth, his parties, his car."[44] Gatsby sees the automobile as a vehicle to carry him down the road to glory, to the fulfillment of the American dream. Yet at the end of that road lies meaningless death. The symbol is circular; the automobile, the dream, and death become one.

As in the rest of Fitzgerald's novels, communication devices in *The Great Gatsby* are letters, books, newspapers, and telephones. None of these devices facilitate communication; they either break it off or they misinform. Gatsby's books stand unread on the shelf; had he read them, his narrow universe might have broadened, and he might have conceived a better dream. Newspapers make a goddess out of the ordinary Daisy, and Gatsby accepts the picture they paint. The telephone never aids communication. Often it interrupts just when people might have a chance of getting to know one another. In the second bloom of the love between Gatsby and Daisy, the telephone rings and juxtaposes the reality of Gatsby's business life with his dream. Finally, nothing communicates except the novel, which makes a human being out of a myth. What Nick learns—and communicates to the reader—as he tells the story of Gatsby is that his subject "can be understood only in relation to the 'last and greatest of all human dreams': the original European vision of" America.[45]

Although the light-dark imagery really did not function fully in *This Side of Paradise* and *The Beautiful and Damned*, Fitzgerald finally establishes this important image pattern and gets full value out of it by making traditional images ironic. Darkness, for example, does not hide Gatsby. Only when night blots out the gaudy frills and trappings of the mythic Gatsby can the real Jay Gatsby appear. Not the cardboard character that Jay Gatsby, third-rate artist with an adolescent imagination, created but a genuine human being emerges from the darkness. While Nick has "unaffected scorn" for the character, he will tell the tale of the human being.

The meaning of the moon, too, is reversed. Earlier a symbol of romance and escape, the moon in *The Great Gatsby* eventually becomes the light for an El Greco nightmare. A helpful stage light for Gatsby, the moon later makes painfully vivid and surreal both death and obscenity. The final view of Gatsby's dream is an obscene word glowing in the moonlight on Gatsby's porch. A monument more fit could not be found; the dream is obscene, no matter how pure the dreamer.

If in earlier novels artificial light represented romance and escape, here it symbolizes the very human attempt to control the environment. Gatsby strives valiantly, but fails. He can illuminate only the merest flicker of a moment; then his lights fail, disappear like the "inessential" houses in Nick's re-creation, his vision, of virgin America. Yet for one brilliant moment, Gatsby apparently fetched order from chaos through artificial light. But Gatsby, as light man for this tiny universe, uses illumination to dazzle and to create a world that never existed. He would mask the flaws in the realization of his shabby dream.

The sun symbolizes the reality that ravages Gatsby's world. All characters try to avoid the sun, and naturally, Tom Buchanan grows muddled when he tries to talk about it. But in chapter 7 even Gatsby, world-champion dreamer, must face truth beneath the squelching sun. Gatsby's dream melts in the heat like the plastic thing it is. And Gatsby dies the next day as the sun shines. But death is not the single reality. Life is real, too, and with the coming of morning, the second rebirth occurs in *The Great Gatsby*. James Gatz became Jay Gatsby in moonlight; Nick Carraway, spectator, becomes Nick Carraway, participating human being, in that morning sun.

Corruption imagery is less pervasive, but more systematically organized in *The Great Gatsby* than in *The Beautiful and Damned*. All corruption stems from three clearly recognizable sources—the valley of ashes, the ravages of man, and moral rot. The valley of ashes seems at first to be a geographically contained area that produces nothing but dust and makes every other area look good. But ashes are everywhere, and everyone must pass through the valley of death; those who make the journey are no longer innocent of foul dust, the single product of the valley. Contamination is circular. The rest of the world created the ash heap, which now contaminates the rest of the world. As the valley produces "foul dust," West Egg produces "meretricious beauty," East Egg an explosive ennui—three products of equal value. Tom would pluck the flower of the valley, Myrtle; Gatsby would win the mindless beauty of East Egg, Daisy; and Myrtle would go anywhere to escape, but finds the only route from the valley is death. Gatsby takes the same route.

As man caused the valley of ashes, of course, he is also responsible for destructive forces loosed against his fellows. He rapes the land, ravages other men. Tom and Daisy leave death and ruin in their wake, and so does Gatsby. His Saturday-night parties leave in chaotic shambles the world he spent the previous week structuring. Boasting that he can repeat the past, he walks among "fruit rinds and discarded favors and crushed flowers.'' And Fitzgerald leaves to the reader's imagination the desolation Gatsby might have caused in building his empire with his partner, Meyer Wolfsheim.

Oddly, characters like Wolfsheim and Tom Buchanan do not contaminate other characters. Corruption is widespread and apparently innate. Corruption imagery, for example, soils Daisy's "white girlhood" long before she meets Tom, and Jordan Baker's moral idiocy certainly cannot be blamed on either Tom or Wolfsheim. Gatsby wears his association with Wolfsheim unself-consciously, and it is his dream, not his business "gonnection," that leads to his moral lapses. Corruption touches everyone and runs from the weakness of Klipspringer to the ruthlessness of Dan Cody, precursor to that ultimate in human corruption, Meyer Wolfsheim. Simply stated, the corrupt American dream inspires deeds of corruption, not of valor. The world cries for purgation, a flood of forty days and forty nights. And there is a purgation of death—the Wilsons, Gatsby. But the valley lives on. Wolfsheim and the Buchanans survive. The single hope is Nick, who has seen the source of Gatsby's vision. Out of the corruption comes death, certainly, but also a new, human Nick whose humanity enables him to tell the story of Gatsby.

The essential image pattern in *The Great Gatsby* is water imagery. Unlike Anthony Patch, Jay Gatsby sees in the ocean and the rains an infinity of possibility. Whereas Anthony cannot fall because he fails to rise, Gatsby climbs to marvelously gaudy height upon the tail of a false dream. Both Gatsby and Nick Carraway come East to build new lives on an egg-shaped island in the sea. The possibilities seem boundless, marred only by the valley of ashes and the ''small foul river'' (p. 23). Compared to the possibilities expressed by spring, by the water of life, the valley seems unimportant; yet the valley of death, not continual resurrection in water, is the reality—what life delivers as opposed to what it promises.

At first, however, water seems an unsullied symbol of rebirth, of the continuing life cycle. But as Nick sees the world of the novel more clearly, water begins to symbolize death. The initial hint comes when Nick and Gatsby pass a corpse on the Queensboro Bridge. This leads the reader to view in a more somber light the rain that falls as Gatsby and Daisy renew their love, as they try one damp afternoon to eradicate five years. The earlier association with death and the general tone of the prose hints that Fitzgerald finds something both futile and grotesque in what Gatsby and Daisy are trying to do.

Fitzgerald uses a flashback to show explicitly that he thought of water in terms of death and rebirth; when James Gatz becomes Jay Gatsby, the dominating symbol is a bizarre moon-water image. The rebirth actually occurs on water; James Gatz rows out, and Jay Gatsby climbs aboard Dan Cody's boat. The rebirth is real, but also the last one Jay Gatsby will have. Time is more powerful than water or dreams. The reader and the protagonist discover simultaneously that time causes the vast difference between what one spring delivers and what a later one delivers. That irony creates the essential differences between *The Great Gatsby* and the first two novels. All was promise to young Amory Blaine, and he never fell. Anthony Patch had no potential, started out too low to fall. But the world, wet and rich in potentiality, belonged to Gatsby. He returned to water on the last day of his life, but found water powerless. Time had already taken his world away.

3

Tender Is the Night

As is common knowledge, Fitzgerald spent the nine years from 1925 to 1934 working on the various versions that eventually became *Tender Is The Night.*. He had more false starts on *Tender Is the Night* than on *This Side of Paradise,* and as the previously cited biographies make clear, his life was in considerably greater disarray after 1925 than before. Matthew J. Bruccoli finds seventeen stages of *Tender Is The Night* in the F. Scott Fitzgerald Papers at the Princeton University Library, dividing these stages into three main groups: "The Francis Melarky or matricide group, the Lew Kelly or shipboard group, and the Dick Diver group. The Melarky group is the earliest; Fitzgerald worked longest with it, and much of it ultimately found its way into the published novel."[1]

The three groups represent essentially different novels and characters with opposite natures; it is thus amazing that Fitzgerald could use any of the material from the earlier versions in the final novel, but he did, and he made them fit. Bruccoli observes that none of the "actions of Melarky which are transferred to Rosemary . . . is inappropriate to her, although she and Francis have entirely dissimilar natures."[2] He further notes that

> the metamorphosis of Francis Melarky into Rosemary Hoyt and Dick Diver is one of the most intriguing aspects of these manuscripts, for it is accomplished without awkwardness. That the experiences of a violent young man should be converted into the experiences of both an ingenuous actress and a profoundly intelligent psychiatrist seems, on the surface, absurd. Yet when it is done, there is no patchwork discernible.[3]

Why does this work? I would submit that in spite of the chaos in his life and even his composition methods, the Fitzgerald who wrote *Tender Is the Night* was a thoroughly mature artist who could establish image patterns that would create inner unity and strength in any work he attempted and out of any chaos he confronted.

Transportation Imagery

As in other Fitzgerald novels the automobilie in *Tender Is The Night* immediately establishes social position. The symbol is so rigid that Fitzgerald possibly meant it as a parody of itself. What else could Nicole and Baby Warren drive but a Rolls Royce? Do they have an ounce of choice? And the Divers drive a "big Isotta."[4] Given their immense wealth, their choices, too, are limited. Diver may understand this, but Nicole and Baby believe money gives them choice. Assuming ostentation in the mere owning of a Rolls, the Warren car is quietly ostentatious, Gatsby's blaringly so. The Warren sisters, like Tom Buchanan, would view a man like Gatsby with smirking scorn. They would recognize that given his limitations, Gatsby could have chosen no other car. The Warrens have taste, certainly, and wealth so thoroughly established that the emblem of their social standing need never be gaudy; but they, as surely as Gatsby, must choose within the limits of their vision. Dick Diver began with a wider vision, with more choices,[5] but he cancelled his options when he chose Nicole and her money.[6] Dr. Richard Diver, the better artist, chose to be Dick Diver, impresario. As a lesser artist, he chose to fashion a world like that created by others; he might have made one uniquely his own. He chose to drive a big Isotta.

As a device for measuring social position, the automobile engenders humor—poignant in that it typifies the tinsel human beings strive for. Generally, though, for Fitzgerald the automobile assumes a darker role. Of all the automobile references in *Tender Is the Night,* few are innocuous. One of these occurs when Rosemary, too sunburned to swim, must hire a car for a tour with her mother. Although the car already has become an ominous image, nothing happens to her on this journey. In this novel, Rosemary is the eternal child,[7] free forever from harm.

The other harmless automobile reference occurs when Dick is still in command of himself, when he can still work miracles for the entertainment of others, especially Rosemary and Nicole. To show his social omnipotence, he commandeers the car of the Shah of Persia. Not unduly impressed, Rosemary takes for granted that this great man, this magical wizard of the social world can do anything (p. 138). Whether or not hints of disaster exist in this scene depends on the reader's view of Dick's motives for taking the car. Does Dick act from a spirit of hilarity or of hysteria? Although a note of depression has infiltrated the Divers and party since they left the beach, this is clearly the act of a man still orchestrating experience for his wife and his friends; he is conducting a merry lark they can look back on and laugh at in years to come. Only later, when Dick is too weary to conduct such pranks, does the disintegration begin to show.

Dick remains impervious to automobiles until he escorts Rosemary home from the houseboat cafe in a taxi. The kiss in the back of that cab lays the groundwork for the scene in Rosemary's room where the eighteen-year-old actress asks Dick to "Take me" (p. 125). Still in control, Dick need not take her. He handles this difficult scene with the grace and charm for which he is famous.[8] But next day, Dick's control is less total. The affair—invigorating to Rosemary, enervating to Dick—gains impetus in the back seat of another cab: they "lurched together as if the taxi had swung them" (p. 136). In this scene, the stage manager is Rosemary, not Dick: "It was time for Rosemary to cry, so she cried a little in her handkerchief" (p. 136).

Quite early in the novel, transportation becomes associated with madness, just as later it will be associated with the grotesque and the violent. The first meaningful reference to a mode of transportation appears in one of Nicole's letters to Diver. She refers to a mysterious "they," the undefined people who follow her down Michigan Boulevard and finally force her into a car full of nurses. Totally unstable, she views both the car and those taking care of her as part of the conspiracy, part of the imagined menace feeding her madness.

The automobile becomes associated with the truly grotesque, however, only when that anachronistic barbarian, Tommy Barban, challenges the whining novelist, McKisco—Diver's small-spirited foil—to a duel as they ride back to the hotel from the Diver villa. It is a night of madness, a darkness crowded with events and people even more crazy than the duel. The grotesque spectacle opens when Barban *seriously* challenges McKisco in Nicole's honor. Solemnly, he proposes a mad act designed to silence Mrs. McKisco's gossip about Nicole's madness. The car stops, and with the formality of a sacred rite, Barban utters the challenge, casts the gage. Terrified, McKisco finds himself absurdly trapped by his wife's impudence, his own petulence. Add to this mad scene the titillated homosexual, Campion, who chatters about the duel, weeps at the loss of his lover, Royal Dumphrey. Some of them drunk, some sick, some merely curious, a caravan of actors and observers drives through the night toward that unlikely combination of serious melodrama and theatre of the absurd. Of those in the caravan, the only casualties are Campion, who faints, and McKisco, who vomits.

The pattern of transportation imagery grows increasingly grotesque. Note the scene at the train station where the Divers and Rosemary go to see Abe off on the first leg of a trip designed to take him to his work in America. Fitzgerald lavishes the best, most graphic prose in this scene on Abe's gigantic hangover and on the alienation he feels toward everyone. Amidst images of sickness, death, and separation, one of the many violent acts occurs: Maria Wallace shoots her British companion. To add either heavy-handed symbolism or grotesque humor to this pivotal scene, Fitzgerald has the bullet obliterate the man's identification card. At any rate, the shot is "part of the device of underlining the turning points of the novel with shots."[9] It also forms part of the emerging pattern of imagery that links transportation with the grotesque, with violence, with death. When Dick's father dies, Dick uses ship, train, and car to return to the U.S. for the funeral. On this journey, Dick attempts both to renew himself by returning to the source of his beliefs and to admit that those roots no longer have anything to do with the present Dick Diver. When Dick makes that admission, one way of life dies, another begins.

Continuing the vein of violence, Nicole explodes in a madness that long had been building as she, Dick, and the children drive back from the fair. Her conduct at the fair, while bizarre, was not dangerous. Riding home, however, violent madness erupts, becomes part of the pattern of automobile imagery when Nicole grabs the wheel:

> The car swerved violently left, swerved right and tipped on two wheels as Dick, with Nicole's voice screaming in his ear, crushed down the mad hand clutching the steering wheel, righted itself, swerved once more and shot off the road; it tore through the underbrush, tipped again and settled slowly at an angle of ninety degrees against a tree. (p. 208)

This mad scene in the car recalls the letter where Nicole was certain she had been abducted.

Nicole's madness coupled with the death of his father hastens Dick's descent. When he stops in Rome, he sleeps with Rosemary, as he had not had to do in Paris. Consistent with the transportation imagery, he thinks taxi drivers have overcharged him, and he engages in a desperate fight. This marks Dick's lowest point to date. Drunk, he finds himself worse off than Anthony Patch, who in *The Beautiful and Damned* dreamed of thrashing a taxi driver. In his dream, Anthony emerged victorious; Dick, badly beaten in a real battle, nearly loses an eye. But psychic wounds make small his physical injuries. His reality is much more sordid than Anthony's dream.

Violence in transportation imagery continues aboard T.F. Golding's yacht. Dick, his charm gone, disgraces himself utterly, then threatens suicide. For a single moment it would seem that he and Nicole might end their lives with a grand romantic gesture:

> Cold in terror she put her other wrist in his grip. All right, she would go with him—again she felt the beauty of the night vividly in one moment of complete response and abnegation—all right, then—but now she was unexpectedly free and Dick turned his back, sighing, "Tch! tch!" (p. 292)

Like the duel, this gesture promises much, produces only an ache, an anxiety. No feeling remains between Nicole and Dick, who is too drunk even to drive home afterwards when they have gone ashore. Tommy Barban takes Dick's place in the driver's seat, as well as everywhere else. As Tommy drives, Dick rests in the back seat in an "appeased sleep, belching now and then contentedly into the soft warm darkness" (p. 293). For Dick and Nicole, only the inevitable break remains. When that comes, bicycles and automobiles race by. The path is circular, and the symbolism is simple; all roads lead to exactly where Dick is sitting right now. Tommy demands Nicole, and the traffic passes. At the end of the affair, Nicole is cured: it is Dick now who is sick. There is no road out. Life goes on.

Communication Imagery

The idea also prevails throughout *Tender Is the Night*—as it did in the previous novels—that significant communication between human beings occurs only when it causes trouble for the protagonist. But as in *The Great Gatsby,* there are exceptions. A telephone can ring just in time to provide needed relief, or, depending on the point of view, just in time to save someone from facing reality. To those who hold the latter view, such a call hinders self-communication, precludes self-knowledge. Yet Fitzgerald would probably subscribe to the Sophoclean view that while self-knowledge gained from trauma may build character, may even enable a person to stand as tall and fall as far as Oedipus, traumatic confrontations do nothing for stability, for mental health. When Collis Clay's call arrives on the heels of three mad, violent events—Maria Wallis has shot the Englishman at the train station, someone has just killed Jules Peterson, Nicole has suffered a serious relapse into mental illness—Rosemary feels great and necessary relief. The call spares her a closer look at a world grown increasingly chaotic. She is saved; her view that events have meaning, that a universal plan exists, remains intact. She can continue her career in the belief that it matters. Dick comprehends absurdity, grows weary.[10]

Not communication, but lack of it, spares Rosemary the knowledge that saps Diver. Yet failure of communication is so common in Fitzgerald that it becomes one of Diver's tribulations. That failure, when not attributable to inadequacy in the language or to paucity of ideas, generally occurs because machines designed to transmit communication break it off instead. Even communication devices that work seem to lay traps for Diver. Such is the case of Nicole's early letters to him. These letters tell him more about Nicole than she would want him to know. They mark the extent of her madness, the progress of her cure. They were "divided into two classes, of which the first . . . was of a marked pathological turn, and . . . the second . . . was entirely normal and displayed a richly maturing nature" (p. 10). These letters intrigue Diver, man and doctor. He is drawn to this writer of the letters, and that causes his downfall, both as man and doctor.

Rarely, however, does a device communicate too much. More commonly, the message is either too dark and deep for words, or the speaker has nothing to say. Nicole's father, for example, carries a secret too dark for communication. No message is safe for this man; the most innocuous utterance might reveal too much. Once sufficiently close to his daughter to know her in the Biblical sense, he can now describe her only through a mixture of clichés: "She was smart as a whip and happy as the day is long" (p. 16). For Devereaux Warren, safety exists only within the cliché. The more weary the phrase, the safer he feels. Part of Fitzgerald's irony here is that because the man can remain inviolate only through silence, the telephone forces him to speak, to reveal his secret. This is absolutely consistent with Fitzgerald's use of devices of communication elsewhere. Had Warren anything to gain from relating his story, Dr. Dohmler could not have used the telephone to bully him into returning to the clinic to confess incest.

The telephone, of course, facilitates communication and enhances Nicole's opportunity for recovery, but it does not help Diver, except as a *doctor* healing a patient. For the *man,* the knowledge gained through this telephone call forms a link in the chain of destruction. Paradoxically, Diver can cure his patient only when he ceases to be a doctor. Their relationship is that of vampire to victim. Healthy and strong in the end, Nicole leaves Dick a bloodless drifter.

While Warren finally had plenty to say, the opposite usually holds true. Communication breaks down because people have said all there is to say, or because they had nothing to say in the first place. When Dick refuses to go to bed with Rosemary, that refusal closes communication. Leaving, Dick "gave her two lines of hospital patter to sleep on" (p. 127). Devereaux Warren hid behind a cliché, one that is the special providence of doltish fathers; Diver makes a graceful exit, uses doctors' banalities to evade the truth that nothing remained to be said. Thus two vastly different men use basically the same tactics, yet they remain moral mountains apart. But Diver nears Warren's position, and his bedside manner loses considerable charm, when he actually does go to bed with Rosemary, who symbolically is as much his daughter as Nicole is Warren's biological daughter.[11]

When Nicole bids farewell to Abe at the train station, even less remains to be said than when Dick left Rosemary to sleep alone. With Abe too deep in drunkenness for human communication, these two old friends can say nothing. Abe feels too sick, too tired to don his traditional mask, that of court jester, which itself severs communication. Too often he has worn the mask, and his friends have grown weary of it. He, too, is tired of it, and there is no longer anything behind the mask. As so often is the case with Fitzgerald characters, there is nothing to say, nothing to be done.

When something might be said, Fitzgerald erects a barrier against communication. This barrier is usually a machine designed to transmit communication, but might even be human. A chaperone, for example, disrupts serious conversation as effectively as does a jangling telephone. Early in their romance Dick and Nicole have a chance to be alone, but the señora, the chaperone, guards against communication of any kind. Only when they bid her "buenas noches" can they talk. This classic dilemma of young lovers is ironic in that the lovers are not young. Nicole's insanity renders her a child, but her experience—what she was born knowing, what she learned—makes *child* a curious term when applied to her. Experience and education should make Dick a man of the world, but he is a born naif, a child. The irony cuts many ways in this scene, and the communication that flows when the barrier departs is disastrous to Diver. He will fall into fatal love.

Generally the telephone acts as a dam against communication, but sometimes the language itself fails. When Baby Warren tries to help Dick after the Roman brawl, she has trouble, partially because she speaks a language different from those she seeks to enlist in her cause. But Baby always speaks a different language, even if every speaker mouths English.[12]

But the telephone, even more than the language or a paucity of ideas, acts as the most common block to communication. Fitzgerald hints often at the unreliability of the telphone. After Maria Wallis shoots the Britisher at the railway station, for example, Nicole wants Dick to telephone for help. Delegating authority in crisis, however, clashes with Dick's style. He will not telephone away his responsibility at this time. He has yet to deteriorate, to reach the point where he allows others to do what he does better than anyone else—create order from chaos.

Superior though he is to the telephone at this point, Dick later will experience comic defeat when he meets Rosemary in Rome. He suffers embarrassment, because he is tired, unshaven, but next day, spruced up, he visits Rosemary's room where she meets him in black pajamas. He has come to make love, and she seems dressed for it, but nothing can start because the telephone transforms each advance into a retreat.

At the first interruption by the telephone, Dick turns from Rosemary to two novels, one by McKisco, one by Edna Ferber. As Rosemary chatters, the waiter removes the breakfast table, which in a sense is removing a barrier. But almost immediately, the telephone rings again. Dick rises, symbolically moves his hat from bed to luggage stand. Rosemary admonishes him not to leave. He stays. When the telephone rings a third time, desperation drives him to McKisco's novel. Once more a frustrated Dick discovers the ironic discrepancy between expectation and actuality.

Not until the next night do they sleep together and finally communicate in the only way left to them. Fitzgerald comments wryly: "She wanted to be taken and she was, and what had begun with a childish infatuation on the beach was accomplished at last (p. 231).[13] This description makes the taking of Rosemary seem for Dick just one more inevitable and loathsome task out of the way. He never touches her again.

While that scene is comic—as comic as a scene can be where an old and dignified friend makes an ass of himself—later problems caused by the telephone are more serious. One such scene occurs when Dick calls the clinic to explain that Nicole's father is dying. Kaethe, his fellow psychologist's wife, receives the call. Dick forgets the most important part of the message, that Nicole should not be told of her father's impending death. Kaethe, whom Nicole has treated superciliously as a peasant, tells Nicole that Warren is near death. Jealous of Dick, disliking Nicole, Kaethe acts from spite, and Nicole suffers because she is not given the complete message.

One comic failure of communication nearly drives the squabbling Divers together again. Their relationship in decline, they return to the Villa Diana where they must endure the indignity of a drunken cook, Augustine, whom they cannot control. Augustine threatens, shouts, wields knives. The scene functions as comic relief for the reader, and would be comic relief for the Divers if they could end it and recall it in tranquility. Trying to close the scene, however, Nicole calls the police, "but was answered with . . . almost an echo of Augustine's laugh. She heard mumbles and passings of the word around—the connection was suddenly broken" (p. 285).

The telephone works no better here than it does in other Fitzgerald novels; it functions only when communication would be detrimental to the protagonist. The telephone works, for example, when it deprives a weary Diver of a night's sleep; it rouses Dick from bed so he can rush gallantly to the aid of Mary North and Lady Caroline Sibly-Biers when they are arrested for dressing as sailors and trying to seduce two young village girls. And the telephone works equally well to arrange the assignation between Tommy Barban and Nicole. For Dick, the benefits derived from Bell's marvelous invention lie buried beneath the liabilities.

Light-Dark Imagery

In *Tender Is The Night* Fitzgerald again uses four major qualities of light—moonlight, darkness (the absence of light), man-made or artificial light, and the natural light of day. In at least two instances, the sun in *Tender Is the Night* is surreal. And more often than in any other Fitzgerald novel, the sun is either obscured or filtered through something, thus giving a different quality to the light.

The moon as a symbol is first introduced in a context of madness. Compounding the significance of the moon, the "Diver's house on the Riviera is the Villa Diana and Nicole plays the virgin moon goddess."[14] Here the moon is both romantic and ominous. Rosemary notes that it "hovered over the ruins of the aqueducts," enhancing their appearance, yet connecting itself with the word *ruins* (p. 71). In the same tone, Rosemary listens to distant music through the "ghostly moonshine of her mosquito net . . . " (p. 71).

When the Diver party reaches Paris, innocent adventure takes on a cast of decadence. The river holds "many cold moons," and life loses romance (p. 121). No longer is Dick firmly in control; Abe's eyes are bloodshot from sun and wine. The decline continues with time. At the bar in Gstaad where the Divers meet Franz and Baby Warren for the Christmas holidays, the moon competes with artificial light. The Tunisian barman

> manipulated the illumination in a counterpoint, whose other melody was the moon off the ice rink staring in the big windows. In that light, Dick found the girl devitalized and uninteresting. He turned from her to enjoy the darkness, the cigarette points going green and silver when the lights shown red, the band of white that fell across the dancers as the door to the bar was opened and closed. (p. 194)

Dick shows more interest in tricks of light and in darkness than in human beings—a trait less than desirable in a psychologist.

Moons in *Tender Is the Night* are often cold. When Dick returns to America for his father's funeral, he finds a "cold moon bright over Chesapeake Bay" (p. 222). Gone are the days when the moon represented romance. This cold moon symbolizes death and madness—the death of his father and the lunacy of his wife. Not until Nicole ends their marriage and begins the affair with Tommy does moonlight regain its traditional romantic role. Nicole and Tommy swim in a "roofless cavern of white moonlight" as the excitement of their love grows

(p. 316). Moonlight marks beginnings, not ends. The moon blesses, makes lovely a young affair, but Dick knows the moon lies. He is no longer enchanted by the moon; Tommy and Nicole are. The moral of the moon and of the novel can be found in Keats' "Ode to a Nightingale": "The fancy cannot cheat so well as she is famed to do."

Man-made light in *Tender Is the Night* usurps the moon's traditional role. At Caux, for example, when Dick and Nicole escape from the others,

> stars began to come through the white crests of the high Alps. On the horseshoe walk over-looking the Lake Nicole was the figure motionless between two lamp stands. (p. 44)

"The necklace and bracelet of light" two thousand feet below further illuminate this clear stage picture (p. 47). When the storm douses the artifical light and the only illumination comes from lightning, they fall in love.

As in moonlight, one can lie to oneself in artifical light:

> Staring . . . across the upshine of a street-lamp, [Dick] used to think that he wanted to be good, he wanted to be brave and wise, but it was all pretty difficult. He wanted to be loved, too, if he could fit it in. (p. 23)

The odd word, *upshine,* draws attention to this passage. With nothing but sky to catch and reflect the light, it dissolves into the universe, showing nothing. By the "upshine" in Zurich, Dick chooses goals, separates his own destiny from that of others. And he makes a mistake. More than anything else, he wants to be loved, but he fails to recognize it in this light. Excessive desire for love is his flaw, the quality that makes him soft.

Generally, artificial light is theatrical. Rosemary finds the Brady studio in half darkness, an appropriate twilight for creating illusions. The stage—bathed in a "white crackling glow" until a bank of lights goes off with a "savage hiss"—connects the snake of evil with darkness (p. 79). The hint of evil taints theatrical lighting and casts a pall over some of Dick's accomplishments. Dick, social magician, creator, has arranged for the lights at his party to emerge slowly as evening deepens to dusk. As great a dispenser of illumination as Jay Gatsby, Dick has arranged for romantic candles, a table lamp of spicy pinks, wine-colored lanterns, and garden lanterns to light his party. He lights the Villa Diana as skillfully as any stage is lighted. Later everything will look sordid in the unreality of lights by night. By that time he can no longer envision possibilities; he is too tired to use his imagination.

Fitzgerald often says as much through darkness as through light. Chapter 1 of book 2, "Rosemary's Angle," opens with a stream-of-consciousness monologue in which light-dark imagery reveals Nicole as one generally happy, but also as one whose mind remains dark and gloomy. She points out that everything got dark after Topsy was born. Also, she says that she and Dick talk, lighting cigarettes deep into night, but when dawn approaches, they dive into pillows and sleep. Even during the best period of their marriage, they function better at night than in daylight.

The duel, too absurd for the light of day, occurs on a "limpid black night, hung as in a basket from a single dull star" (p. 97). On that night, Rosemary's chauffeur drives through "banks of darkness and thin night" (p. 97). Back at her hotel, Rosemary dreams, "cloaked by the erotic darkness" (p. 97). Darkness symbolizes not only the madness of the duel (a throwback to the dark ages), but the madness of Nicole, whose attack has occasioned the duel. Ironically and appropriately, a false dawn appears before the duel. It is not a real dawn, and to Tommy Barban, not a real duel. In darkness, one pretends.

Darkness even cloaks the war wounds of Amiens. By day the scars show clearly,

> but after dark all that is most satisfactory in French life swims back into the picture—the sprightly tarts, the men arguing with a hundred violas in the cafes, the couples drifting head to head, toward the satisfactory inexpensiveness of nowhere. (p. 120)

So far as the narrator is concerned, the best the French have to offer is illusion, one that won't tolerate the light of day.

Illusions of love also wane by light, thrive by night. When Dick and Rosemary kiss in the dark taxi, Dick is "chilled by the innocence of her kiss, by the glance that at the moment of contact looked beyond him out into the darkness of the night, the darkness of the world" (p. 125). Although they have no sexual intercourse, Rosemary loses the innocence of her kiss, becomes "one acquainted with the night." Night's illusion is the worldly "darkness of the world." Looking at Rosemary, Dick sees that "night had drawn the color from her face" (p. 125). Now, her lover notes, she possesses "all the world's dark magic" (p. 126).

When Dick arrives at Innsbruck at dusk, darkness offers balm for the wounds inflicted by reality.[15] In total blackness, he recalls better days with Nicole, nights bright with moonlight, mornings adrip with dew. But the surcease of pain is temporary, and Dick soon learns, in Rome, how unsavory are the denizens of darkness: "There were no women in the streets, only pale men with dark coats buttoned to the neck, who stood in groups beside shoulders of cold stone" (p. 239). Muddled, drunk in darkness, Dick fights taxi drivers and the police who arrest him, take him to a "bare barrack where carabinieri lounged under a single dim light" (p. 243). Even under this single dim light, the truth about Dick is clear enough. No more does he create, no more does he control others; he fails even to control himself. As Baby Warren tries to rescue what remains of Dick, her nerves "cringed faintly at the unstable balance between night and day" (p. 246). Outside the light creeps slowly, but within the jail, prisoner Diver sits in still, "violent darkness" (p. 246). From this darkness floats Dick's disembodied voice, "shouting and screaming" (p. 246).

Night, once reserved for love and joy, now cloaks nightmarish episodes. Darkness covers Dick's fight with taxi drivers, the McKisco-Barban duel, Peterson's death, Abe's fights and problems, the lesbian episode involving Mary North and Lady Sibley-Biers, and the near double suicide on T.F. Golding's yacht. After the strident evening on T.F. Golding's yacht, Dick rides in the back seat as Tommy Barban usurps the wheel. Drunk, Dick belches "now and then contentedly into the soft warm darkness" (p. 293). This drive tolls the death knell on his marriage; from this point, Barban sits in the driver's seat. It all happens at night. The greatest illusion, the most bitter irony, is the title of the novel: *Tender Is the Night*.

Nor is day tender. Neither day nor night provide refuge; that's the rub, the bitter, direct sunlight of reality. Sometimes, however, day fosters temporary illusion; in *Tender Is the Night*, Fitzgerald uses more indirect light, more shadows and filtered sun, than in his other novels. At first glance, for example, the clinic hardly seems a "refuge for the broken, the incomplete, the menacing. . . . " (p. 9). Sunshine makes it seem the paradigm of healthful settings. Despite the sun outside, however, smoke hazes Franz' office, causing immediate tension between sun and smoke. Dick opens the French windows to let the smoke out, to invite the sun in. The cone of sunshine mingles with smoke, causes Dick's mind to leap to his lovely patient, Nicole. In spite of the darkness in her mind, her beauty identifies her with sunlight. Dick, artist and doctor, must let out the darkness, the smoke, and bathe her continually in sun. When darkness comes, Dick must provide the sun himself.

Essentially, that is the purpose of the clinic and Dr. Diver—to fence out life's viscissitudes and allow the patients to mend in summer sun. Yet shadows snake through the bars:

> The veranda of the central building was illuminated from open French windows, save where the black shadows of stripling walls and the fantastic shadows of iron chairs slithered down into a gladiolus bed. (p. 24)

Snakes crawl this Eden; shadowy serpents explore the flower bed. Fitzgerald links shadows with evil masked as beauty—again, Nicole. Having set up this association, the narrator explains that Dick and Nicole "went down two steps to the path, where, in a moment, a shadow cut across it—she took his hand" (p. 25).

The reader seldom sees Nicole clearly because the light is seldom direct. One time Nicole looks lovely because rain blurs the sun: "her face, ivory against the blurred sunset that strove through the rain, had a promise Dick had never seen before" (p. 33). Blurred herself, she confuses Dick. Once, when Dick knows she cares for him, Nicole puzzles him by breaking a date. He feels caught in the middle of "centripetal and centrifugal" forces (p. 36). Confused, he goes to the tram depot, watches "spring twilight gilding the rails" (p. 36). This romantic twilight image only deepens his confusion. Yearning for substance, not shadow, he feels no comfort until the "substantial cobblestones of Zurich clicked once more under his shoes" (p. 36).

To Rosemary, when she first appears on the Riviera, Dick is sun itself. The sun blinds her, but her eyes gradually adjust to the ''brutal sunshine'' (p. 58). As the sun dazzles her, so—at first—does Dick. The creator of fabulous images captivates and blinds the young girl. While he retains the energy to work magic tricks of charm and sociability, she cannot see him clearly; but his light wanes with age, weariness. The one-time patron saint of social light suffers for blinding Rosemary, as he suffers for dazzling Nicole. In the beginning of both romances, Fitzgerald juxtaposes shadow and sun. As Rosemary tells her mother that she loves Dick, ''a heavy pattern of beams and shadows swayed with the motion of the pines outside'' (p. 68). These shadows are less ominous, less serpentine than those associated with Nicole, yet the pattern exists.

Finally, though, nothing escapes the direct light of sun. Sun slays illusion, and if there is any advantage to the direct light of reality, it is this: ''If the day is harsh, it has vigor; the night is the time of ease and also weakness.''[16] Dick ignores daylight until he grows soft and ineffectual. Typical of the Fitzgerald hero, he does not court the light of reality. When he meets it, he is soft.

With more subtlety than is his wont with images, Fitzgerald plants the first inference that danger lurks in light of day as Dick rides the funicular up to Caux and notes that on this bright day the sun is straight up. For the moment it casts no shadows on the ''white courts of Kursal'' (p. 40). On this shadowless day, he finds that Nicole's destination matches his own. As they approach Caux, ''the thousand windows of a hotel burned in the late sun'' (p. 42). And then suddenly, ''they were on top of the sunshine'' (p. 42). This romantic Icarian image, which recalls the earlier scene where Dick stares into the upshine of a street lamp, foreshadows a fall.

At the Villa Diana, the Divers seem to live in sunshine. On the surface, those who bask in the sun are in every way superior to those who have no tan. The McKisco party—two homosexuals, a pseudo artist, and two gabby women—pales next to the attractive Divers, but the Divers really spend little time in the sun. They retreat to the shade of the umbrella to talk, and finally, their basis in reality becomes more tenuous than that of the McKisco party, especially McKisco himself, who actually produces a novel, no matter how limited its merit. The only one who stays in the sun too long is the uninitiated Rosemary. Burned, she must separate herself from the swimming Divers for a couple of days.

The sun shows too much, characterizes too well for the comfort of those who luxuriate in illusion. Much better is Nicole's vegetable garden in ''the fuzzy green light'' (p. 83). Sickly and green like the garden, this light resembles Nicole. And if Dick had braved the sun, he never would have allowed himself the luxury of love with the child, Rosemary. If he looked closely, he would shun love with Nicole. But they all fall in love. Dick and Rosemary emerge at twilight from the ''perverted'' house on Rue Monsieur. They are lovers engaged in a twilight love—a desperate man grasping at a young girl as his youth and idealism flee, a young girl charmed by an older man. Time will rob Diver of both youth and charm, will cure Rosemary of her love for him.

After Dick confesses to Rosemary's mother that he loves her daughter, he shuts out the afternoon light, supposedly so he can work. In reality, though, he blocks out the light so he can maintain the illusion that he can have a meaningful love affair with this young girl. Later he will be jealous of her, and once more he will want to shut out the light: "Do you mind if I pull the curtain" recurs in Dick's mind like a T. S. Eliot refrain. The answer to the line is, "Please do, it's too light in here" (p. 180). Maddened by jealousy—"How many men"—Dick would blot out the reality of sex, the reality that Rosemary has a life that he does not share.

The sun also shows madness. A very strange sun—a sun with a face on it—blazes on the Diver's tiny Renault as they head for the carnival where Nicole suffers the breakdown that nearly proves fatal to the whole family. Grief, to Nicole, is a "terrible dark unfamiliar color" (and this color of darkness blots the surreal sun). Another surreal sun image is the violet dawn of the morning when Baby Warren tries to extricate Dick from Italian authorities. Her experience with the American Embassy in Rome is frustrating and bizarre, and in this surreal sun she learns for the first time that even the Warren money is not omnipotent. Along the same lines, Dick sees through only one eye after the fight. Even in the sunshine that falls through the window at the guard house, Dick has a vision problem. The reader, however, sees Diver clearly.

The final indication of the extent of Diver's fall is the contrast between Dick and Tommy Barban. Whereas Dick looks pale and wan even in the romantic lights of the night, Tommy stands strong, in spite of his sore throat, even in sunlight. Tommy can flourish in the direct light of reality because for him reality remains forever simple. Soldier and barbarian, Barban has none of the niceties of civilization to confuse him. Dick no longer sees these refinements, once his supreme gift, as having value, and now he stands pale next to Tommy: "The three of them stood in sunlight, Tommy squarely before the car, so that it seemed by leaning forward he would tip it upon its back" (p. 297). Dick will tip no cars. Losing his own strength does not mean he will gain Tommy's.

By the end of the novel, Dick is a Sisyphus weary beneath the white sun of the Riviera. For a moment he regains his old charm, talks to Mary North as he once talked to everyone; but he cannot maintain the charade. He sees the absurdity: "Then, as the laughter inside of him became so loud that it seemed as if Mary must hear it, Dick switched off the light and they were back in the Riviera sun" (p. 133). For Dick, the light of reality releases absurd interior laughter. He sees that he has cast the splendid furniture of his life not in a mansion, but a void. He has nothing to do but carry his unfinished, unfinishable treatise forever and discuss it in dark rooms. Future romances will be tawdry, and he will move from town to town, and every town will be the same.

Dirt-Disease-Decay Imagery

From the early pages, disease and decay imagery dominates *Tender Is the Night.* Dick, for example, always immerses himself in sickness; a doctor at a clinic for the diseased rich, he courts disease when he marries his patient. Even before that, as he burns his textbooks for heat, Dick sells himself the illusion that he knows and will know forever what the books say, that he no longer needs them. As fire reduces them to ashes, Dick notes that he lives and studies in Vienna, a city "old with death" (p. 4). He knows, too, that he must be broken, that if he is intact as a human being, he is also incomplete; life will break him one way or another (pp. 4-5). Treating death and disease, the doctor cannot afford illness. Down with flu, Dick cannot answer one of Nicole's letters. This failure to answer drives Nicole frantic. Dick must remain well to aid the ailing; yet he is human.

No one in *Tender Is the Night* is completely well, totally immune to disease. Even Baby Warren, with walls of money to insulate her against the world, must endure illness. During her debutante days, when an attack of appendicitis upset her social schedule, her socially ambitious mother forced her to dance all night with an ice pack strapped beneath her dress. Early next morning, she underwent surgery. But it is Dick, the doctor, who suffers the most serious disease—ennui. By the end of the novel, this enervated man lacks the energy to function as a doctor. Even before that, when Tommy Barban comes to him with a sore throat, Dick can only suggest that Barban gargle something. The doctor can prescribe, but has no medicine in stock to administer. Practically everything is gone by this time, including his charm, energy, and love. He loses his status as healer, and Nicole takes over; Nicole has the medicine, a special camphor rub, that will cure Tommy's throat. Dick can only ask Nicole not to give Tommy the entire jar.

Dick loses his function when he cures Nicole. Bitterly, he says to Barban that the healthy "Nicole is now made of—Georgia pine, which is the hardest wood known, except lignum vitae from New Zealand" (p. 294). She is hard now; Dick is soft. Effecting her cure, Dick falls victim to debilitating weariness. Nicole's father, too, fits into the universal pattern of illness. An alcoholic, his liver fails. Abe North, as much of an alcoholic as Warren, falls seriously ill as he prepares to leave for America. He coughs "hard and retchingly," and his body is "bathed in sweat" (p. 144). The pattern of sickness is complicated by mad events; as Abe rides obliviously from the station, Maria Wallis commits murder in full view of everyone. This world gone mad contrasts absurdly with the controlled world Diver tried to create. As Yeats said, "Mere anarchy is loosed upon the world." Even the beach created by the Divers has been "perverted to the tastes of the tasteless" (p. 299). Transience tempers everything Dick creates; he builds no permanent fortress against disease and rot, no battlements against chaos.

After the shooting at the station platform, everyone, including Dick, strongly senses the end of something, but no one can quite articulate the problem. Fitzgerald underscores the feeling, however, with this image of corruption as they leave the train station:

> As they came out, a suspended mass of gasoline exhaust cooked slowly in the July sun. It was a terrible thing—unlike pure heat it held no promise of natural escape but suggested only roads choked with the same foul asthma. During their luncheon . . . Rosemary had cramps and felt fretful and full of impatient lassitude . . . (p. 148)

In keeping with the general theme of illness, Mary North's new husband has a son suffering from an Asiatic disease that cannot be diagnosed. When the Divers visit Mary, their son Lanier reports that he had to bathe in the dirty water of the ailing boy. The squabble that arises from this confusion crumbles what remains of the friendship between the Divers and Mary North.

In the restricted Diver universe, Nicole's garden[17] serves as the soundest model for corruption. Everything grows quickly, rots quickly; this mirrors the life they created on the Riviera. Dick states succinctly what ails the garden, even though he cannot apply his knowledge to his own life: "'Nicole's garden,' said Dick. "She won't let it alone—she nags it all the time, worries about its diseases. Any day now I expect to have her come down with Powdery Mildew or Fly Speck, or Late Blight" (p. 85). Nicole's treatment of her garden identically matches Dick's treatment of Nicole.

But Nicole survives. The marriage is very good for her, bad for Dick. It fosters decay. As Nicole's husband, he watches his ambition rot. Early in their married life, he abandons his treatise so he can spend his days watching Nicole—who tries unsuccessfully to translate a chicken recipe. Both suffer because Dick believes in the work ethic (p. 57). Nicole does, too, possibly. Because of this marriage, Dick burns out his vitality, or more precisely, has it consumed by the vampire, Nicole.[18] Dick works unstintingly to protect Nicole from the reality she cannot tolerate. He makes everything seem more important than it is, and then he deteriorates into depression when he considers the "waste and extravagance involved" (p. 84).

Waste and extravagance would be meaningless if it were not for time, and here, in a typical Fitzgerald touch, time is the great promoter of decay. In the mere space of a night, even the child, Rosemary, wilts like a flower: "Her face was pale with fatigue in the false dawn. Two wan spots in her cheek marked where color was by day" (p. 140). Fading by night, brightening by day—that is her future. She will be like her mother. Contrasting youth and age and uttering a grim prediction of decay to come, Fitzgerald describes the mother of the lovely Rosemary as having a face

> of fading prettiness that would soon be patted with broken veins; her expression was both tranquil and aware in a pleasant way. However, one's eyes moved on quickly to her daughter, who had magic in her pink palms and her cheeks lit to a lovely flame, like the thrilling flush of children after their cold baths . . . . (pp. 58–59)

Few people articulated more often than Fitzgerald that most things break, that one can miss the glory of a rose in the blink of an eye. A thief, time robs everyone. As Dick's father ages, time deteriorates his handwriting. Dick's moral capital, his father, gradually fades into old age, dies, leaving Dick bankrupt.

Yet time is not the sole villain; deterioration is too pervasive for that. It occurs even in the heart of the illusion, the movie set. When Rosemary visits Brady, she encounters "the bizarre debris of some recent picture, a decayed street scene in India, a great cardboard whale, a monstrous tree bearing cherries large as basketballs" (p. 79). The decaying set varies wildly from nature, but no more so than the world Diver builds to protect Nicole, who, like many Fitzgerald characters, takes offense at natural odors, at the natural processes of life. Franz's wife, Kaethe, gives off an odor, "an ammoniacal reminder of the eternity of toil and decay," that repels Nicole (p. 258). Odors, realities, natural processes form no part of Nicole's world; Diver, plus the vast resources of the Warren money, protect her from life.

But Dick fails to protect Nicole from the ubiquitous moral decay. He cannot protect her from the "ill-smelling, handsome man" who comes to her in search of Abe North. Nor can he protect her from Abe, nor Abe from himself. After total dissipation, Abe breaks down morally. He is a musician who no longer functions as such; and worse, he has fallen to the point where he casts off *all* responsibility: "He shook off all facts as part of the nightmare" (p.164). Dick, too, sheds responsibility. When he and Franz dissolve their partnership, Dick feels relief: "Not without desperation he had long felt the ethics of his profession dissolving into a lifeless mass" (p. 274). Like Abe, Dick first sheds the ethics of his profession, then all ethics.

Dick falls victim to a pervasive corruption, to a general deterioration that matches Nicole's madness in that it renders impossible the control of his own life. The most overt early sign that Dick no longer controls himself occurs at the studio where he goes unannounced to meet Rosemary. Everything begins to go awry, and of course he does not find Rosemary. When he steps into a bistro to call her, he has to squeeze "in an alcove between the kitchen and the foul toilet" to use the phone (p. 154). This ample, if none too subtle, comment sets Diver's situation as he runs over Paris seeking a child lover.

Before Dick deteriorates, his foil, Abe, leads the way. Dick's collapse is neither so evident nor so violent as Abe's, yet Abe must be considered in any judgment rendered upon Dick; Abe represents the outer limits of purposeless dissipation, and his fate is always a possibility for Dick. Possibly the most sordid result of Abe's irresponsibility is the death of Peterson, the black man murdered in Rosemary's room. Jules Peterson's face, "harassed and indirect in life, was gross and bitter in death . . . The shoe that dangled over the bedside was bare of polish and its sole was worn through" (p. 172). This murder—directly attributable to Abe's carelessness—matches the nightmarish quality of the murder on the station platform. It culminates in Nicole's second attack of madness in a fortnight. Having relinquished all sense of responsibility, Abe begins to create havoc and death. Although Dick will cause no deaths, his dissolution, his falling into an alcoholic haze of irresponsibility, largely parallels Abe's. Nicole speaks truly when she complains of the change in Dick: "You used to want to create things—now you seem to want to smash them up" (p. 286). That is the fundamental change, as total as a genetic change, or an altered chemical compound. It is Dick Diver's loss.

Dick's nihilistic bent is as thorough, if less dramatic, as Abe's. Rather than causing murder, for example, Dick simply becomes less completely proper, a sin in Fitzgerald's lexicon of evils. He hangs his dirty shirts so he can wear them again. Still perceptive, he recognizes what he is doing, even slightly despises himself for it: "You'll wear a shirt that's a little dirty where you won't wear a mussed shirt" (p. 172). Thus he maintains minimum standards. Significantly, though, he obviously concerns himself more deeply with appearance than with reality. The physical state—especially the state of dress in the case of Diver—always mirrors the mental state.

Beyond question, Dick's mental state is precarious. At the clinic where he functions as money's partner to the hard-working Franz, he experiences a symbolic dream of war that starts off with orderly pageant and ends in a "ghastly uprising of the mutilated" (p. 196). Dick has been treating the mutilated, has lived as husband-doctor to one of the mutilated for years. The mutilation is both mental and physical. The extreme example of the physical deterioration mirroring the mental and spiritual one is the American painter gone mad: "On her admittance [to the clinic] she had been exceptionally pretty—now she was a living, agonizing sore," a victim of nervous eczema (p. 199). Nicole's mind has become distorted, ugly, like this woman's body. She suffers the monomaniac's delusion, perhaps precipitated by Rosemary, that all women are interested in Dick, and that Dick inevitably returns this interest. Just before her delusion turns so murderous that she tries to kill the whole family by wrecking the car, she raves, "'Home!' she roared in a voice so abandoned that its louder tones wavered and cracked. 'And sit and think that we're all rotting and the children's ashes are rotting in every box I open? That filth!'" (p. 207). Earlier, even, the danger signals had been rife:

> Twice within a fortnight she had broken up: There had been the night of the dinner at Tarmes, when he had found her in the bedroom dissolved in crazy laughter telling Mrs. McKisco she could not go into the bathroom because the key was thrown down the well. . . .
> The collapse in Paris was another matter, adding significance to the first one. It prophesied possibly a new cycle, a new pousse of the malady. (p. 180)

No one can maintain the pace; in the four years since he last saw Rosemary, Dick ages. When he sees her in Rome after the death of his father, he tries to hide his "unshaven face, his crumpled slept-in collar" (p. 224). He had been at an "emotional peak at the time of the previous encounter; since then there had been a lesion of enthusiasm'' (p. 225). Through weary eyes, he is critical; looking at Rosemary he notes that the corners of her lips are chapped. It is striking that Dick should note such a small imperfection, especially as he is on the brink of his most serious plunge into depravity, the brawl with the taxi drivers of Rome.[19] Whereas the woman suffering from nervous eczema physically mirrors Nicole's deteriorated state of mind, Diver, after his sordid brawl, reflects himself:[20] ''He felt his nose break like a shingle and his eyes jerk as if they had snapped back on a rubber band into his head. A rib splintered under a stamping heel'' (p. 244). This is Diver.

The most pervasive imagery of disease and decay, however, takes the form of perversion. Lehan points out that

> *Tender Is the Night* is full of perversion and abnormal love; Campion, Dumphry, and Francisco are all homosexuals. Mr. Warren is guilty of incest; and Mary North and Lady Caroline turn out to be lesbians. Fitzgerald says that ''it was as if for the remainder of [Dick's] life he was condemned to carry with him the egos of certain people, early met and early loved and to be only as complete as they were complete themselves. There was some element of loneliness involved—so easy to be loved—so hard to love'' (p. 245). *Tender Is the Night* is a novel about the failure of an individual—it is also a novel about the failure of society. In many ways, the world failed to come up to Dick's expectation of it. That's why innocence had such appeal.[21]

This novel explores the perversion of innocence. Dick becomes both violated and violator. The spoiled priest, the near holy innocent, becomes corrupt: ''When Dick violates [Rosemary], he destroys his last image of innocence—of freshness.''[22]

None of the homosexuals play important roles in the novel, yet they are so prevalent as to be a part of the atmosphere. For the male homosexuals, Fitzgerald harbors something akin to good-natured contempt. Francisco is charming and amusing, if worthless and utterly lost. In essence, Dumphry and Campion[23] play clown roles: when Royal Dumphry dumps Luis Campion, Rosemary finds Campion ''weeping hard and quietly and shaking in the same parts as a weeping woman. . . . His face was repulsive in the quickening light'' (pp. 98–99). A sign of the corruption and perhaps a product of it, Campion and Dumphry are presented as repulsive, but Fitzgerald's portrait is so condescendingly humorous that the homosexuals present no real threat. The clown Campion, for example, abhors violence, but runs like an excited child to the duel. He even brings his movie camera. Rosemary describes him as ''so terrible that he was no longer terrible, only dehumanized'' (p. 107). As McKisco vomits following the duel, the intrepid Campion faints. Rosemary tries to kick him back to consciousness.

As Campion represents sexual perversion of the human being, the house of ''oddly beveled mirrors'' is a perversion of taste; it functions as a foil to the safe and tasteful world created by the Divers. A creation gone wild, the house is something that was once good that is now soured: ''It was a house hewn from the frame of Cardinel Retze's palace'' (p. 133). It stands as a sinister warning that the Diver world can and will be perverted.

But finally, no perversion approaches that of Lady Caroline Sibley-Biers. Tommy Barban, disparaging the title, refers to her as "the wickedest woman in London" (p. 289). The narrator points out that she is "fragile, tubercular—it was incredible that such narrow shoulders, such puny arms could bear aloft the pennon of decadence" (p. 289). Dick detests her, as he shows when she dismisses the lesbian episode as a mere lark:

> Dick nodded gravely, looking at the stone floor like a priest in the confessional—he was torn between a tendency to ironic laughter and another tendency to order fifty stripes of the cat and a fortnight of bread and water. (p. 322)

Dick and the landlord, Gause, extricate Mary and Lady Caroline from the predicament only to have Lady Caroline refuse to pay Gause the money he has put up for her bail. Gause gives her a well-deserved kick in the rump, and he and Dick ride back home, disgusted in silence. The episode adds one more log of moral decay to an already dense, rotting forest. Gloom so thoroughly pervades that even the Jaun-les-Pins Casino affords no joy; it is "still sobbing and coughing with jazz" (p. 325).

More than anything else, however, this novel deals with the corrupting influence of the sire on the offspring, or the corrupting of innocence. Of all the fathers in *Tender Is the Night,* only Dick's father is a good influence. Dick declines rapidly; when his father dies he loses his last connection with decency. But Dick inherited from his father a kind of innocence that begs corruption, considering the kind of world he lives in. Leaving his father's home, his country, "Dick got up to Zurich on fewer Achilles' heels than would be required to equip a centipede, but with plenty—the illusions of eternal strength and health, and of the essential goodness of people" (p. 5). These weaknesses are also strengths. Like every tragic hero, Dick climbs high because of his flaw and then paradoxically tumbles because his flaw imposes limitations upon him. Dick's father did not prepare him to live in the twentieth-century world, a world pervaded by corruption.[24] Conversely, he did not drive his son to homosexuality or incest.

Francisco's father, like Dick's father, is a man with a stern moral code. Francisco's father, however, lacked human understanding, compassion. Obviously, Francisco has no chance. His father drives him to alcohol, to homosexuality. By the time Dick tries to play surrogate father, Francisco is irretrievable. Committed to debauchery, Francisco's current paramour is Royal Dumphry. He has no more chance than Von Cohn Morris, an alcoholic kleptomaniac whose parents are hardcore temperance fanatics. Morris' father, ignorant and simplistic, blames the ills of the entire universe on alcohol. And Francisco's father,

> Señor Pardo y Cuidad Real, a handsome iron-gray Spaniard, noble of carriage, with all the appurtenances of wealth and power, raged up and down his suite . . . and told the story of his son with no more self-control than a drunken woman. (p. 261)

The stern-father/effeminate-son relationship takes second billing to the incest motif in *Tender Is the Night's* long catalogue of corruption. Robert Stanton characterizes manifestations of this motif as older-man/young-girl relationships. The first and most damaging of these relationships—Devereaux Warren's incestuous affair with Nicole—sets the tenor for all affairs between a young woman and older man.[25] Specifically, incest between Warren and his daughter establishes expectations in the reader when Diver becomes romantically involved with Rosemary Hoyt, who has just starred in *Daddy's Girl.*[26] Fitzgerald describes Dick's attitude toward Rosemary as "paternal" (pp. 85, 124). Dick refers often to Rosemary's youth: "When you smile . . . I always think I'll see a gap where you've lost some baby teeth" (p. 125). And after Rosemary leaves the Riviera, Dick emphasizes the immaturity of all other women.[27]

With Nicole, too, Dick plays the role of father, the provider of safety and security. Dick is, in fact, a "'spoiled priest,' the father of all of his friends; he creates the moral universe in which they live."[28] But Dick, the father, loses control; he can no longer control Nicole's life, nor as a psychiatrist can he want to. In the affair with his other daughter symbol, Dick knows full well that Rosemary is in control.

Symbols of disease and decay—especially perverted sex—pervade *Tender Is the Night* so completely that Fitzgerald is not merely describing one man's world, but Everyman's. Dick, the doctor, would embrace the world of victims until he becomes victim himself. A product of his times, Dick is one of many who shifts from the "past culture of his father to an unworthy future."[29] This idea becomes clear at his father's grave. America, too, opts for an unworthy future:

> In embracing Rosemary, ... Dick Diver is a symbol of America and Europe turning from a disciplined and dedicated life to a life of self-indulgence, dissipation, and moral anarchy—a symbol of the parent generation infatuated with its own offspring. Dick's collapse, appropriately, occurs in 1929.[30]

Dick cuts himself loose from everything at his father's grave. Consciously, he severs himself from any moral anchor when he speaks over the corpse of his father: "Good-bye, my father—Good-bye, all my fathers" (p. 222). Shortly after that he reaches Rome, sleeps with Rosemary, fights with Italian taxi drivers and police. A quibble centering on a taxi fare reduces the former paragon of decorum to beaten brute: "The world reeled; he was clubbed down, and fists and boots beat on him in a savage tattoo" (p. 244).

Diver can no longer see, and appropriately, he nearly loses an eye in the fight. This is the climax of the novel; the rest is a long denouement, a playing out of various humiliations. At the Italian court the crowd mistakenly believes Dick is the man who raped a five-year-old girl. He mockingly confesses. When Nicole accuses him of seducing the fifteen-year-old daughter of a patient, he feels guilt even though he is innocent. Finally he must leave Lockport because of an entanglement with a girl who worked in a grocery store. His medical treatise will never be finished because he suffers too many diseases himself. Upon occasion he can recall the old charm, but not for long because he no longer believes in himself.

Corruption is pervasive; thematically and structurally, images of corruption bind the novel together: "There are . . . no 'marginal' episodes in the book, if practically all of them serve to illustrate a widespread condition of moral disorder and social corruption."[31] And they do, of course. *Tender Is the Night* is a novel literally held together by corruption imagery.

Water Imagery

Water imagery shows Eliot's truth, "April is the cruelest month." It is the beginning of the cycle, a time filled with hope for renewal, for resurrection by water. Yet all people fall victim to this cycle, and April's promises mean nothing. Love and hope spawned in fertile April rains dry up and wither by December. The cycle of death and rebirth continues until one April there is drowning, but no resurrection; even water has lost its power of renewal, and all that remains is sterile existence. This idea is a major theme in *Tender Is the Night.* It is this idea that emerges from a careful study of water symbolism, which is prominent throughout the novel, and upon which Fitzgerald lavishes some of his most poetic lines.

Chronologically in the 1934 version, and both chronologically and structurally in the 1951 Cowley edition, *Tender Is the Night* begins during an April filled with promise: "It was a damp April day" and Dick Diver has already achieved moderate and seemingly effortless success. He has taken degrees and impressive scholarships from the best universities—Yale, Oxford, Johns Hopkins—and he has studied for several years with the best Viennese psychiatrists. More important, Diver has potential. He has already done some original and creative work in psychiatry, and he seems capable of greater, more vital work. Also, the Swiss setting for his work is the very portrait of vitality: "The sun swam out into a blue sea of sky and suddenly it was a Swiss valley at its best—pleasant sound and murmurs and a good smell of health and cheer" (p. 9).

In this setting the relationship between Nicole and Diver promises to be rewarding and fertile, in spite of the tension created by Nicole's mental condition and strengthened by the warnings of medically-qualified men that this love should not be encouraged. Nicole is young and beautiful, and Dick seems practically invincible—in spite of the author's warning that "Dick got up to Zurich on less Achilles heels than would be required to equip a centipede, but with plenty—the illusions of eternal strength and health, and of the essential goodness of people" (p. 5). This could be a strength rather than a weakness; only after Dick gets rid of these Achilles heels, in fact, does he lose the will to struggle.

At this time, though, their love takes root and flourishes in the rejuvenating spring rains. Describing the potential in the love of Dick and Nicole, Fitzgerald says,

> Her face, ivory gold against the blurred sunset that strove through the rain, had a promise Dick had never seen before: the high cheekbones, the faintly wan quality, cool rather than feverish, was reminiscent of the frame of a promising colt—a creature whose life did not promise to be only a projection of youth upon a grayer screen, but instead, a true growing; the face would be handsome in middle life; it would be handsome in old age: the essential structure and economy were there. (p. 33)

Disregarding this promise and acting upon the advice of his colleagues, Diver tries to step out of Nicole's life; but he can do this only when the rain ceases to fall, and even then, the break is temporary. Surrounded by beauty and by the fertility of spring, the love between Nicole and Dick is too firmly rooted to be blighted by the cold logic of clinicians.

After a short separation, Diver and Nicole meet casually on a funicular on the way up to a mountain spa. Soon, in the rain, they are alone together, and the romance is sealed when the "storm came swiftly, first falling in torrents from the mountains and washing loud down the roads and stone ditches" (p. 48). Torrents of water seem to bless and baptize their love. And the romance that began in April culminated in marriage in September.

In book 2, the Divers have created a world of their own on the French Riviera. Into this world a host of new characters are introduced. These characters could be classified as the tanned (Diver's party) and the untanned (McKisco's party), and the worth of each character corresponds closely to his skill in the water. Of the untanned, few actually go into the water, and McKisco, obviously the best of the lot even though he is characterized as a scrawny and irritable paradigm of sterility, nearly drowns each time he encounters water. McKisco's homosexual friends, Dumphry and Campion, seldom leave shore.

The tanned have an entirely different attitude toward water; at home in the sea, they swim almost ritualistically. Swimming is a part of their world, a part of their every day. One such swim is viewed through the eyes of Rosemary, who

> felt that this swim would become the typical one of her life, the one that would always pop up in her memory at the mention of swimming. Simultaneously the whole party moved toward the water, super-ready from the long, forced inaction, passing from the heat to the cool with the gourmandise of a tingling curry eaten with chilled white wine. The Diver's day was spaced like the day of older civilizations to yield the utmost from the materials at hand, and to give all the transitions their full value, and she did not know that there would be another transition presently from the utter absorption of the swim to the garrulity of the provincial lunch hour. (pp. 76–77)

The swim is a ritual, a daily return to water. Among those who dive, there is an almost religious love for water; even Abe North, a man destroyed by bitterness and alcohol, swims well, and he does not plunge totally into depravity until after he leaves the sea.

On the surface, the difference between the tanned and the untanned is apparent. Those who swim, those who are renewed by water, have an intense vitality. They are graceful, interesting, charming people. Those who avoid water are petty, dull, carping people. Ironically, however, neither group is productive. The swimmers have potential and capability: Abe North *was* a promising and brilliant musician; Dick Diver *was* a promising and brilliant psychiatrist. But after promising, like April, neither of these men delivered.[32] The Divers, of course, are socially creative. When they throw a party, everything is right—nothing is gauche, nothing vulgar. They have managed to create a social world in which they can live, yet it is a false world and one destined to end. Beautiful people grace the Diver party, but no one on the beach does more than McKisco, and his contribution to the civilized world certainly is meager enough. Mrs. McKisco describes her husband's unwritten novel as being "'on the idea of Ulysses. . . . Only instead of taking twenty-four hours my husband takes a hundred years. He takes a decayed old French aristocrat and puts him in contrast with the mechanical age'" (p. 66).

Even Rosemary, prototype of youth and fertility, cannot really be called productive. Her sole triumph is a movie called *Daddy's Girl*. That name alone, perhaps, comments sufficiently upon the quality of the picture, but Fitzgerald slams the point home, eliminates all conjecture concerning Rosemary's acting ability with these lines: "Daddy's girl. Was it a 'itty-bitty bravekins and did it suffer? Ooo-ooo-tweet, de tweetest thing, wasn't she dest too tweet?" (p. 130). That line makes the reader squirm; but all too clearly Rosemary, as an artist, is McKisco's equal. Unlike Nicole, with classic beauty and grace, Rosemary is simply cute, sweet, a pretty child with neither beauty, sex appeal, nor talent. Yet for the moment, at least, she has a kind of warmth, a charming innocence. Unquestionably, she is a positive character, and her affinity for water is graphically described:

> Rosemary laid her face on the water and swam a choppy little four-beat crawl out to the raft. The water reached up for her, pulled her down tenderly out of the heat, seeped in her hair and into the corners of her body. She turned round and round in it, embracing it, wallowing in it. (p. 60)

This description of total immersion in water strongly resembles that of a woman and her lover. If ever renewal by water worked, it should work for Rosemary, and if Dick's problem could be reduced to Nicole's illness and the Warren money, Rosemary should provide the solution to that problem. But Rosemary solves no problems, no matter how fertile and vital she herself might be. If anything, she acts as the catalyst to Diver's decline.

Dick Diver, Abe North, Nicole, Rosemary Hoyt, and even Tommy Barban, however, are more admirable than McKisco. Those who dive into water have an essential vitality that McKisco lacks. McKisco, the intruder in a world fashioned by the Divers, is in all ways a little man. Unsatisfied with everything, he can neither change the real world, nor create a world of his own. And significantly, in that grotesque scene where he and Tommy Barban prepare to duel, McKisco refuses Abe North's suggestion that he take a swim to freshen up: "'No—no, I couldn't swim.' He sighed. 'I don't see what it's all about,' he said hopelessly" (p. 104). True enough, he does not see what it is all about.

Book 3 opens on a note of depression and thoughts of death. The water here is a small stream on a World War I battlefield. Dick, awed and depressed by the field where many men lost their lives for a romantic cause says, "'See that little stream—we could walk to it in two minutes. It took the British a month to walk to it—a whole empire walking very slowly, dying in front and pushing forward behind'" (p. 117). Later, in the rain, they find a girl seeking her brother's grave. And finally, on a houseboat cafe, the first really ominous note concerning Abe North is sounded: "Since reaching Paris Abe North had had a thin vinous fur over him; his eyes were bloodshot from sun and wine. Rosemary realized for the first time that he was always stopping in places to get a drink" (p. 121). Gone from the Riviera, away from the daily, ritualistic swim, the Diver party loses some of its class. Abe North is drunk, not socially and pleasingly tight; Rosemary's love for Dick is beginning to make her unhappy; Mary North is beginning to worry about her husband; Nicole's nerves are beginning to tighten. In Paris they no longer dive into water. They float on water in a houseboat cafe, but they are not in it. And here, with a third of the novel finished, water begins to symbolize death without resurrection.

When the group leaves the beach, even Diver begins to lose some of his poise. He loves Rosemary, but the time when that love could flourish is gone. The rains come, and Diver has some hope, but he is tired, older than he was a few days earlier when he left the Riviera. He meets Rosemary alone, but the meeting is strained, and when he asks her to sit on his lap, "She came over and sat there and while the dripping slowed down outside—drip—dri-ip, she laid her lips to the beautiful cold image she had created" (p. 167). After a moment of passion, Diver recalls his responsibility toward Nicole: "'The rain's over,' he said, 'Do you see the sun on the slate?'" (p. 167).

The image is harsh, as stark as reality, and the events that follow are equally stark: Rosemary, making love, realizes that both she and Dick are acting; Peterson is murdered in Rosemary's room; Nicole suffers an attack of insanity. Each of these events, in its own way bizarre, signifies the end of something. The party is over, everyone drifts away, leaving Dick and Nicole alone together. Like the end of *The Great Gatsby,* this scene occurs in August, and "there was a hint in the air that the earth was hurrying on toward other weather; the lush mid-summer moment outside of time was already over" (p. 175).

Bleak winter follows autumn. "In November the waves grew black and dashed over the sea wall onto the shore road, such summer life as had survived disappeared, and the beaches were melancholy and desolate under the mistral and rain" (p. 187). In this atmosphere, Nicole supposedly is cured; at least she is well enough to travel, and the outward symptoms of her disease have disappeared. The cure, however, is effected in an atmosphere of gloom, and the rain that falls is not the regenerating water of life, but the freezing water of death and winter. Under such unfavorable conditions, Nicole's recovery is expensive. Only at the cost of a love fertilized in the life-giving water of spring is she cured in the sterile, "black" waves of winter.

Expensive though it is, Nicole's recovery is not permanent. Another spring and summer, less promising than the first, finds the Divers back in Zurich, with Dick, Franz, and the Warren money nearly equal partners in a clinic for the diseased rich. Nicole, unfortunately, is one of the diseased rich, and when her illness takes a violent turn that could have killed the whole family, Dick decides he must get away, both from Nicole and from the clinic. Free from both, he recalls better days. He can remember a spring "when the grass was damp and [Nicole] came to him on hurried feet, her thin slippers drenched with dew" (p. 218).

Ominously, Dick's holiday begins in October. Again, the rain is not the water of life, but "black sleet and hail and mountain thunder" (p. 219). Dick wants to climb a mountain in this weather, but the guide refuses, and the vacation becomes a holiday of death. Dick learns that his father has died peacefully and that Abe North has died violently in a brawl. He returns to America to attend his father's funeral. From the voyage to Virginia across the Atlantic Ocean and the Chesapeake Bay, Dick gains only a sense of loss, of isolation, nothing else. The trip over water to his homeland does not rejuvenate him. His father dead, his roots severed, Dick declines rapidly, sinks to new lows.

The funeral over, Dick returns to Europe where he again meets Rosemary. Once in the summer she had begged him to sleep with her. He refused. Now, in November, he sleeps with her without the slightest hesitation. The decline has begun in earnest; no longer a paragon of grace, Diver descends to a street brawl with taxi drivers and petty Italian officials. Completely out of control, he shows how far he has fallen, how different he is from the Diver by the sea: "There was dirty water in the gutters and between the tough cobblestones; a marshy vapor from the Campagna, a sweat of exhausted cultures tainted the morning air" (p. 242).

Another April and Dick and Nicole have been some months away from the clinic. No rains fall during this bleak spring, and Dick, master of every situation, barely escapes with his life during an argument with the cook. The argument breaks the tension, but only momentarily. The Divers have grown so tired of each other that not even a common cause can bring them together for long. Tension mounts quickly in the Diver household and soon, whether to break the monotony of a cool feud, or simply in remembrance of better days on the beach, the Divers, against Nicole's will, return to the water to attend a yacht party held by T. F. Golding. On the yacht, Nicole meets Tommy Barban, and Dick gets drunk and disgraces himself. He has become as petty as McKisco and as much of a drunk as Abe North. Here on the yacht, however, Dick and Nicole have one last, brief moment when they are really together, not just in each other's presence. Though perfunctorily nasty to Nicole, Dick has surrendered to life. He contemplates jumping into the sea. He takes Nicole's arm, and for the one moment when she is prepared to make the fatal dive with him, they are spiritually, if terrifyingly, together. But they do not jump. Death would follow this dive, but not resurrection, and Dick gives up the idea. When he breaks his hold on Nicole's wrists, the two, for all practical purposes, have parted forever. They have broken a bond.

Early in summer, Dick makes one final return to the water. He and Nicole meet Rosemary on the beach that Dick had built and over which he had reigned with easy grace a few years earlier. The beach has changed, much as the Divers have changed: it has been "perverted . . . to the tastes of the tasteless," and "few people swam any more" (p. 299). Dick, of course, still feels drawn to water, but Nicole "noticed that this summer, for the first time, he avoided high diving" (p. 300).

Unfortunately he does not avoid the aquaplane. Two years earlier, he had lifted a 200-pound man above his head with ease; now he cannot lift a 150-pound man. After three attempts—and three failures—he is exhausted. Nicole

> saw him slide under the water and she gave a little cry; but he came up again and turned on his back, and the Mexican swam near to help. It seemed forever till the boat reached them, but when they came alongside at last and Nicole saw Dick floating exhausted and expressionless, alone with the water and the sky, her panic changed suddenly to contempt. (p. 300)

For the first time, Diver has humiliated himself in water. He is not renewed, but destroyed, and no resurrection occurs. He floats "exhausted and expressionless, alone with the water and the sky." He is the victim of the unrelenting cycle of seasons, of the April that promises so much only to return again and again and to deny little by little the promises she made.

The water symbolism in *Tender Is the Night* is ironic, just as the name "Diver" is ironic. Almost instinctively, Dick seeks rebirth in water. At first, water seems to provide the renewal he needs, but water falls helpless before time. Diver seeks, he dives in vain, because water cannot return what passing seasons have taken away. He is a diver—like the deep divers in *Moby Dick*—and like Ahab, he finally discovers that nothing beneath the surface of the sea can help him. Figuratively, Dick dives deeply into water, but in reality, his dive simply takes him from a higher to a lower social and spiritual level.

Like *The Great Gatsby* and, in a sense, every Fitzgerald novel, *Tender Is the Night* illustrates once more the author's belief in the "futility of effort and the necessity of struggle."[33] That, essentially, is the theme supported by water symbolism in *Tender Is the Night*. Man is defeated the moment he draws his first breath, but the actual fall begins only when he grows too weary to struggle. This is exactly what happens to Dick Diver. Diver's story, of course, is not the story of every man, but it was the story of Fitzgerald and is the story of a large segment of humanity. By strict definition, the story is not tragic. Diver ends not like a day with a flash of brilliant purple and orange, but slowly, agonizingly, painfully. The turning point comes when he leaves the sea, but even this is not a sudden reversal of fortune. In a sense, he drowns rather than falls.

As the story of one man, the novel is not tragic, but as the story of many of the best, most fascinating members of the human race, *Tender Is the Night* gains tragic implications. Diver and those like him are fated to fall, and nothing can be done about it. The specific circumstances leading to Diver's fall are Nicole's illness and the Warren money, but any set of circumstances would have worked equally well. Diver's real enemy is time; life so thoroughly exhausts him that finally he can find no spring of renewal. No matter how much of his former self he retains, his chief asset, his charm, is gone.[34] Without charm, without vitality, without grace, Diver must lose because he is defenseless. To Nicole and to his friends he gave freely of these qualities, and though they may be renewed, once the killing cycle of seasons has evolved too many times, even water, the traditional symbol of life and rebirth, cannot resurrect them. In *Tender Is the Night,* and perhaps in life, the only people not defeated are those with nothing to offer. The McKiscos endure unchanged, outlasting the Dick Divers, the Abe Norths, and all people with potential for greatness. Franz and the McKiscos are durable; they persist because they have nothing to lose. Those with something to lose expend their energies and fall victims to time.

The view of life is more complex in *Tender Is the Night* than in *The Great Gatsby.* One can watch Gatsby follow a materialistic, death-dealing dream epitomized by the car and say, "just here Gatsby went wrong." But Dick Diver's world is not one characterized by life or death struggles and choices. His is a world full of absurdity and erupts in violence, madness, and loss. So, too, do trains. The transportation imagery proves that all roads are circular in *Tender Is the Night;* all lead back to an enervating, chaotic limbo.

The communication imagery proves that in *Tender Is the Night* Fitzgerald maintains the philosophy established in *The Great Gatsby.* Attempts to communicate are futile, almost laughably so. When communication does occur, it destroys the protagonist. Because Nicole and Diver communicated too well, Dick finds himself in the untenable role of psychiatrist-lover. This destroys him. Generally, though, no communication takes place. Causes of the breakdown range from failure of language to paucity of ideas to telephones that inhibit rather than facilitate communication. With his use of the telephone in *Tender Is the Night,* Fitzgerald has added an element he did not use in the communication imagery in *The Great Gatsby*—humor. In Rosemary's apartment the telephone rings three times to promote social intercourse over sexual intercourse. These interruptions leave Diver frustrated until the next night. And when the Divers try to call for help as the drunken cook, Augustine, assails them with a knife, they get not aid, but laughter followed by a broken connection from the police station. Again, attempts at communication are laughably futile.

Tracing the light-dark imagery, one first notes that *Tender Is the Night* shows a moon symbolic of madness, a cold moon that shines down on absurdity and death.

Its traditional role as symbol of romance is usurped by man-made light. Dick, like Gatsby, tries to control his own world through artificial lights, and like Gatsby, he succeeds—for a while. Dick believes in the magnificently tasteful and secure world he has created for Nicole. He lives in that world as if there were not another world lurking just outside his cast of light. And when he must face reality, he has basked too long in the light of wine-colored lanterns. He is too soft, too weary to struggle. Life from this point is mere existence; Dick drifts rather than steers.

Darkness is the essential correlative to madness in this novel. Forbidden love—Devereaux Warren for Nicole, Dick for Rosemary—takes root in darkness and leads to frequent outbreaks of lunacy. The night becomes a cover for unnatural acts, death, violence, and absurdity.

As in *The Great Gatsby,* sunlight is the ray of reality that cuts through the beautiful sham and leaves it a shambles. Again, all characters try to avoid the sun, but none succeed. Dick, creator of false worlds, must finally stand in the bright sun on the Riviera and survey his kingdom. What he sees releases dark laughter in his head. He has confronted absurdity. Sisyphus continued to push the rock; Dick will not even have that much purpose in his life. He can no longer commit himself to labor for nothing.

Dirt-disease-decay imagery is almost as important in *Tender Is the Night* as in *The Beautiful and Damned.* In *Tender Is the Night,* Dick Diver, a doctor trained to combat disease, marries his patient and renders himself vulnerable to disease. He throws his energies and gifts into protecting one woman, into eliminating corruption from the world he created for Nicole, when he might have worked for humanity. His other work slides; Nicole becomes a vampire who gets well at Dick's expense and leaves him enervated. Dick creates a world as alien to nature as is a movie set. Both Dick's world and the movie set glitter for a moment before they begin to rot.

To a great extent, *Tender Is the Night* is about moral rot, a softening of the will, a loss of control. Dick Diver and Abe North, for example, lose their functions in society and drift into a limbo of irresponsibility. Both stop creating and begin to destroy. Dick, once the most civilized of men, suddenly foregoes decorum. It is a sign of his deterioration, just as the American artist dying from eczema symbolizes Nicole's mental state.

The greatest moral rot, however, shows up in the guise of perversion. The pattern begins with the incestuous affair between Nicole and Devereaux Warren. Every father, with the exception of Dick's, violates the innocence of his child. Nicole's father traumatizes her into madness; Dick gets an innocence from his father that makes him unable to live in the world of his choice. Von Cohn Morris' father pushes him to alcoholism, and Francisco's father drives him into homosexuality. Fathers corrupt sons and daughters and the cycle continues. Moral decay prevails, and no apparent remedy exists.

The real core of *Tender Is the Night,* however, is water imagery, not dirt-disease-decay imagery. Water imagery shows that if Gatsby failed because time rendered his absurd dream grotesque, Dick Diver should have succeeded because he had more to give and his demand from life was considerably more sane than was Gatsby's. Diver simply wanted to be good, and—he wanted to be loved. For love he was willing to give and give and give of himself. He would be the father, the healer, the priest with perpetual energy. Setting his goal, he heeded the promise of April. Winter would come, but with spring and the ritualistic swims, Dick Diver would be rejuvenated and would give more. His love and his life are blessed in water and they seem eternal. And while Dick and his party reside by the sea, there indeed seems scant reason to doubt eternal youth.

Away from water, though, Diver no longer has the energy to control his own small universe, and the whole party begins to fall apart. The rain falls on a graveyard, and the river flows by the battlefield of Amiens. Tension mounts: Nicole cracks; Abe proves himself an alcoholic with no purpose beyond the next bottle; Rosemary and Dick embark upon a doomed affair. The promises of April fade and with them goes joy. Sun glaring on slate replaces the rain as Dick and Rosemary discover they are playing at love, someone shoots Peterson, and Nicole escapes into a second attack of madness.

Rain from this point is of the winter variety, bringing madness, death. Abe North and Dick's father die as October rains fall. Dick crosses the Atlantic to return to his father's funeral, to the ideals that made him strong. But he can only bid farewell to all his fathers. He cuts himself free to drift. Rootless, he returns to Rome where he sleeps with Rosemary and fights with taxi drivers. He can neither live on land nor die on water; his proposed double suicide—a leap into water from T. F. Golding's yacht—leaves both Dick and Nicole alive, but strikes a final blow to their love. Yet Dick does not know the game is over. He returns once more to the Riviera where he had been so thoroughly in command that he needed no crown. The water that once nourished him now exhausts him, leaves him humiliated. April has paid her promise, and time has defeated him. Too weary for the struggle, his sole choice is to stand on the beach and listen to mad, ironic laughter in his head. For him, the beach is barren.

4

The Last Tycoon

The Great Gatsby and *Tender Is the Night* were the products of arduous and extensive revision, the kind of revision that insured that every iteration of a given image not only fit into the pattern but deepened our emotional grasp of the theme. As a painter does with each single brush stroke, Fitzgerald, with each instance of a recurring image, made the world of the novel clearer. He did not live long enough to finish, let alone revise, *The Last Tycoon;* nevertheless, the image patterns in this great fragment serve as the sinews and nerves that provide a sound inner structure for the novel and would have continued to do so had Fitzgerald lived to finish it.

Once again the five major image groups serve as microcosms of the novel as a whole. They carry themes, define the world of the novel. The single difference is that in *The Great Gatsby* and *Tender Is the Night* Fitzgerald employed a different sort of irony. In these novels the golden world of possibility seemed real until about midpoint. Then image patterns made it clear that what appeared to be a world teeming with life actually contained the seeds of death at the core. In *The Last Tycoon* Fitzgerald does not bother to try to convince his readers that this is a story of life and opportunity. From the fully developed airplane imagery in the opening pages he lets his readers know that this is a story of death. He trades his usual irony, carefully created by the image patterns, for a dramatic irony. Images tell immediately that Stahr will die; the reader knows, but Stahr thinks he is at the top of his form. The dramatic irony in this fragment is quite likely the kind of irony Fitzgerald intended. To have achieved the kind of irony he used in *The Great Gatsby* and *Tender Is the Night,* he would have had to restructure *The Last Tycoon;* he could not start with the obvious death imagery created by the airplane and convince the reader that this is a story of young love and possibility. Stahr is old and worn beyond his years when the novel opens. Fitzgerald's job is to establish him as a great man and then to force him into a rapid Icarian plunge.

Transportation Imagery

Compared with the airplane that serves as setting for the beginning of *The Last Tycoon* (discussed in the Introduction), neither train nor automobile form vital symbolic transportation patterns in this last, unfinished novel. The train's single function is to transport to Hollywood the American, the fiancé who will destroy Stahr's dream of marrying Kathleen Moore, the woman who might have given his life meaning. Although the disintegration of his plans for a life with Kathleen contributes largely to Stahr's fall, the train forms no image pattern because it appears only once. In one respect, though, it is consistent with transportation imagery in other Fitzgerald works; because it brings trouble to the protagonist, the train is right on time; help is always late, but trouble arrives on schedule. Such is the Fitzgerald universe.

Automobile imagery in *The Last Tycoon* is nearly as simple as the train imagery. True to his practice in the other novels, Fitzgerald uses the automobile here to establish social position. Wylie White, a writer out of place in Hollywood, drives a second-hand car that once belonged to a top executive. White, who plays his cynic's role badly, aspires to the executive position he pretends to despise. His choice of car hints at pitiable aspirations as well as dreary failure. By contrast, Stahr shows little interest in the kind of car he drives until he visits Kathleen, the girl who reminds him of his dead wife, actress Minna Davis. To impress Kathleen, Stahr calls for her in a roadster he had not driven for years. The roadster, like Kathleen, creates a tangible link between past and present. Through the automobile, Stahr establishes his social position and the dignity of the occasion; and like Gatsby, he attempts to relive a cherished moment from the past.

The automobile also symbolizes escape, even though that escape is seriously qualified, as signalled by the death by car of Celia's boy friend. But for the moment, this car transports Stahr and Kathleen safely from the congested schedule of Hollywood to his unfinished house. There they enjoy the leisure of life, of love. After a day together—one that threatened to end like an unresolved chord—Stahr suggests that Kathleen not disappear into her house, that they go somewhere else:

> With relief, she caught at the exact phrasing—to get away from here immediately, that was accomplishment or sounded like it—as if she were fleeing from the spot of a crime. They were in the car, going down hill with the breeze cool in their faces, and she came slowly to herself (p. 86).

This romantic interlude gives them a brief, lovely moment, but the escape, like Stahr, is doomed. From the opening of the novel, Stahr is dying. Images of hope mislead.

Communication Imagery

Earlier Fitzgerald novels had rendered communication devices ominous. This makes the "wholly admirable" Robinson, the man Stahr relies on to rectify the damages of the earthquake, suspect because he worked as a telephone repairman, a lineman, before he migrated to Hollywood. A highly-skilled, reliable craftsman, Robinson repaired telephone wires even during Minnesota blizzards. He seems an excellent human being, but any uneasiness about his connection with the telephone company proves will-founded. In his outline, Fitzgerald was thinking of having Robinson deeply involved in the plot to murder Stahr.

Fitzgerald saw ironic futility in most attempts to use communication devices to deliver important messages. Typical of this is the letter that arrives, but is ignored. The letter of warning from Manny Schwartz comes from a disinterested man and contains a true message, but does not alert Stahr to the danger from powerful men like Brady. Believing the image he has created to communicate himself to the rest of the world, Stahr considers himself invulnerable. He ignores the Schwartz letter. Like Schwartz, though, he weakens, and those words from that miserable suicide comprise a warning he might well have heeded.

The communiqué gone awry appears as often in Fitzgerald's fiction as does the letter ignored. In *The Last Tycoon*, the *essential* letter has lost all meaning before Stahr reads it. Before Stahr earns her love, Kathleen writes to explain that she can never love him, that she has promised to marry another. True enough when she wrote it, the letter lies by the time Stahr finds it: Kathleen loses the letter in Stahr's automobile; Stahr reads it only after it has lost all validity; and Fitzgerald gets away with one of the oldest tricks of both comedy and melodrama. It appears neither contrived nor comic, and oddly enough, not melodramatic. A narrative voice that seems sane—Fitzgerald's always does—can utter fantastic pronouncements without being called to task.

When communication seems to occur, the very presence of a mechanical device makes the message suspect. The weary Stahr, for example, hears by telephone of the damage caused by the earthquake. This knowledge, an incitement, a challenge that shakes him back to life, makes his eyes shine. And the catastrophe that enlivens him also introduces him to Kathleen, a woman who promises to bring possibility and meaning to his future. But the promise is false; their love is doomed, as Stahr is doomed. What seems the road to happiness becomes merely the intersection where Stahr turns the wrong way. Yet he has no way to go. In charge of the disaster, Stahr is an Oedipus who does what must be done. Every move brings him nearer destruction, and like Oedipus, he does not know that he may be the very source of corruption he seeks to eradicate. In one sense, he has done what he can for Hollywood and now must step aside. If nothing else, the labor unions make his paternalistic attitude anachronistic.

Inefficient at first, the telephone ultimately hastens Stahr toward his destiny. Trying to contact the girl who reminded him of his dead wife, Stahr telephones all over Hollywood. When he finds one of the women who rode the floating Siva, she turns out to be the wrong one. When he finds the right one, he sets up an affair destined to fail and to contribute to his own doom.

At their first meeting, Kathleen Moore and Stahr communicate as lovers do, without words. The relationship begins in an atmosphere of heightened romance tempered by irony. Their eyes have spoken, have promised love, but "practically, vulgarly, he did not have her telephone number—or even her name; but it seemed impossible to ask for them now" (p. 66). Communication falls just short. The eyes work, but the telephone does not.

In this final Fitzgerald novel, there is one communication reference that runs counter to our pattern. It occurs when Stahr cavalierly delays a conference of powerful movie magnates to receive the call that squelches the rumor that camera man Pete Zavras is going blind. Knowing that Zavras sees as well as anyone, Stahr can get work for the talented man. In this unusual instance, the telephone interrupts something of lesser importance to enable Stahr to do something really worthwhile, at least in human terms. The rule in Fitzgerald novels, though, is that the mechanical device actually interrupts human communication.

The rule holds true when Stahr tries to reveal himself to Kathleen, or at least tries to explain his self-concept. He is chief clerk, he says, the man who knows where everything is; but a newsboy hawking his communication sheet interrupts their communication: "Mickey Mouse Murdered! Randolph Hearst declares war on China!" (p. 79). Newspapers often interrupt communication. The break here is so complete that Stahr gives no further insight into himself.

The most humorous telephone interruption occurs when Stahr and Kathleen break off communication so Stahr can take a call from a talking gorilla, whom a man named Lew claims is the president. The irony is hardly subtle when Stahr prepares to speak to President McKinley, whom he obviously respects, only to hear the growls of a gorilla. The communication is as absurd as might be expected: "Hello, orang-outang—God, what a thing to be!—Do you know your name? . . . He doesn't seem to know his name" (pp. 83-84). Oddly, comparing the head of the country—as Stahr is head of his company—with an orang-outang humanizes Stahr, even though it certainly diminishes him and effectively concludes rational communication. This incident, however, gives Kathleen a clearer view of Stahr than rational communication ever can:

> He was annoyed with Lew because he had thought it was the president and had changed his manner, acting as if it were. He felt a little ridiculous, but Kathleen felt sorry and liked him better because it had been an orang-outang. (p. 84)

She knows him better, but not well enough to prevent the accidental end of their affair.

Stahr is not the only one to have a highly interesting and emotional moment deflated by the reality of a telephone call. Even Celia, the narrator who participates in the story to a lesser degree than does Nick in *The Great Gatsby,* must suffer an ill-timed call. While Celia is discussing Stahr's new love with Jane Melody, an ancient writer friendly to her, the telephone rings. Celia waits nervously while Jane chats at length with the dullest director in the stable. Celia is in love with Stahr and waits greedily for every morsel of information concerning him. And finally the telephone call ends. Then to her distress, Celia finds that Jane knows nothing about the woman in Stahr's life, not even her name. The telephone call delays Celia's learning that there is nothing to be learned, nothing to be said. This, too, is consistent with Fitzgerald's ironic view.

Light-Dark Imagery

Not surprisingly, Fitzgerald saw little need for the natural light of day in his novel set in Hollywood. Bright afternoon sun accentuates Stahr's pallor, his frailty. And as Stahr and Kathleen drive to his unfinished house on a Sunday afternoon, they don sun glasses, which Fitzgerald calls "cheaters," to block out the sun (p. 80). When they leave Stahr's home the first time, sun shines on their backs. Love can, does flourish by backlight. As they near Kathleen's house, the sun gives way to artificial lights from houses in the canyon. Lights dot the hillside, and Stahr turns on his own headlights. In the romantic twilight, they decide to return to the beach.

Most light in this novel is artificial, man-made. The first reference to it occurs on the airplane. As the stewardess explains to Celia that decent people wrap their gum in paper before throwing it away, the two sit in a half-light that represents a hiatus:

> It was vaguely like a swanky restaurant at that twilight time between meals. We were all lingering—and not quite on purpose. Even the stewardess, I think, had to keep reminding herself why she was there. (p. 4)

No one creates half-light; it just exists. But when Stahr creates light the feeling of hiatus explodes. Sometimes Stahr creates light to cut through illusion as he does when rumor robs Pete Zavras of his livelihood by whispering him blind. Usually, though Stahr dispenses illusion, not truth. Back in the projection room, he reverts to his main role. Pitching the room into blackness, he becomes creator of illusion. But illusions are fragile, so much so that a street light burns away one of Stahr's. Beneath that lamp he sees that Edna Smith, the girl who rode the head of Siva with Kathleen, looks nothing like Minna Davis his dead wife. He explains his mistake to her: "It was dark and the light was in my eyes" (p. 63).

Stahr was seeking not Edna Smith, but Kathleen Moore, who, appropriately, lives at the point of highest light on the hill. They are obviously right for each other from the first. After making love, Kathleen

> lay in the darkness, thinking irrationally that it would be such a bright indefatigable baby, but presently she let him help her up. . . . When she came back into the room, it was lit from a single electric fixture. (p. 88)

Light breaks the illusion until Stahr substitutes candles for the single bulb. In this light, Kathleen looks more like Minna Davis than Minna Davis ever did. Aglow in candle light, Kathleen conforms to Stahr's image of his dead wife, not to the real Minna Davis.

Absolute dark plays a larger role in *The Last Tycoon* than in other Fitzgerald novels. For some characters in other novels, dark holds terrors, but for Manny Schwartz, a man beaten and verging on suicide, black night provides a modicum of cheer. Ugly to himself, he has no wish to see. And Celia, even in total darkness, feels the forces of nature, the green of the trees when she, Wylie White, and Schwartz taxi toward the Hermitage. Not hideous monsters, but a life force emanates from the darkness. Celia has no fear of the night, which makes darkness imagery different from that in *This Side of Paradise,* and *The Beautiful and Damned,* where Amory Blaine and Anthony Patch fear the dark. Celia has no fear of life, while Anthony, and perhaps Amory, shy from it. Schwartz, of course, recoils from life, but if death lurks in darkness, it is all the better for him.

Stahr fears nothing. An insomniac, he barely knows the difference between night and day. He reserves both for work. He does notice, however, when the earthquake cuts the electric lights, casting the lot into darkness. And even though he wants to break the pattern of his life when he meets Kathleen, wants her to be a trollop so he can seek love in the dark like other men, he does not want to put out the candles. Much as he would like to, he cannot stop being Monroe Stahr for even a moment. He must have light, a light that he himself provides. He fears no darkness, yet as an artist, he must control through light.

When Stahr and Kathleen date, Stahr usually provides light from a romantic source, but there is no light on the night before she marries her old fiance, the American. The moon is down, and in the dark they fool themselves into the belief that they will be married. Even as they plan the future, however, the American rides by train back into their lives. The shared dreams, which neither articulates because of awkwardness, die at birth. Yet on this dark night they fool themselves, just as Stahr still fools some people in the dark after reaching a stage of impotent exhaustion. This occurs when he argues with the young communist, Brimmer. Most of the conversation occurs beneath a floodlight, but occasionally Stahr steps out of the light. Celia describes him on these occasions as "watching in dark, dangerous majesty" (p. 126). He still fools Celia.

But the moon provides the major light source in *The Last Tycoon.* Fitzgerald first uses the moon to show how thoroughly Celia rests under Stahr's spell. As the plane approaches the landing strip lined with lights, Celia sees the orange moon over the ocean and subconsciously almost credits Stahr for creating the whole scene. Great though he is, Stahr made no moon, not even the landing field. Still he stands above all other Fitzgerald artists;[1] he created the standards for the movie industry, a spectacularly impressive feat despite its flaws. Truly Stahr is a god creating, but not so much of a god as Celia would make him because he creates only illusion. Appropriately, the illusory light of the moon washes his Hollywood lot on the night of the earthquake: just before the quake, Celia finds a man "washing down a car in a wonderful white light—a fountain among dead industrial shadows" (p. 121).

The first two moon images establish Celia's feeling toward Stahr. The next sets a contrasting view of her father when she finds in his office photos of the studio ghosts—Stahr's dead wife, Minna Davis, and Will Rogers—and the present greats. To enhance the illusion, the "one-way French windows were open and a big moon, rosy-gold with a haze around, was wedged helpless in one of them" (p. 22). While this may be the very moon of Queen Mab, Brady's magic remains circumspect, confined to his office, or at most to the industry. Only Stahr really weaves spells in moonlight. He touches the American essence, its myth and fairy tale. Beneath the moon, the back lot looks like the pages of fairy tales come to life. Celia compares the back lot, Stahr's domain, to an attic where "at night . . . in an enchanted sort of way," the stories and characters are alive (p. 25). Spot lights that compete with the moon break the spell and isolate danger points caused by the flood.

Yet a touch of magic still graces this night. Stahr finds in Kathleen Moore a vision of his dead wife when he sees her eyes "across four feet of moonlight" (p. 26). The dying man in moonlight reaffirms his love for his dead wife. Poe might have written the image. Silver light shines on death.

Calling on the girl he thinks reminded him of Minna Davis, Stahr deludes himself. He indulges in the illusion that the moon at the end of the boulevard was a "different moon every evening, every year" (p. 62). But other lights compete with the moon—street lights, stop lights on automobiles, flood lights that rake the sky: "On an empty corner two mysterious men moved a gleaming drum in pointless arcs over the heavens" (p. 62). Not without hubris, Stahr imagines that he practically created the moon, but he has nothing to do with the other lights. They are variables out of his control; when he meets Kathleen and a spark of love passes between them, he proves so inept in a situation he has not created that they nearly part without fanning the fire. As they walk out of the shadow to his car, there is a "foot of moonlight between them" (p. 66).

Along with the moon, Fitzgerald includes most other symbols of love when he moves the couple back to Stahr's house. They run into rain and fog, which blinds them: "The road lost its boundaries. . . . " (p. 87). Landmarks disappear, or become merely a "sheen of light" (p. 87), and Stahr and Kathleen drive without direction until the fog lifts and the moon lights them on their way. They barely see "each other's eyes in the half darkness" (p. 87). At Stahr's house they make love, climax a love born in rain and moonlight, spawned in the half dark when they could not see each other's eyes. Time takes a breath, stops, creates a hiatus in the half dark. The moon fosters the illusion that these are young lovers, and Kathleen and Stahr act as if they are. The reader knows better.

A typical Fitzgerald moon image illuminates the grunion run. On that "fine blue night," the moon sheds enough light to force Kathleen to shade her eyes (p. 92). The night glows silver until Stahr reads Kathleen's farewell letter. Then "the skies paled and faded—the wind and rain turned dreary, washing the silver fish back into the sea" (p. 98). The moon fades and the weather turns bleak, rends the magic from the night. Pathetic fallacy, certainly, but it shows that for Stahr, Kathleen is the only source of light. No Kathleen, no moon, no life-sustaining illusion.

Dirt-Disease-Decay Imagery

Like every Fitzgerald novel except *This Side of Paradise*, *The Last Tycoon* depicts the destruction of a man in many ways superior to his fellows. The destruction motif opens with a characterization of Manny Schwartz, foil to Monroe Stahr in the sense that what happens to Schwartz can and finally will happen to Stahr. From the beginning of the novel, Schwartz appears as one reeling from a fatal blow:

> He was obviously a man to whom something had happened. Meeting him was like encountering a friend who has been in a fist fight or collision, and got flattened. You stare at your friend. . . . He answers something unintelligible through broken teeth and swollen lips [when you ask what happened]. He can't even tell you about it. (p. 7)

Hollywood destroys man; Schwartz, once on top, now looks as if a "great truck had backed up over him" (p. 8). Stahr's invention, Hollywood, engenders death, destruction, loss of self. Even Wylie White, who never really belonged to the city, nearly lost his identity during his first Hollywood party. And Stahr, from his first appearance in the novel, is a man worn out, dying. A bad heart combined with the rate at which he pushes himself suggests a death wish. At the very least this compulsive worker is killing himself, whether he intends to or not. He has no strength for anything but work. He says he would marry Celia were he not "too tired to undertake anything" (p. 71). And he *is* too tired, even though he overcomes his intense weariness for a while with Kathleen. His very tiredness, however, casts an ironic pall on his affair with Kathleen. Weariness and overwork become synonomous with Stahr. It makes little difference because,

> He was due to die very soon now. Within six months one could say definitely. What was the use of developing the cardiograms? You couldn't persuade a man like Stahr to stop and lie down and look at the sky for six months. He would much rather die. . . . Stahr apparently derived some rare almost physical pleasure from working lightheaded with weariness. It was a perversion of the life force. (p. 108)

Hollywood itself represents a perversion of the life force. In this regard, while the earthquake and subsequent flood can destroy the Hollywood lot, can rearrange everything, the flood does not make the lot any more chaotic than normal. (Compare the description of the lot during the flood with that of the lot during a normal working day, "A Producer's Day"). Chaos is normal, and one reason is that Stahr finally does not reign alone. He must struggle against Brady, whose moral degeneration allows him to plot murder and to carry on an illicit affair with his secretary. When his secretary, Birdie Peters (a flesh-covered skeleton in the closet), tumbles naked from Brady's closet, Celia feels she has experienced a "little immersion in the family drains" (p. 104). Brady, of course, is not the only corrupt executive. Marcus exemplifies another kind of corruption on the board of directors. While his mind deteriorates, his power remains constant. This powerful old man can change the lives of others; he cannot be removed simply because of senility.

Deterioration follows logically from the fantastic pace most people maintain. Stahr drives himself unmercifully, asks and gets the impossible from his people. Celia's account of "A Producer's Day" depicts a bustle of activity seemingly calculated to destroy the human animal. The pace reaches such frenzy that it rapidly wears out the furniture in the projection room. What it does to the people who work hard enough to wear out the furniture is clear enough. Hollywood finally emerges as a wearying joke—like the sign gracing the back of the man at the dance where Celia must watch herself lose Stahr to Kathleen Moore. The sign proclaims that at "midnight in the Hollywood Bowl Sonja Henie was going to skate on hot soup. You could see the sign as he danced becoming less funny on his back" (p. 72).

Images of disease and decay carry the destruction motif, which is underscored throughout by various vain attempts at healing. Were it not already too late, for example, the love between Stahr and Kathleen might heal this dying man. Kathleen certainly tries to provide an environment free of germs. When the two first meet, Stahr cannot enter her home because she has just cleaned house and an ammonia smell pervades everything. This odd image for a love nest projects a hospital perfectly. They never use the sterile walls of Kathleen's home, but make love in the rain at Stahr's unfinished house. This love generates hope, but produces no cure.

Stahr acts as both creator of Hollywood and as healer when his monster goes awry. Patiently he nurses, coaxes the English writer, Boxley, into producing some sort of viable Hollywood script. Stahr, who spends precious hours with Boxley, fails. How he fares with the sex life of the impotent actor remains a mystery. Stahr listens sympathetically, but when a man can get up nothing but his grosses ("up twenty-seven thousand"), the producer seems an unlikely advisor. Only Pete Zavras, a camera man rumored to be nearly blind, benefits noticeably from Stahr's help. And Stahr can aid this man only because nothing ails him. When something goes seriously wrong with a character in Fitzgerald's fiction, human beings cannot help each other. In spite of the futility of the effort, Stahr must try to act as physician and father confessor to the sick and the well, to the whole crippled lot.

What Stahr can do, and what Hollywood does well, is cover the ravages of disease and decay. Note the simple solution when a low gown displays "the bright eczema" on the chest and back of a supposedly-lovely actress:

Before each take, the blemished surface was plastered with an emollient, which was removed immediately after the take. Her hair was of the color and viscosity of drying blood, but there was starlight that actually photographed in her eyes. (p. 51)

Time will force her to join Martha Dodd, once a bright star, but now obscure and attempting to crawl back to the top. Unwilling, unable to accept the end of her career, Martha has a "washed-out look about the eyes" (p. 101). Bewildered by her loss, Martha describes her life and home when she made money from Hollywood and Hollywood made more from her:

> "I had a beautiful place in 1928," she told us, "—Thirty acres, with a miniature golf course and a pool and a gorgeous view. All spring I was up to my ass in daisies." (p. 101)

Impersonal Hollywood creates gods and goddesses from ordinary people; but when their eyes fade, Hollywood casts them adrift like toothless Eskimoes of ancient days, afloat and alone on an iceberg. Some come back, but not through their own efforts, nor through compassion in the movie industry. Those who reach the top again do so through mindless accident. Adrift for years, washed-up cowboy actor Johnny Swanson becomes a hot property when, by purest accident, he mistakenly receives an invitation to act as pall bearer at Stahr's funeral.

Hollywood crushes everyone, weak and powerful. Human resources decay. Age destroys those "discarded flowers" of the acting profession—Johnny Swanson, Martha Dodd, Evelyn Brent (p. 102). Nor is Hollywood any country for writers: Boxley feels the torment of frustration because he cannot achieve the practiced excellence of a hack; Wylie White, out of his element, suffers disillusionment, loses his identity, and falls prey to cynicism; and who is Jane Melody?

> A dried-up little blonde of fifty about whom one could hear the fifty assorted opinions of Hollywood—"a sentimental dope," "the best writer on construction in Hollywood," "a veteran," "that old hack," "the smartest woman on the lot," "the cleverest plagiarist in the biz"; and, of course, in addition she was variously described as a nymphomaniac, a virgin, a pushover, a Lesbian and a faithful wife. (p. 36)

Writers live without identity and their purpose is nebulous. Executives are corrupt or leaning that way. Brady will survive because of his absolute corruption, and in Fitzgerald's outline, Stahr, by the end, has been reduced to Brady's tactics for dealing with foes. He would have Brady killed.

Even by the end of chapter 6, Stahr has degenerated into a parody of himself; when he meets Brimmer, the young communist, Stahr gets drunk and plays "the wicked overseer to a point he would have called trash if he had watched it on the screen" (p. 125). Not used to alcohol, Stahr drinks badly and, like every Fitzgerald hero except Gatsby, gets into a drunken brawl symbolic of his loss of control. No longer capable of holding an industrial empire together, Stahr falls before Brimmer's blow. Chaos reigns:

> The ping-pong balls lay around in the grass like a constellation of stars. . . . There was no mark on Stahr—he must have been hit in the side of the head. He went off behind some trees and was sick, and I heard him kicking up some earth over it.

Stahr is sick unto death, reduced to scratching dirt over his mess like a dog. Illness and decay plague him. Stahr might say, with Yeats in "Sailing to Byzantium," "This is no country for old men." No longer can he command. And though he was the best of all of Fitzgerald's artist gods, he can no longer create.[2]

Water Imagery

A storm vital and violent enough to force to earth a plane carrying Wylie White, Celia Brady, Monroe Stahr, and Manny Schwartz opens *The Last Tycoon*. The storm grounds the plane in Nashville, Tennessee, city of Wylie's birth. The combination of storm and the season of spring make the inference clear: Fitzgerald is at least toying with the idea of rebirth. But contradictions exist. The airplane, for example, early becomes associated with death. While no cause-effect relationship links death to the airplane, air travel always makes Celia think of her dead sister, makes her "somewhat solemn and subdued" (p. 4). Further, the journey by air increases in her the "sense of that sharp rip between coast and coast" (p. 4). The spring deluge spews torrents. In symbolic contradiction, however, the Hollywood crowd flies west in an airplane, a machine that accrues associations of death until finally the purpose of death imagery becomes apparent: Stahr plunges to his death in a plane.

That defeated shell, Manny Schwartz, serves as constant reminder of death on this water-washed plane. Like Stahr, he once had power, once made decisions, but now he can decide only that life is not worth living. A tumbled titan in the business world, Schwartz functions as a foil to Stahr. This airplane carries Schwartz to his place of death, just as another will plummet the already fallen Stahr to his death at the proposed close of the novel.

Associations of death are inherent even in the mythology surrounding Stahr, former boy genius. Stahr is the kind of man who dares, who decides, who makes things happen. Consequently, things happen to him. No docile, aging statesman who has conquered and retired, no warrior elevated above the fray, no gladiator retreated to the grandstand to watch and comment philosophically, Stahr, though ill and sapped of energy, remains a combatant until the end. A defiant Prometheus, he takes risks; but most clearly, the man is Icarus soaring too near the sun. As established earlier, Stahr essentially is a plane. As such he is burdened with every association of death that the plane picks up in *The Last Tycoon*. He is an Icarus who must fall.

The death and flying imagery early associated with water makes clear Fitzgerald's choice to abandon the pattern of first establishing water as a symbol of vitality, or rebirth, only to reverse the role of water in later pages. Standard operating procedure for Fitzgerald was to change water from a symbol of life to an ironic symbol that merely promised life, but never delivered when pitted against that constant ravisher, time. He did this in *The Great Gatsby* and *Tender Is the Night*. From the opening of *The Last Tycoon*, though, water as symbol of fertility and possibility is countered by images of death. The storm that forces Wylie White down to his place of birth rains not the water of life, but of death. Thoughts of death and the actual death of Manny Schwartz reverse traditional life imagery.

The storm in chapter 1 introduces the motif of violent natural phenomena altering people's lives. Even more violent than the storm is the earthquake in chapter 2. Tawdry, artificial Hollywood, of course, ignores natural phenomena; during the earthquake, the voice singing "I love you" repeats the phrase continuously even as the earth trembles; Stahr, too, ignores this most violent of nature's manifestations. He sleeps through everything.

While he disregards rumblings from the bowels of the earth, Stahr cannot ignore the flood caused when the pipes break. That flood, in fact, constitutes one of the more ironic water images in Fitzgerald. During the flood, Stahr believes he sees a ghost, the image of his dead wife, Minna Davis:

> On top of a huge head of the goddess Siva, two women were floating down the current of an impromptu river. The idol had come unloosed from a set of Burma, and it meandered earnestly on its way, stopping sometimes to waddle and bump in the shadows with the other debris on the tide. (p. 25)

From flooding chaos springs love. An artificial river bears the artificial head of Siva, paradoxical god of destruction and reproduction. Astride Siva rides a woman apparently created in the image of Stahr's dead wife. This love for an image from the past ironically comes to a man too tired, too sick for love. Hatched in a grotesque water image, this love between Kathleen and Stahr is doomed from the beginning.

The earthquake virtually ends the need for water symbolism. Celia writes specifically about Stahr—"A Producer's Day"—and little water, symbolic or otherwise, flows through the ordinary life of Monroe Stahr. Drawing on resources he no longer has,[3] Stahr has spent his quota of energy. In this account of Stahr's typical day, the first water reference is to "early snow on a location in Canada with the company already there" (p. 29). Nothing dramatic, no life or death struggle, no rebirth or failed resurrection. Just a simple bother, a thing that halts productions.

Fitzgerald began *The Last Tycoon* by using water imagery ironically, and he continued that trend with the next water image in the sequence, which occurs in chapter 4:

> On the screen a troop of French Canadians pushed their canoes up a rapids. The scene had been photographed in a studio tank, and at the end of each take . . . the actors on screen relaxed . : . and illusion ceased. (p. 53)

"Illusion" is the essential word. In this novel, water fathers many illusions, as it does in all mature Fitzgerald works.

Chapter 5 opens with Celia laboring under the delusion that she can capture Stahr. She uses water in a traditional way to connote freshness: "I had gotten into riding clothes to give the impression I'd been out in the dew since early morning"

(p. 68). "Illusion" fits this traditional reference, too. Celia has not been out in the dew; she merely wants to give that impression. Besides, this romantic cliché has little to do with the reality of life, even in Hollywood.

When Stahr and Kathleen visit Stahr's partially finished home, Fitzgerald relies on water to enhance the love theme. Stahr first recalls happier times when he used to swim. Now his legs are too thin. And the handball court where he once maintained physical fitness was "washed away in a storm" (p. 79). Not rebirth in water, then, but decay engendered by the ravages of water. By this time water has been established as an agent of whatever power plagues mortals with cosmic jokes.[4] This impression gains substance from the love scene on Stahr's beach:

> A headwind blowing out of the sun threw spray up the rocks and over the car. Concrete mixer, raw yellow wood and builders' rubble waited, an open wound in the landscape, for Sunday to be over. (p. 81)

Scarcely a utopian setting, this view and this spray serve admirably to baptize the love of the man who invented Hollywood.

But it is not a mocking rain that falls as Stahr and Kathleen return to the beach home to consummate their love. It is as vital a rain as ever drenched young lovers: "At Santa Monica a sudden gust of rain bounced over them" (p. 86). They shield themselves from the rain, however, and drive on into fog, an admirable image for young love:

> Fog fizzed in at the chink, and Kathleen took off the rose-and-blue hat in a calm, slow way that made him watch tensely. . . . She shook out her hair, and when she saw that Stahr was looking at her, she smiled. (p. 87)

Sensual and suggestive, this image foreshadows love; except that the lovers are neither young nor innocent—of paramount importance to Fitzgerald—nothing in the tone or in the situation indicates doom for this love. And when they finally return to Stahr's house, they "found the dripping beams of a doorway and groped over mysterious waist-high obstacles to the single furnished room odorous of sawdust and wood" (p. 87). Here the water image hints not at a wound across the landscape, as shown on the initial trip to the partially-finished house, but at something being created. Like more youthful lovers, Stahr and Kathleen make love while the rain falls. The rain ceases as it must, but bodes no ill because they turn from rain to the sea, to the grunion hunt that leaves the "sand alive" (p. 92). This is the greatest fertility image of them all. The grunion return annually, emphasizing the cycle, the power of water to renew life each spring.

Kathleen and Stahr rush barefoot along the "foaming edge of water" and get soaked by many a "wave of spray" (p. 92). To top it off, they meet a magnificent, if improbable, Emerson-reading black man who comes to the sea to catch grunion and read essays, probably "Nature." Central to this scene is the natural setting, which plays no role at all in Hollywood. Love forms and is bathed in these waters; yet the cosmic joke surfaces—the joke that might have been expected, considering Fitzgerald's use of water imagery to this point. The joke is the letter that Kathleen wrote to inform Stahr of her engagement to the American. As he reads the letter, in true Hadryesque fashion

> the skies paled and faded—the wind and rain paled and turned dreary, washing the silver fish back to sea. It was only one more day, and nothing was left except the pile of scripts upon the table. (p. 98)

Magic has been ripped from an enchanted day.

The above water images are consistent with the pattern, but the one featuring Stahr as a helmsman tending a frantic ship falls outside the frame. Fitzgerald probably would have cut it, or at least repaired it. This image originates with Boxley, the writer, and is filtered through Celia:

> He knew that Stahr, the helmsman, was finding time for him in the middle of a constant blow—that they were talking in the always creeking rigging of a ship sailing in great awkward tacks on open sea. (p. 105)

Not satisfied with this conceit, Fitzgerald continues in another vein: "Or else—it seemed at times—they were in a huge quarry where even the newly-cut marble bore the tracery of old pediments, half-obliterated inscriptions of the past" (p. 105). In the final draft, Fitzgerald would not have been ambivalent about which image to use. He probably would have cut the water-helmsman conceit because it is out of character for him; it does not fall in line either with the promise soon to be blighted, associated with water in Fitzgerald novels, or with the cynical lack of promise associated with water in *The Last Tycoon*. It is not a deterministic image in that it implies that man can steer. Besides, the image is much too clumsy for Fitzgerald's final product.

More in line with the consistent use of water imagery in this novel is the ironic comment that occurs when Stahr and Kathleen, after their separation, seem to have solved their problems. Driving aimlessly and falling in love again, or perhaps simply renewing their love, they "pass over suicide bridge with the new high wire" (p. 114). Hardly subtle, but this image is consistent with what water imagery has come to symbolize in *The Last Tycoon*.

The final water image in the uncompleted manuscript occurs during the ill-fated meeting between the world-weary Stahr and the young communist, Brimmer. They argue in the Brady back yard where "fresh water from the gasping sprinklers made the lawn glitter like spring" (p. 123). Ironically, it is not spring, but midsummer. And like everything else in Hollywood, the water comes not from natural sources, but from "gasping sprinklers." The meeting ends badly, absurdly, with Stahr drunk and goading Brimmer into a fight that Brimmer wins, is destined to win.

As is often the case, water in the latter part of a Fitzgerald novel is ominous. Water from the gasping sprinkler bodes no good for anyone; the meeting ends as might be expected, with Stahr sick in the bushes. The problem runs much deeper than the alcohol he has just imbibed.

In *The Last Tycoon*, neither car nor train is important. It is now the airplane that has become the symbol of death. Having connected flying and death, Fitzgerald then connects flying with Stahr. Stahr becomes an Icarian figure who will indeed plunge to his death from the sky. He is doomed from the opening page of the novel, and Fitzgerald leaves little doubt that an airplane will be the instrument of death.

From the very first novel Fitzgerald has insisted on the futility of trying to communicate. To try to communicate is equally absurd in *The Last Tycoon*. Boys selling newspapers shatter attempts to communicate. A telephone call from a talking orang-outang breaks off communication between Stahr and Kathleen Moore. And a letter that tells what once was truth, but is valid no more, causes a major plot complication. This is the letter that Kathleen Moore wrote to Stahr telling him that she could not love him because she planned to marry the American. But Kathleen loses the letter, and Stahr reads it. For once a letter communicates, but too late, only after the truth it had to tell was false. The very devices of communication seem almost malevolent in all Fitzgerald novels. The universe is perversely absurd, and to try to communicate merely heightens the madness.

The light-dark imagery is perfect for a novel about the man who created illusions for a nation. *The Last Tycoon* tells the story of the best artist in Fitzgerald's cast of characters. Gatsby created illusion only for Daisy, Dick Diver only for his small circle of intimates, but Monroe Stahr spun out illusion for a nation. The sun of reality is unwelcome in Hollywood, and when it appears, Stahr and Kathleen Moore, the woman he loves, don sunglasses to shut it out.

Stahr's story is that of the man who makes man-made light on a large scale. He would control even more than Gatsby or Diver. Not even in love does Stahr stop being the artist, the god who would control. He wants to take Kathleen in darkness, pretending she is a whore. But the artist in him demands candles, control through light.

The moon, too, is a major source of light and producer of illusion. The moon bathes the back lot and the shards of myth that lie out there in random array. Stahr can put these bits of myth together and fashion the imagination of a nation. And the moon helps. The greatest myth fostered by the moon, however, is that Stahr and Kathleen Moore are young lovers. The illusion sustains life for a while, but when Stahr reads Kathleen's letter telling of her fiancé, the American, the moon loses its magic. Without the illusion, Stahr loses the will to struggle. He succumbs as Dick Diver did before him.

Underscoring Stahr's downfall is dirt-disease-decay imagery. *The Last Tycoon* shows a system that grinds people down. It will wear out Monroe Stahr, but he deserves it because he invented the system. Stahr works so hard within the system he created that he is killing himself. Fitzgerald calls Stahr's slaving for the system a "perversion of the life force" (p. 108). Whether that is true or not, the system certainly does not deserve Stahr's kind of dedication, for it is corrupt all the way through. Of the executives, Brady is a prime example. His lechery becomes minor compared with the greed that will lead him to scheme, to plot the murder of Stahr. Brady's corruption is active. Old Marcus's is passive, but still dangerous. Marcus maintains power in Hollywood even though age has left him feebleminded.

In a Hollywood swamped with disease, Stahr is the chief healer. Yet Stahr, dying himself, cannot help those with real problems. What he can do is cover up the blemishes long enough for the camera to fool the world. But he cannot fool himself; he sees the corruption. And he falls victim. In an industry that crushes and corrupts everyone, Stahr cannot escape. Once a god, Stahr has reached a level by the end of chapter 6, the last chapter Fitzgerald wrote in fairly polished draft, where he gets drunk, fights, vomits, and covers his mess like a dog. And by the end of the novel he is no better than Brady. Stahr plots to have Brady killed, just as Brady had plotted his death. Although Stahr regrets his plot against Brady, he is in essence a morally dead man before his plane crashes.

Water imagery serves an entirely different function in *The Last Tycoon* than in *The Great Gatsby* and *Tender Is the Night.* By the time he was writing *The Last Tycoon,* Fitzgerald had abandoned the technique of making images appear positive at first only to have them prove negative later in the novel. The violent storm in *The Last Tycoon,* for example, is never the image of fertility it would have been in the middle novels. Death images counter the vitality inherent in the storm. Celia is preoccupied by thoughts of death, and the airplane, as well as the Icarian Stahr, become practically synonymous with death. And of course the storm forces the airplane down into the city of Wylie White's birth, Manny Schwartz's suicide.

The flood caused by pipes broken during the earthquake is the second major water image. The artificial river, a result of the flood, carries an artificial head of Siva, god of destruction and reproduction. On this head rides Kathleen Moore, whom Stahr mistakes for his dead wife. Trying to recapture his past when life had meaning, Stahr falls in love with the ghost of his dead wife. The grotesque water images, plus images of death in chapter 1, offer little hope that this love will flourish, will make Stahr a new man.

Only when water has been discredited as an image of life does Fitzgerald stage what seems to be a traditional love scene in the rain. The grunion run on the beach is an even-clearer fertility symbol than the rain. Here is where young love flourishes, but the lovers are not young. (Youth is more important to Fitzgerald than to most men.) After a brief separation, Stahr and Kathleen—supposedly planning marriage—drive across Suicide Bridge. The image is hardly subtle, no more than the final water image—"gasping sprinklers" as the young communist, Brimmer, batters the aging Stahr. Water imagery has shown the reader from the beginning that Stahr is doomed. But Stahr tries to live in his watery element as if he had a future, and Fitzgerald thereby gains dramatic irony.

Conclusion

Looking back over Fitzgerald's five novels as a whole—his most important and ambitious work during his two productive decades, 1920-1940, certain generalizations come to mind. I have identified the major categories of images as transportation, communication, light and dark, dirt-disease-decay, and water imagery. Each of these image patterns appears in all of Fitzgerald's novels and each sheds specific light on the work that could be found only through that image pattern. Take transportation imagery. Usually it would be dangerous to classify as imagery a commodity like transportation, which for most writers amounts to little more than a device to help carry out stage directions. Characters who move further than center stage require transportation. When he needs only to move characters from one place to another, Fitzgerald, like any author, is capable of sending his people on nonsymbolic travels in nonsymbolic conveyances. In the early pages of *The Beautiful and Damned,* for example, Fitzgerald ships Anthony Patch from New York to Rome. Neither the journey nor the passage by water seems symbolically significant; it is structurally significant, however, that this trip balances against the sea voyage made by Anthony and Gloria at the end of the novel. Neither the jaunt to Rome in the beginning nor the ocean voyage at the end will change Anthony, although he entertains high hopes for both. In the end he still must tolerate being Anthony Patch—his problem from first to last. More often than not, though, both the trip and the mode of travel form meaningful patterns.

The car, the airplane, the boat, the train—these are the dynamic machines, the artificial arteries that pump life through the industrialized urban world. And they work. In Fitzgerald's fiction, trains run on time, taxis come when summoned. They kill, too, and that is all important; beyond question, the dynamic machines are snakes in the garden, yet paradoxically, they are necessary in Fitzgerald's Eden. Fitzgerald would be bored, would make veritable hell of a pastoral paradise. Fitzgerald's Eden cannot exist without these dynamic machines of transportation that both create and perpetuate a way of life. But in the act of creation, these machines sometimes destroy. They kill, become symbols of death even as they function.

Yet they do function. Fitzgerald maintains an ambivalent attitude toward the machines that create and destroy, just as he might strike an ambivalent stance toward a tragic flaw. The machine, in fact, may be the tragic flaw of civilization. As is ever the case with tragedy, though, the flaw provides the strength that first lifts the hero to heights rare among mortals. Thus it is possible, even sane, to admire and at the same instant deplore the hubris of an Oedipus. So is it possible to love and hate the dynamic machinery of transportation, which undeniably nurtures society even though it may destroy the Myrtle Wilsons, the Gatsbys, the Monroe Stahrs of the world.

But Fitzgerald shows no love, no admiration for the static machinery of communication, the telephones, the newspapers, the letters designed to help man commune with man. These static devices do not function, and there lies all the difference. Transportation machines transport; communication devices and machines actually break off communication, or worse, feed false information that destroys human understanding and human bonds. Image patterns indicate that Fitzgerald knows that machine or no machine, device or no device, communication will not take place:

Fitzgerald uses these static devices of communication, these artificial aids in understanding and in creating community among men, to illustrate a world view where absurd and unpredictable coincidence influences the lives of all characters. Through the failure of these devices, Fitzgerald proves himself philosophically akin to Thomas Hardy, whose characters often miscarry vital messages.[1] For Hardy and Fitzgerald, coincidence and communication gone astray amount to more than fictional technique; both involve a world view. Hardy believed that malevolent accidents stem from a lack of design in the universe. What might one expect from an idiot universe running pilotless and wild? Even though Fitzgerald might see a universe equally as chaotic as Hardy's, Fitzgerald's seems less *randomly* absurd because he at least proffers tangible villains. One of these is the machine.

The machine in Fitzgerald's fiction may be the ornament and emblem of civilization, may even constitute the necessary ingredient for society's survival; nonetheless, it is unreliable to the point of near malevolence. Meant to serve humanity, the machine often does just the opposite. And the static machinery of communication does not even perform its primary function, which darkens the irony and makes Fitzgerald more true to form in dealing with static devices than with dynamic machines. While the engines of communication promise much, Fitzgerald from first to last novel remains a writer with little hope for either communication or communion in the community of man.

The light-dark imagery supports A. H. Steinberg's characterization of Fitzgerald as a "watchman of the night."[2] Fitzgerald describes the moon of romance, the joy, the evening's ecstasy. But he also focuses a bright sun on illusions that wilt in the light of day. Knowing day as intimately as night, he uses light and dark throughout his novels both as symbols and as controls for the reader's emotions. Richard D. Lehan points out that while *This Side of Paradise* lacks sense of place, it has at least "a heightened sense of feeling—the mood of youth under moonlight."[3]

In *The Beautiful and Damned* and later novels, Fitzgerald firmly establishes the night as romance, day the opposite: "The day is reality, harsh, harsh, and vigorous; the night is illusion, tender, joyful but devitalizing."[4] That specific reference to *Tender Is the Night* applies equally well to *The Beautiful and Damned*. In both, "the night is the time of enchantment, masking the ugliness of reality that the day exposes."[5]

Light-dark imagery broadens into an unobtrusive symbolism that never threatens the poetry of Fitzgerald's brilliant visual pictures. No realist, not one to depict scenes as the normal eye views them, he describes a lighted landscape of the mind. Nuances of shadow and light create the essence of that landscape. Wright Morris, for example, notes in *The Great Gatsby* a

> serene, almost elegaic air; there is nothing frenetic or feverish about it, and the fires of spring, no longer burning, have filled the air with the scent of leaf smoke. The dark fields of the republic are bathed in a moonlight of nostalgic haze.[6]

Like a great photographer, Fitzgerald knows the importance of light and shadow. With stagelights blazing or casting shadows, symbol and scene merge. The heat and intense sunlight during the confrontation scene in *The Great Gatsby*, for example, combine to form a "glittering hell,"[7] all that remains of Gatsby's dream.

The dirt-disease-decay imagery highlights a side of Fitzgerald's work and philosophy that receives little attention. For one reputed to write exclusively about the golden life, the free-flowing wealth of the boom, Fitzgerald soils his fictional universe with a surprising amount and variety of dirt, disease, and decay images. Of course only those who have not read Fitzgerald, or who "know" what they will find when they "read" him, could reduce him to a mere historian of glitter. Beyond question, he described the surface world brilliantly. Yet he remained too much of a moralist[8] to halt his investigation of life at the surface level, no matter how attractive that surface was.[9] He loved the boom, hated it, loved the American dream, hated it. Commenting on one of Fitzgerald's major preoccupations in fiction, Marius Bewley says, "The American dream, stretched between a golden past and a golden future, is always betrayed by a desolate present—a moment of fruit rinds and discarded favours and crushed flowers."[10] Fitzgerald never neglects the fruit rinds. Waste and violence lurk behind the party scenes, and the aftermath concerns him as much as the golden festivity itself."[11] Bewley speaks directly to the point:

> The great achievement of [Gatsby] is that it manages, while poetically evoking a sense of the goodness of that early dream, to offer the most damaging criticism of it in American literature. . . . [But] the criticism manages to be part of the tribute.[12]

Water imagery tells more about *The Great Gatsby* and *Tender Is the Night* than any other image pattern. Forever fascinated by the promise of life, Fitzgerald mines symbolic gold both from spring and from the water that drenches that season; spring embodies the epitome of promise, of hope, of rebirth, but for Fitzgerald few promises are kept. The cycle of seasons dictates that winter returns, and the most glowing promise of spring fails to stave off the season of death. The brighter the spring, the more blighted the winter. Time is the great enemy, the weed that chokes the romantic.[13] After too many springs, the resurrecting water brings no more life, but only death and dying. Fitzgerald knew well that "One generation passeth away, and another generation cometh: but the earth abideth forever." He knew also that "To everything there is a season, and a time to every purpose under the heaven: A time to be born, and a time to die; a time to plant and a time to pluck that which is planted." Though he knew these truths from Ecclesiastes, the pattern established in his water imagery shows that he found them counter to the promises of spring, that he discovered in them a great source of irony.[14] Perhaps he learned late that love, life, art—all things of value—are mortal, and that mortality is the ulitmate negation of promise. As these lines concerning a peak period of his life indicate, he knew well how fleet is time:

> And lastly from that period I remember riding in a taxi one afternoon between very tall buildings under a mauve and rosy sky; I began to bawl because I had everything I wanted and knew I would never be so happy again.[15]

Fitzgerald always saw bust inherent in boom, believed in Pozzo's despairing dictum: "They give birth astride a grave, the light gleams an instant, then it's night once more."[16] Nowhere does he voice this belief more clearly than through his use of water imagery. Torn two ways, Fitzgerald desires intensely to believe in the promise, but he knows for sure that winter follows spring, as this discussion of the boom years suggests:

> America was going on the greatest, gaudiest spree in history and there was going to be plenty to tell about it. The whole golden boom was in the air—its splendid generosities, its outrageous corruptions and the tortuous death struggle of the old America in prohibition. All the stories that came into my head had a touch of disaster in them—the lovely young creatures in my novels went to ruin, the diamond mountains in my short stories blew up, my millionaires were as beautiful and damned as Thomas Hardy's peasants. In life these things hadn't happened yet, but I was pretty sure living wasn't the reckless, careless business these people thought—this generation just younger than me.[17]

Tracing these five image patterns through the novels is not to say that other categories might not have been chosen. Atmosphere and weather, for example, or color imagery could have been worth a chapter. That would have changed the focus, but not the essence of this study. As the reader has noted by now, weather falls naturally under the category of water imagery and color emerges at least peripherally from the discussion of light and shade. Other possibilities include imagery growing out of references to music, flowers, art, artifact, animals, and most certainly alcohol. Again, though, focusing on the patterns created by these images would not have changed the essence of this study. Nor, I think, would the inclusion of the short stories add anything but bulk to my argument.

Before laying this study to rest, I would like to stress four points: Fitzgerald never stopped developing as an artist; he probably would have continued to write witty, forgettable novels like *This Side of Paradise* and *The Beautiful and Damned* had he not espoused the traditional techniques of those who use imagery to create a unified artistic whole, both thematically and structurally; in creating *Tender Is the Night*, Fitzgerald wrote a novel as rare and fine as any he ever wrote, a novel that in many ways surpasses *The Great Gatsby;* and finally, while Fitzgerald wove the patterns of many images through his later works, the theme always caused one cluster of images to dominate all the others in each novel.

The first and most important conclusion to emerge is that Fitzgerald's use of imagery becomes more sophisticated and more skillfully integrated into his fiction with each succeeding novel. Patterns, for example, occur but rarely in *This Side of Paradise*, perhaps because Fitzgerald shows only what it was *like*, not what it *meant*, to attain manhood just before the fabled twenties. Fitzgerald superimposes his protagonist on a time, a place, and as young men do, Amory survives without visible scars. This episodic novel portrays chronologically the education of a young man, but because that education remains incomplete, because it never bares that final Fitzgerald truth—that enervating formula of the futility of effort vs. the necessity of struggle—the novel drifts down roads without destination, paths without pattern. In later novels, image patterns establish the ironic plight of a romantic idealist trapped in a practical, corrupt world; and they form the very structural nerves and sinews that carry the reader, if not the protagonist, to a tragic realization. But here, image patterns do not perform that function.

Obviously, neither *This Side of Paradise* nor *The Beautiful and Damned* would make good subjects for an imagery study. They do, however, provide excellent foils for the imagery techniques Fitzgerald used in his later, better work. I have written so much about *This Side of Paradise* only because I believe in negative examples. Analyzing why image patterns fail to emerge here—with the possible exception of water imagery—shows more clearly why they do emerge in the novels that follow. The same holds true of *The Beautiful and Damned*, where patterns exist, but remain unimpressive. And to prove that image patterns alone cannot pump life into a work, *The Beautiful and Damned* is dull compared to *This Side of Paradise*, in spite of its more consistent complex of image patterns. Yet this novel promised greater things, looked ahead to the irony and art that would supplant paradise and damnation.

The second point I would like to stress deals with why *The Great Gatsby* and the later novels thoroughly dwarf the first two novels. What really happened, it seems, is that Fitzgerald switched allegiance from that group of writers who *tell* a tale, from those who write novels that *tell* what happened only in a physical or intellectual way. Abandoning the traditions of the intellectual Wells and the popular Mackenzie, Fitzgerald allied himself with the greatest writers in literary history, those who tell what happened, certainly, but more significantly, *show* what it was like to be there, how it felt, how the weather was, how the moods ran, and—what it all meant.

Those writers subordinate the intellectual and physical sides of experience in favor of the emotional and psychological, and they do so particularly through the use of imagery, which to the fiction writer is the equivalent of a point of argument to the essayist or the debater. The essayist, through a series of logical arguments, leads the reader to an intellectual position. Even readers who will not accept that position know how the writer arrived there if the argument is sound. The logic produced through image patterns, however, leads not to an intellectual position, but to an emotional awareness. Images create the world of the novel, and logical patterns of imagery make all facets of that world cohere, make the work of art a unified whole. More basically, images show what the world is like and, in Fitzgerald's case, show how it is to be Nick, or Gatsby, or Diver, or Stahr.

Sophocles was one of the first to use images to bring out truths that logic cannot reach. Homer did it, and most certainly Shakespeare. With *The Great Gatsby,* Fitzgerald joins this tradition wherein writers intensify experience through an elegance of language and patterned imagery. He enters the stream represented by John Keats, whose command of language ranges from the musical lyric in a minor key as in "La Belle Dame Sans Merci" to the dramatic *Hyperion,* a poem with the power of deep-gutted rolling thunder. Fitzgerald knew and admired T. S. Eliot, too; waste-land imagery permeates and unifies each of the last four novels. Fitzgerald, in fact, is so much a part of the tradition represented by Eliot that the author of *The Waste Land* praised *The Great Gatsby* as the first step forward by the American novel since Henry James. And James, of course, is the obsessed image hunter's delight: "*The Great Gatsby* is Jamesian in its figurative language, but the density of imagery is somewhat less. . . ."[18]

Fitzgerald also follows the tradition of James Joyce. Despite the obvious failings of the apprentice novels, the youthful Fitzgerald, who admired art so much that in a moment of excess he once offered to leap through a window in homage to Joyce's art,[19] might indeed have the energy to write *The Great Gatsby, Tender Is the Night,* and *The Last Tycoon.*

Obviously, then, Fitzgerald did not invent the use of patterned imagery, nor was he the sole American to take advantage of this technique. Hawthorne, Twain, Poe, and Stephen Crane used it early, Hemingway and Faulkner would later. Fitzgerald shares the tradition with most Americans of any stature. And with Europeans like Flaubert. But of all the writers in that tradition, Joseph Conrad most influenced Fitzgerald. In *Heart of Darkness,* for instance, Conrad goes so far as to set up a color chart to aid image seekers; he lists the colors on the map of Africa and tells what each color means. These colors appear later in the patchwork quilt costume of the harlequin, showing that the mixture of elements in the man paralleled the mixture in the country. In other works Conrad was less blatant, but used the same techniques.

The way, finally, to tell whether a writer works from the tradition represented by Fitzgerald's first two novels, or from that represented by his last three is to ask this question: in reading the novel, was I impressed mostly by the physical actions and by the "message," or did I find in this work a profoundly moving emotional experience, a knowing that runs deeper than intellect? If the experience was emotionally moving, then in all probability the use of imagery contributed to the impact. That is why, I take it, that Jane Austen can generate excitement from what are potentially the dullest tales in human history while Sir Walter Scott, starting with exciting tales of action, sometimes loses his reader in a slough of ennui.

Fitzgerald does not bore his reader, never in the last three works. *The Great Gatsby*, of course, has received the most attention, but as a third point of emphasis, I should like to reiterate that Fitzgerald wrote more than one excellent novel. In terms of image patterns, at least, *Tender Is the Night* equals, perhaps surpasses *The Great Gatsby*. The deserved praise directed toward *The Great Gatsby* might with equal justice be aimed toward *Tender Is the Night*. William H. Hildebrand, for example, aptly describes the function of imagery in *The Great Gatsby*, but his appraisal applies equally well to *Tender Is the Night:*

> If it is true, as I think it is, that a work of art is born in its images, then it is also true that intricately patterned novels like *The Golden Bowl* and *The Great Gatsby* are borne along on their images, that is, that the emotional logic of the story is to be found in the logic of the images.[20]

In that same vein, Charles Samuels says of *The Great Gatsby* that

> Its fundamental achievement is a triumph of language. . . . Throughout, *The Great Gatsby* has the precision and splendor of a lyric poem, yet well-wrought prose is merely one of its triumphs. Fitzgerald's distinction in this novel is to have made the language celebrate itself. Among other things, *The Great Gatsby* is about the power of art.[21]

Tender Is the Night is too large a work, a work that attempts too much to have the precision of a lyric poem. Yet it, too, makes the "language celebrate itself." And in both novels, images broaden into symbols and symbols make the abstract concrete. Though Fitzgerald did not have time to revise, or even finish his last novel, *The Last Tycoon* also achieves much of its impact because of the intricate patterns that had begun to form.

The fourth and final point I would like to make is that after *This Side of Paradise*, a novel generally devoid of image patterns, Fitzgerald allowed the theme to determine which of the clusters of images would be more important than any other. He always formed patterns from a number of different images, but one set of images dominated each of the later novels. In *The Beautiful and Damned*, for example, the main source of cohesion stems from dirt-disease-decay imagery. The theme that life is meaningless, that the world of the novel will indeed destroy and damn the beautiful, dictates that the imagery of decay be foremost. Both *The Great Gatsby* and *Tender Is the Night* explore the ironic contrast between the enormous promise life seems to offer and the unromantic reality. Water imagery best exemplifies this irony because in these two novels, Fitzgerald establishes water first as an apparent symbol of life, energy, rejuvenation, then shows that promise to have been false. Time cancels all hope. And because much of *The Last Tycoon* deals with the creation of illusion in Hollywood, the imagery of light and shade, of artificial light and moonlight forms the most important and coherent patterns in that novel. As always in a Fitzgerald novel, many image patterns conspire to create a unified whole, but theme and subject matter determine which of these clusters of images will be most important, which will create the symbols that light the way through the novel.

Notes

Introduction

1. G. Wilson Knight, *The Wheel of Fire: Interpretations of Shakespearian Tragedy with Three New Essays* (London: Methuen & Co., Ltd., 1959), p. 3.

2. *The Letters of John Keats*, ed. Maurice Buxton Forman (London: Oxford University Press, 1960), p. 67.

3. Milton Hindus, *F. Scott Fitzgerald: An Introduction and Interpretation (New York: Holt, Rinehart & Winston, 1968)*, p. 37.

4. Anna R. Gere, "Color in Fitzgerald's Novels," *Fitzgerald/Hemingway Annual* (1971), p. 333.

5. Wolfgang A. Clemen, *The Development of Shakespeare's Imagery* (Cambridge: Harvard University Press, 1951), p. 3.

6. If the best writers attract excellent criticism, Fitzgerald is a fine writer indeed. There are many studies of imagery, especially color imagery in *The Great Gatsby*. Because of the number of such articles, I chose to avoid color symbolism.

7. See Susanne K. Langer, "The Dramatic Illusion," *Feeling and Form* (New York: Charles Scribner's Sons, 1953), pp. 306–25. Langer's opposition of literature as a continual past striving toward the present against drama as a continual present striving toward the future seems to create a problem. It begs the question, how can anyone use the techniques of Shakespearean critics to discuss novels when the two genres are utterly different? I accept Langer's definitions unequivocally, but reject the problem. Whether the genre be fiction or drama, imagery moves through the work as a thread that creates atmosphere, theme, and ties beginning to end. It does this regardless of whether the progression be from past to present, or from present to future.

8. Caroline F. E. Spurgeon, *Shakespeare's Imagery and What It Tells Us,* (Cambridge: Cambridge University Press, 1971). First published in 1935.

9. Caroline F. E. Spurgeon, *Leading Motives in the Imagery of Shakespeare's Tragedies* (New York: Haskell House, 1970), p. 3. First published 1930.

10. Robert B. Heilman, *This Great Stage: Image and Structure in King Lear* (Baton Rouge: Louisiana State University Press, 1948), p. 4.

11. Ibid., p. 8.

12. Robert L. Gale, *The Caught Image: Figurative Language in the Fiction of Henry James* (Chapel Hill: University of North Carolina Press, 1964), p. 4.

13. See E. H. Gombrich, *Meditations on a Hobby Horse* (London: Phaidon Press, Ltd., 1963), pp. 30–44. Gombrich asks rhetorically "whether it really matters all that much if we know what the work of art meant to the artist" (p. 31). He answers, only if we assume "this private, personal psychological meaning . . . is alone the real, the true meaning" (p. 31).

14. See Arthur Mizener, *The Far Side of Paradise* (Boston: Houghton Mifflin, 1965); Henry Dan Piper, *A Critical Portrait* (New York: Holt, Rinehart and Winston, 1965); Andrew Turnbull, *Scott Fitzgerald* (New York: Charles Scribner's Sons, 1962); Matthew J. Bruccoli, *Some Sort of Epic Grandeur: The Life of F. Scott Fitzgerald* (New York: Harcourt Brace Jovanovich, 1981); and André Le Vot, *F. Scott Fitzgerald: A Biography*, tr. William Byron (New York: Doubleday, 1983).

15. Moody E. Prior, *The Language of Tragedy* (New York: Columbia University Press, 1947), p. 2.

16. Ibid., p. 8.

17. See Robert F. Goheen, *The Imagery of Sophocles' Antigone* (Princeton: Princeton University Press, 1951). Goheen analyzes monetary, military, sea and sailing, marriage, disease and cure, and sight imagery. A sample of the kind of light his study sheds on *Antigone* is the conclusion that Creon perceives everything in mercantile terms. Creon has the assurance and strength often commensurate with a limited view, but that limitation causes his downfall (p. 16). Creon also uses metaphors that "tend to reduce other people . . . to the level of slaves" (p. 20).

18. Clemen, *The Development of Shakespeare's Imagery*, p. 4.

19. Una Ellis-Fermor, *The Frontiers of Drama* (Suffolk: Methuen & Co. Ltd., 1964), p. 78.

20. William Flint Thrall and Addison Hibbard, *A Handbook to Literature*, revised and enlarged by C. Hugh Holman (New York: The Odyssey Press, 1960), p. 478.

21. Hazel Greenberg, "Cluster Imagery in the Novels of Edward Lewis Wallant" (Unpublished Ph.D. dissertation, Department of English, Southern Illinois University, 1972), p. 37.

22. See Sergio Perosa, *The Art of F. Scott Fitzgerald*, trans. Charles Matz and Perosa (Ann Arbor: University of Michigan Press, 1965), pp. 152–78. Perosa argues cogently that in the later stories and in *The Last Tycoon*, Fitzgerald was moving toward a more spare style, a technique more in the manner of Hemingway. If this is true, perhaps *The Last Tycoon* would not have been as imagistically complex as the novels during the middle years. One should bear in mind, however, that Fitzgerald never lavished as much revision and thought on a story as on a novel. *The Last Tycoon* could have resembled *The Great Gatsby* more closely than Perosa's study would suggest.

23. Matthew J. Bruccoli and Margaret M. Duggan, eds., *Correspondence of F. Scott Fitzgerald* (New York: Random House, 1980), p. 112. In July 1922, Fitzgerald expressed his desire to "write something *new*—something extraordinary and beautiful and simple + intricately patterned."

24. F. Scott Fitzgerald, *Afternoon of an Author*, ed. Arthur Mizener (New York: Charles Scribner's Sons, 1957), p. 132.

25. Kenneth E. Eble, "The Craft of Revision: *The Great Gatsby*," *American Literature*, 36 (November 1964), 317.

26. Victor A. Doyno, "Patterns in *The Great Gatsby*," *Modern Fiction Studies*, 12 (Winter 1966–67), 425.

27. Henry Dan Piper, *F. Scott Fitzgerald: A Critical Portrait* (New York: Holt, Rinehart and Winston, 1965), p. 109.

28. *The Letters of F. Scott Fitzgerald*, ed. Andrew Turnbull (New York: Charles Scribner's Sons, 1963), p. 186. Hereafter cited as *Letters*. Note Sanford Pinkster, "Seeing *The Great Gatsby* Eye to Eye," *College Literature*, 3 (Winter 1976), 69: "Fitzgerald's last-minute choice, however instinctual, was based on the book he had already written. Put another way: an effective literary symbol is never an isolated or accidental phenomenon. It requires a context, a pattern of interlocking images."

29. C. Day Lewis, *The Poetic Image* (London: Johnathan Cape, 1947), p. 88.

30. Edward A. Armstrong, *Shakespeare's Imagination: A Study of the Psychology of Association and Inspiration* (London: Lindsay Drummond, 1946), p. 111.

31. James E. Miller, Jr., *The Fictional Technique of Scott Fitzgerald* (New York: New York University Press, 1964), pp. 1–44.

32. *Letters*, p. 168.

33. Ibid., p. 183.

34. Frances Kroll Ring, "Footnotes on Fitzgerald," *Esquire*, 52 (December 1959), 150.

35. Matthew J. Bruccoli, *The Composition of Tender Is the Night: A Study of Manuscripts* (Pittsburgh: University of Pittsburgh Press, 1963), p. 138. Bruccoli's meaning of "symbolic commentary" differs slightly from mine. His sense of the phrase includes only those instances where minor scenes or actions comment symbolically on major scenes. Fitzgerald certainly uses that technique, but images definitely provide even more important comment than that emerging from simple juxtaposition of scenes.

36. Piper, *A Critical Portrait*, p. 143.

37. See Leo Marx, *The Machine in the Garden* (New York: Oxford University Press, 1964).

38. F. Scott Fitzgerald, *The Last Tycoon* (1941; rpt. New York: Charles Scribner's Sons, 1969), p. 4. All quotations are from this edition. Page numbers hereafter cited in parentheses.

39. Stahr, of course, reacts with as much panic as anyone else when outside forces like the labor movement and the Communist Party threaten the empire he created. He is confused, no longer in control. Drunk, sick, he stoops to a fight with the Communist, Brimmer. The Stahr who vomits behind the bushes is a mere shadow of the man who revolutionized the movie business.

40. The Icarian images are Celia's. Her love for Stahr makes her far from objective. Only lovers and worshippers can speak seriously in heroic terms.

41. Stahr learned that in this kind of world, the man in charge makes a completely arbitrary decision because one decision is as good as another. He understood the futility of wasting time after he has studied all the facts and found them to be of no help. His example is that of a railroad man who has to send a train through any of a half-dozen gaps, all of which are equally good. Explaining his philosophy to the pilot, Stahr says, "You choose some one way for no reason at all—because that mountain's pink or the blueprint is a better blue" (p. 19).

42. See Wright Morris, *The Territory Ahead: Critical Interpretations in American Literature* (Forge Village, Mass.: Atheneum, 1961), p. 160. "But Fitzgerald *knew*. That was the hell of it. He was the first of his generation to know that life was absurd."

43. Jackson R. Bryer, "Style as Meaning in *The Great Gatsby:* Notes Toward a New Approach" in *Critical Essays on F. Scott Fitzgerald's "The Great Gatsby,"* ed. Scott Donaldson (Boston: G. K. Hall & Co., 1984), pp. 117–24.

44. Kermit W. Moyer, *"The Great Gatsby:* Fitzgerald's Meditation on American History" in *Critical Essays on F. Scott Fitzgerald's "The Great Gatsby,"* ed. Scott Donaldson (Boston: G. K. Hall & Co., 1984), pp. 218–28.

45. For an excellent discussion of how attention to small details of technique and style can illuminate theme, see Jackson Bryer, "Style as Meaning in *The Great Gatsby,"* pp. 124–28.

46. Clemen, *The Development of Shakespeare's Imagery,* p. 3.

Chapter 1

1. James L. West III, *The Making of "This Side of Paradise"* (Philadelphia: University of Pennsylvania Press, 1983), pp. 12–19.

2. Ibid., p. 45.

3. See Clinton S. Burhans, Jr., "Structure and Theme in *This Side of Paradise," Journal of English and Germanic Philology,* 68 (October 1969), 608–9. Burhans argues that Fitzgerald uses the people Amory looks up to as a structural as well as thematic device.

4. F. Scott Fitzgerald, *This Side of Paradise* (1920; rpt. New York: Charles Scribner's Sons, 1970), pp. 86–87. All quotations are from this edition. Page numbers hereafter cited in parentheses.

5. Sister M. Bettina, SSND, "The Artifact in Imagery: Fitzgerald's *The Great Gatsby," Twentieth-Century Literature,* 9 (October 1963), 140. "Fitzgerald in his imagery counterpoises the real and the artificial." The artifact and the real thing, like the tenor and vehicle in a metaphor, blend and comment on each other, thus serving Fitzgerald's purpose as satirist and illustrating the famed double vision first mentioned by Malcolm Cowley. The result of this double vision is a man like Nick Carraway, a man both involved and aloof from the scene. In *This Side of Paradise,* Fitzgerald uses the artifact, the automobile to satirize Amory and to point out a salient characteristic of the young man; he is absolutely of the city and apart from his natural surroundings.

6. Joseph Conrad, *Heart of Darkness* from *Three Short Novels* (New York: Bantam Books, 1971), p. 4: "'And this also,' said Marlow suddenly, 'has been one of the dark places of the earth.'"

7. See *Letters,* p. 67. Fitzgerald confesses to Scotty that he was like Amory in this respect: "And after reading Thoreau I felt how much I have lost by leaving nature out of my life."

8. See Lillian Hellman, *An Unfinished Woman: A Memoir* (Boston: Little, Brown and Co., 1969), pp. 67–68. Ms. Hellman describes a ride with Fitzgerald in which he drove much as Beatrice did. Apparently such drives were common during his final years in Hollywood. See Aaron Latham, *Crazy Sundays: F. Scott Fitzgerald in Hollywood* (New York: Viking Press, 1970), pp. 19–20.

9. F. Scott Fitzgerald, *The Beautiful and Damned* (1922; rpt. New York: Charles Scribner's Sons, 1950), p. 26. All quotations are from this edition. Page numbers hereafter cited in parentheses.

10. Barry Edward Gross, "The Dark Side of Twenty-five: Fitzgerald and *The Beautiful and Damned," Bucknell Review,* 16, iii (December 1968), 47.

11. They could hardly have been more out of place than in Marietta, as the automobile imagery indicates: "Marietta offered little social life. Half a dozen farm estates formed a hexagon around it, but these belonged to ancient men who displayed themselves as inert, grey-thatched lumps in the backs of limousines. . . . " (p. 186).

12. See Sidney Finkelstein, "Alienation as a Literary Style: F. Scott Fitzgerald and T. S. Eliot" in his *Existentialism and Alienation in American Literature* (New York: International Publishers, 1965), p. 172. Speaking of Fitzgerald's kind of alienation, Finkelstein says there are many passages in *The Great Gatsby* where "we see the people vividly, but cannot feel them as people, with an inner life. . . . In depicting the estrangement of the people from one another, Fitzgerald expresses also his own detachment from them."

13. This "terrifying place" apparently is the Waldorf, but it could be any place. Certainly the most terrifying place is inside Beatrice's head, where the sun never penetrates.

14. One of Clara's distinctive traits is that she can "cast her lights and shadows around the rooms that held her," illuminating and highlighting like a candle the most commonplace of people (p. 139). Monsignor Darcy, too, had a facility for making "religion a thing of lights and shadows, making all light and shadow aspects of God. People felt safe when he was near" (p. 266).

15. This scene is much more convincing than the similar moonlit scene between Amory Blaine and Eleanor Savage in *This Side of Paradise*, but it is even less probable.

16. West, *The Making of "This Side of Paradise,"* p. 47. West notes that the recycling of old scenes from "The Romantic Egotist" may be responsible for the awkward and unbelievable juxtaposition of the traumatic death of Dick Humbird and his joyous infatuation as he dances with Isabelle the next night.

17. See Robert F. Sklar, *F. Scott Fitzgerald: The Last Laocoön* (New York: Oxford University Press, 1967), p. 48. Sklar sees more to the devil scene than I do and perhaps writes about it more graphically than Fitzgerald did:

> The images of decay and fire, death and hell—the calcium pallor of the street where the showgirls live, temptation like a warm wind, the divan 'alive like heat waves over asphalt, like wriggling worms'—build up to the climactic moment when Amory sees the face of Dick Humbird. . . . Humbird had been condemned to Hell; and seeing Humbird's face contorted with evil saves Amory from a similar end.

Certainly that is what Humbird's evil face should have done. I would contend, though, that the symbols do not function at this point and that Sklar describes what should have been rather than what actually was.

18. *Letters,* p. 304.

19. Ibid.

20. Sklar, *The Last Laocoön,* p. 135. Sklar points out that an early title for this novel was "Education of a Personage."

21. Oddly, two obscure images do function well in *The Beautiful and Damned*— ladder imagery and food and eating imagery. See John Ditsky, "F. Scott Fitzgerald and Jacob's Ladder," *Journal of Narrative Technique,* 7 (Fall 1977), 226–28. Ditsky examines ladder imagery in *The Beautiful and Damned* and *The Great Gatsby*. See also George J. Searles, "The Symbolic Function of Food and Eating in F. Scott Fitzgerald's *The Beautiful and Damned,*" *Ball State University Forum,* 22 (Summer 1981), 14–19.

22. The lovers obviously hope, but the reader, more sophisticated, reads the signs.

23. André Le Vot, *F. Scott Fitzgerald: A Biography,* tr. William Byron (Garden City: Doubleday, 1983), pp. 98–99.

Chapter 2

1. Le Vot, *F. Scott Fitzgerald: A Biography,* p. 152.

2. William Baer and Steven McLean Folks, "Language and Character in *The Great Gatsby,*" *The Language of Poetry,* 6 (1975), 18–25.

3. Bruce Bawer, "'I Could Still Hear the Music': Jay Gatsby and the Musical Metaphor," *Notes on Modern American Literature,* 5 (Fall 1981), Item 25.

4. Lawrence Jay Dessner, "Photography and *The Great Gatsby,*" *Essays in Literature,* 6 (Spring 1979), 79–89.

5. F. H. Langman, "Style and Shape in *The Great Gatsby*" in *Critical Essays on F. Scott Fitzgerald's The Great Gatsby,* ed. Scott Donaldson (Boston: G. K. Hall & Co., 1984), p. 43. "The whole novel is strung together by repeated phrases, by motifs, ideas that appear and modulate and return." See also Jackson Bryer, "Style as Meaning," ibid., p. 24.

6. "The Romance of Money" from *Three Novels of F. Scott Fitzgerald,* ed. Malcolm Cowley (New York: Charles Scribner's Sons, 1953). See also Vincent Kohler, "Somewhere West of Laramie, On the Road to West Egg: Automobiles, Fillies, and the West in *The Great Gatsby,*" *Journal of Popular Culture,* 7 (Summer 1973), 152–58.

7. Daniel J. Schneider, "Color Symbolism in *The Great Gatsby,*" *University Review,* 31 (Autumn 1964), 18.

8. F. Scott Fitzgerald, *The Great Gatsby* (1925; rpt. New York: Charles Scribner's Sons, 1960), p. 27. All quotations are from this edition. Page numbers hereafter cited in parentheses.

9. Howard S. Babb, "*The Great Gatsby* and the Grotesque," *Criticism,* 5 (Fall 1963), 339. Babb points out as examples of the grotesque the description of McKee's picture and the "gossip columns which lie side by side with a book concerning religion—all of these contrasts hooting at the vulgarity of Mrs. Wilson."

10. Matthew J. Bruccoli, "A Note on Jordan Baker," *Fitzgerald/Hemingway Annual* (1970), 232–33. "The name Jordan Baker is contradictory. The Jordan was a sporty car with a romantic image. . . . The Baker was an electric car, a lady's car—in fact an old lady's car. . . . This contradiction is appropriate to her character: although she initially seems to share Nick's conservative standards, he is compelled to reject her because of her carelessness." See also Laurence E. MacPhee, "*The Great Gatsby*'s 'Romance of Motoring': Nick Carraway and Jordan Baker," *Modern Fiction Studies,* 18 (Summer 1972), 208. MacPhee suggests that Fitzgerald derived Jordan Baker's name "from two of the best-known trade names in motoring, the Jordan "Playboy" and Baker "Fastex" velvet, a luxury upholstery fabric for automobiles." See also Roderick S. Speer, "*The Great Gatsby*'s 'Romance of Motoring' and 'The Cruise of the Rolling Junk,'" *Modern Fiction Studies,* 20 (Winter 1974–75), 540–43. Agreeing with MacPhee's thesis that Fitzgerald was both aware of and influenced by romantic automobile advertising when he wrote *The Great Gatsby,* Speer points out that Fitzgerald contributed a serialized article called "The Cruise of the Rolling Junk" to *Motor Magazine.* This article, according to Speer, evinces Fitzgerald's "constant sense of the disappointment always lurking at the fringes of idealism and enthusiasm." This theme "bears directly on that endangered romanticism . . . which lies at the heart of *Gatsby.* . . . " (pp. 540–41). Indeed, much of the point of the automobile imagery is that the car, envisioned by the characters as a romantic means of escape, leads in reality down a one-way road toward death.

11. Henry Dan Piper, "The Untrimmed Christmas Tree" in *Fitzgerald's "The Great Gatsby,"* ed. Henry Dan Piper (New York: Charles Scribner's Sons, 1970), p. 98. In an earlier version,

Gatsby's car was an even more blatant symbol of death than it is here: ''In one draft, when Gatsby proudly shows Nick his oversized yellow sports car ('the death car,' as the New York newspapers will later call it after Myrtle's death), Nick is automatically reminded of a hearse.''

12. Kenneth S. Knodt, ''The Gathering Darkness: A Study of the Effects of Technology in *The Great Gatsby,''* *Fitzgerald/Hemingway Annual* (1976), 130–38.

13. Notice that during the face-to-face confrontation where Gatsby shows Daisy proof of his absolute devotion, the telephone rings, breaks the spell. (This business call offers just one of the many hints of Gatsby's sinister activities.)

14. See E.C. Bufkin, ''A Pattern of Parallel and Double: The Function of Myrtle in *The Great Gatsby,''* *Modern Fiction Studies,* 15 (Winter 1969–70), 517–24. Bufkin observes that ''a minor character may be a major character's double by reenacting the major character's traumatic experience. Gatsby and Myrtle, sharing many features, are . . . doubles in this sense. . . . '' (p. 518). Myrtle's affair with Tom parallels and comments morally on Gatsby's affair with Daisy (p. 520). And the physical violence Tom inflicts on Myrtle at the New York apartment foreshadows the psychic violence he will inflict on Gatsby during the confrontation scene in New York (pp. 521–22).

15. See Marius Bewley, ''Scott Fitzgerald and the Collapse of the American Dream'' in his *The Eccentric Design* (New York: Columbia University Press, 1959), p. 269. ''In *The Great Gatsby,* the tawdry romance with Daisy . . . is the means Fitzgerald uses to show Gatsby the intolerable cheapness of his dream and illusion.'' Bewley obviously thinks Gatsby finally understands, that he gains tragic knowledge. Nick would lead the reader to the same conclusion. Fitzgerald does not say.

16. A.E. Elmore, ''Color and Cosmos in *The Great Gatsby,''* *Sewanee Review,* 78 (Summer 1970), 427.

17. Lehan, *F. Scott Fitzgerald and the Craft of Fiction,* p. 120.

18. Dale B.J. Randall, ''The 'Seer' and 'Seen' Theme in *Gatsby* and Some of Their Parallels in Eliot and Wright,'' *Twentieth Century Literature,* 10 (July 1964), 52.

19. Sadao Nishimura, ''Symbols and Images in *The Great Gatsby,''* *Kyushu American Literature,* 24 (July 1983), 92–95.

20. Schneider, ''Color Symbolism in *The Great Gatsby,''* 14. Silver symbolizes ''both the dream and the reality, since as the color of the romantic stars and moon . . . it is clearly associated with the romantic hope and promise that govern Gatsby's life, and as the color of money it is obviously a symbol of corrupt idealism.''

21. David R. Weimar, ''Lost City: F. Scott Fitzgerald'' in his *The City as Metaphor* (New York: Random House, 1966), p. 95. Fitzgerald's attraction for cinema shows up in his prose, in the visual pictures he paints and lights.

22. Kenneth Eble, *F. Scott Fitzgerald* (New York: Twayne, 1963), p. 90. ''With the beginning of Chapter Seven, the novel gains momentum and the mood changes. The lights in Gatsby's house fail to go on. Heat and sweat become the dominant images.''

23. Bufkin, ''A Pattern of Parallel and Double,'' 517–24.

24. See ''Third Act and Epilogue,'' *The New Yorker,* 30 (June 1945), 54. See also Lehan, *Fitzgerald and the Craft of Fiction,* p. 110.

Nick as ironic narrator is constantly tugged at—attracted and repelled by the same experience. The only character in the novel who puts experience to the scrutiny of an active conscience, Nick can say at one and the same time that "there was something gorgeous about" Gatsby and that Gatsby "represented everything for which I have an unaffected scorn."

25. For an interesting view of depravity in the novel see Keath Fraser, "Another Reading of *The Great Gatsby,*" *English Studies in Canada,* 5 (Autumn 1979), 330–43.

26. See John M. Howell, "The *Waste Land* Tradition in the American Novel." (Ph.D. Diss., Department of English, Tulane University, 1963), pp. 9–31: Robert J. Emmitt, "Love, Death, and Resurrection in '*The Great Gatsby*" in *Aeolian Harps: Essays in Literature in Honor of Maurice Browning Cramer,* eds. Donna G. Fricke and Douglas D. Fricke (Bowling Green: Bowling Green Univesity Press, 1976); James E. Miller, Jr., "Fitzgerald's *Gatsby:* The World as Ash Heap" in *The Twenties: Fiction, Poetry, Drama,* ed. Warren French (Deland, Fla.: Everet/Edwards, 1975); Letha Audhuy, "'*The Waste Land*': Myth and Symbol in *The Great Gatsby,*'" *Etudes Anglaises,* 33 (1980), 41–54; and Christine M. Bird and Thomas L. McHaney, "*The Great Gatsby* and *The Golden Bough,*" *Arizona Quarterly,* 34 (Summer 1978), 125–31.

27. Daniel J. Schneider, "Color Symbolism in *The Great Gatsby,*" 14. White, the traditional color of purity, is used ironically in the cases of Daisy and Jordan. "Daisy is the white flower—with the golden center," and brass buttons both grace and tarnish her dress. Off-whites, brass and variants of yellow, symbolize money, greed, corruption.

28. Joan S. Korenman, "A View from the (Queensboro) Bridge," *Fitzgerald/Hemingway Annual* (1975), 93–96.

29. Dalton H. Gross, "The Death of Rosy Rosenthal: A Note on Fitzgerald's Use of Background in *The Great Gatsby,*" *Notes and Queries,* 23 (January-December 1976), 22–23.

30. See Douglas Taylor, "*The Great Gatsby:* Style and Myth," *The Modern American Novel: Essays in Criticism,* ed. Max Westbrook (New York: Random House, 1966), p. 66:

> The most eloquent irony of the novel is generated by the subtle interplay between, on the one hand, the elegance and charm of Daisy's world as opposed to the cunningness of its inner corruption and, on the other hand, the gaudy elaborateness of Gatsby's efforts to emulate its surface as contrasted with the uncontaminated fineness of his heart.

31. See David L. Minter, "Dream, Design, and Interpretation in *The Great Gatsby,*" from *Twentieth-Century Interpretations of The Great Gatsby,* ed. Ernest Lockridge (Englewood Cliffs, N.J.: Prentice-Hall, 1968), p. 83:

> The whole of Gatsby's story, including both his dream and his absurd plan for realizing it—his plan for procuring a fortune, a mansion, and a bride—is redeemed from corruption and waste, from failure and absurdity only through Nick Carraway's effort imaginatively to interpret it and render it.

32. Taylor, "Style and Myth," p. 63.

33. See Robert Ornstein, "Scott Fitzgerald's Fable of East and West" from *Twentieth-Century Interpretations,* ed. Ernest Lockridge (Englewood Cliffs, N.J.: Prentice-Hall, 1968) p. 58:

> It may seem ironic that Gatsby's dream of self-improvement is realized through partnership with Meyer Wolfsheim, but Wolfsheim is merely the post-war successor to Dan Cody and to the ruthlessness and greed that once exploited a virgin west. . . . The racketeer, Fitzgerald suggests, is the last great folk hero, the Paul Bunyan of an age in which romantic wonder surrounds underworld "gonnection" instead of raw courage and physical strength.

34. For a discussion of alienation in Fitzgerald, see Sidney Finkelstein, "Alienation as a Literary Style: F. Scott Fitzgerald and T.S. Eliot" in his *Existentialism and Alienation in American Literature* (New York: International Publishers, 1965), pp. 165–83.

35. Jeffrey Steinbrink, "'Boats Against the Current': Mortality and the Myth of Renewal in *The Great Gatsby*," *Twentieth Century Literature*, 26 (Summer 1980), 157–70. "Repeatedly," Steinbrink notes, "Fitzgerald allows us (and perhaps himself as well) to entertain the hope that it *is* possible to make a 'fresh start'—to undo the calamaties of the past or to relive its quintessential moments" (p. 159). Yet in the end Fitzgerald makes us "realize and accept the unlikelihood of regeneration or renewal in an entropic universe" (p. 159).

36. Lionel Trilling, *The Liberal Imagination* (Garden City, New York: Anchor Books, 1953), p. 239.

37. Daniel J. Schneider, "Color Symbolism in *The Great Gatsby*," 14. White is the major color associated with the Buchanans and their estate. "White traditionally symbolizes purity, and there is no doubt that Fitzgerald wants to underscore the ironic disparity between the ostensible purity of Daisy and Jordan and their actual corruption."

38. Gatsby is ill at ease with the whole business. Witness his half-lies, the party for Daisy at Nick's. His very formality is wooden, plainly a mask to hide the living human being beneath the aloof exterior.

39. Richard C. Carpenter, "Fitzgerald's *The Great Gatsby*," *Explicator*, 19 (June 1961), Item 63. Carpenter points out the "incongruous serenity" of Gatsby dead, floating peacefully in his pool. He also notes the contrast between Myrtle's death and the restfulness of Gatsby's. He contrasts the mattress carrying Gatsby with the funeral barge of the archetypal hero, the young man from the provinces. Civilization has sunk this low; Gatsby, his hopes, his dreams, the optimism of a nation are headed, with autumn debris, toward the drain.

40. F. Scott Fitzgerald, *The Crack-Up*, ed. Edmund Wilson (New York: New Directions Paperback, 1957), p. 69.

41. The theme is not substantially different from the one so tediously uttered in *The Beautiful and Damned*.

42. *The Crack-Up*, p. 70.

43. Charles Weir, Jr., "An Invite with Gilded Edges," in *F. Scott Fitzgerald: The Man and His Work*, ed. Alfred Kazin (New York: Collier Books, 1962), p. 143.

44. Leo Marx, *The Machine in the Garden* (New York: Oxford University Press, 1964), p. 358.

45. Ibid., p. 356.

Chapter 3

1. Matthew J. Bruccoli, *The Composition of "Tender Is the Night": A Study of the Manuscripts* (Pittsburgh: University of Pittsburgh Press, 1963), p. 17.

2. Ibid., p. 29.

3. Ibid., p. 35.

4. F. Scott Fitzgerald, *Tender Is the Night* (1934; rpt. New York: Charles Scribner's Sons, 1960), p. 96. All quotations are from this edition. Page numbers hereafter cited in parentheses. I am using this chronological structure partially on the authority of a letter Fitzgerald wrote to Perkins:

> But I am especially concerned about *Tender*—that book is not dead. The depth of its appeal exists—I meet people constantly who gave the same exclusive attachment to it as others

had to *Gatsby* and *Paradise*, people who identified themselves with Dick Diver. Its great fault is that the *true* beginning—the young psychiatrist in Switzerland—is tucked away in the middle of the book. If pages 151–212 were taken from their present place and put at the start, the improvement in appeal would be enormous. In fact the mistake was noted and suggested by a dozen reviewers. (*Letters*, p. 308).

Malcolm Cowley used that letter to justify publishing this chronological edition and that is my rationale for using it. See, however, Lucy M. Buntain, "A Note on the Editions of *Tender Is the Night*," *Studies in American Fiction, 1* (Autumn 1973), 208–13, and Brian Higgins and Hershel Parker, "Sober Second Thoughts: The 'Author's Final Version' of Fitzgerald's *Tender Is the Night*," *Proof*, 4 (1975), 111–34.

5. Wayne C. Booth, *The Rhetoric of Fiction* (Chicago: University of Chicago Press, 1961), pp. 193–94:

> The world surrounding Dick, in its empty modernity, is used both to heighten our sense of his unique value and to increase our sense of his vulnerability. Dick is, in fact, caught between two worlds: the world of his aspirations—romantic, a bit "Victorian" (p. 236), as he said, believing in "good instincts," honor, courtesy, and courage (p. 221)—and the postwar world of Baby Warren—valueless, drifting, incapable of understanding the achievement that Dick cares for, willing, in fact, to buy Dick as a husband for Nicole in the hope of using him to cure her.

6. See G.C. Millard, "F. Scott Fitzgerald: *The Great Gatsby, Tender Is the Night, The Last Tycoon*" in *Tender Is the Night: Essays in Criticism,* ed. Marvin LaHood (Bloomington: Indiana University Press, 1969), p. 39. Millard sees as a major thread in the novel the "theme of money sapping initiative out of the characters."

7. Edwin Fussell, "Fitzgerald's Brave New World" in *The Great Gatsby: A Study*, ed. Frederick J. Hoffman (New York: Charles Scribner's Sons, 1962), p. 228. Fussell notes the profusion of childhood images surrounding Rosemary.

8. See Piper, *A Critical Portrait,* p. 215:

> Externally, Dick appears to Rosemary to be in perfect control of himself and the society he dominates. But what if he begins to doubt the absolute value of the career to which he has dedicated his talents? Not only is charm amoral, but its exercise requires the suspension of moral judgement. What is charm, after all, but the giving away of yourself in little pieces until finally there is nothing left of the individual you once were . . .? Once [Dick's] immaculate purpose is blunted, he is no longer able to function in his chosen social role.

9. Bruccoli, *The Composition of "Tender Is the Night,"* p. 138. See also William E. Doherty, "*Tender Is the Night* and the 'Ode to a Nightingale'" in *Essays and Criticism,* p. 195. Doherty suggests that shots force Diver back to reality at the three climaxes of the novel. These climaxes come when "Dick falls in love with Nicole, when Abe leaves on the train from Paris, and when Tommy becomes Nicole's lover."

10. Morris, *The Territory Ahead,* p. 163. "It was neither fatigue nor the aimless wandering, but the paralysis of will that grew out of the knowledge that the past was dead, and that the present had no future" that destroyed Diver.

11. See Robert Stanton, "'Daddy's Girl'": Symbol and Theme in *Tender Is the Night*," *Modern Fiction Studies,* 4 (Summer 1958), 140. Having suggested that Warren's relationship with Nicole

establishes the pattern for all older men with younger women, Stanton points out multiple references to Rosemary's immaturity and to Dick's paternal interest in her. He continues, saying

> in embracing Rosemary . . . , Dick Diver is a symbol of America and Europe turning from a disciplined and dedicated life to a life of self-indulgence, dissipation, and moral anarchy—a symbol of the parent generation infatuated with its own offspring. Dick's collapse, appropriately, occurs in 1929.

12. F. Scott Fitzgerald, "The Rich Boy," *Babylon Revisited and Other Stories* (New York: Charles Scribner's Sons, 1960), p. 152. Like Anson Hunter, Baby Warren is one of the very rich who are "different from you and me."

13. This is exquisite comic understatement. This summary, repeating nothing, adding no new details, points out that the affair is so unimportant that it *can* be summarized. Some might complain that the scene is prudishly timid, not comic. Although Fitzgerald often proved himself capable of prudery, that would seem a strange conclusion at this point.

14. John Grube, "*Tender Is the Night:* Keats and Scott Fitzgerald" in *Tender Is the Night: Essays and Criticism,* p. 180.

15. Thomas Deegan, "Dick Diver's Childishness in *Tender Is the Night,*" *Fitzgerald/Hemingway Annual,*" (1979), 129-33. Under stress "Dick wishes to withdraw from the bright light of human contact into the tender night of illusions."

16. Doherty, "*Tender Is the Night* and 'Ode to a Nightingale,'" p. 198.

17. Suzanne West, "Nicole's Gardens," *Fitzgerald/Hemingway Annual* (1978), 85-95.

18. *Letters,* p. 81. Fitzgerald wrote these lines to Scotty: "I think the pull of an afflicted person upon a normal one is at all times downward, depressing and eventually somewhat paralyzing, and it should be left to those who have chosen such duties as a life work."

19. Robert Roulston, "Dick Diver's Plunge into the Roman Void: The Setting of *Tender Is the Night,*" *South Atlantic Quarterly,* 77 (Winter 1978), 85-97. Rome typifies the decay of Western civilization. It is here that Dick and society become the most debased.

20. Robert A. Ferguson, "The Grotesque in the Novels of F. Scott Fitzgerald," *South Atlantic Quarterly,* 78 (Autumn 1979), 460-77. The grotesque, the incongruent, the threat of violence and occurrences of actual violence run through the fiction of Fitzgerald like threads "through fabric."

21. Lehan, *F. Scott Fitzgerald and the Craft of Fiction,* p. 135.

22. Ibid.

23. Bruccoli, *The Composition of Tender Is the Night,* p. 96. The name Campion—originally Brugerol—is a "pun on the slang term for homosexual behavior, camping."

24. In one sense Dick's father left Dick in a predicament similar to that of one of his patients, "an American girl of fifteen who had been brought up on the basis that childhood was intended to be all fun." She has just hacked off her hair with nail scissors:

> There was nothing much to be done for her—a family history of neurosis and nothing stable in her past to build on. The father, normal and conscientious himself, had tried to protect a nervous brood from life's troubles and had succeeded merely in preventing them from developing powers of adjustment to life's inevitable surprises. (p. 202)

25. Stanton, "'Daddy's Girl': Symbol and Theme in *Tender Is the Night,*" 136.

26. Ibid., 137.

27. Ibid.

28. Ibid., 138.

29. Ibid., 140.

30. Ibid.

31. Perosa, *The Art of F. Scott Fitzgerald,* p. 127.

32. John Lucas, "In Praise of Scott Fitzgerald," *Critical Quarterly,* 5 (Summer 1963), 136:

> In this novel an individual's identity is recognized through and defined by his function: it is Dick's function to be a doctor, this is his identity, his nature; Abe North's function is to be a musician, it is *his* identity, *his* nature: when their functions are usurped their identities are shattered, and they break down.

33. *The Crack-Up,* p. 70.

34. Piper, *A Critical Portrait,* pp. 205–28.

Chapter 4

1. See Barry E. Gross, "Scott Fitzgerald's *The Last Tycoon:* The Great American Novel?," *Arizona Quarterly,* 26 (Autumn 1970), 198:

> Gatsby and Diver are also artists and men of action. But Gatsby creates and acts in a world of his own and Diver in a limited world not worthy of his devotion; Stahr, however, reaches millions of people, creates and acts in a world potentially significant, potentially valuable.

2. Like Gatsby and Dick Diver, Monroe Stahr lives in a world he himself created. Stahr is the best artist of the three; to a certain extent both Gatsby's adolescent heaven and Diver's controlled, cultured, absolutely safe utopian refuge are borrowed from other sources. While Stahr's world may be even less real than the other two, it at least is a unique work of art. Although perhaps sterile—an accusation leveled frequently at art for art's sake—it is entirely original. And its man-god creator stands firmly in control for a long time. Gatsby, Diver, and the best artist, Stahr, build and control their own worlds. In each case these worlds offer an escape, a fortress against reality. Fitzgerald admires each of these creators while perhaps not admiring their creations.

3. *The Crack-Up,* p. 72. Fitzgerald had thought deeply about this problem, considered it the essence of his own crack-up: "After about an hour of solitary pillow-hugging, I began to realize that for two years my life had been a drawing on resources that I did not possess, that I had been mortgaging myself physically and spiritually up to the hilt."

4. A cosmic joke—grim humor apparently caused not by man, but by malevolent universal forces—frequently appears in the guise of good fortune. The classic example of the cosmic joke, as I am using the term, occurs in *The Mayor of Casterbridge* when Michael Henchard, buffetted and beaten by evil fortune, chooses to drown himself, to put a quiet, lonely period to a stormy, futile life. Yet he is foiled by an image of himself in the water, the dummy used earlier in the skimmity ride. Henchard reads the presence of the dummy as a sign from the gods—a sign that he rests under the special protection of Providence. This is similar to the scene in *King Lear* where the blind Gloucester is told by his son, Edgar, that he stands on the edge of a cliff. The land lies level, and Gloucester, trying to leap off the cliff, merely falls on his face. Both Henchard and Gloucester are spared but to suffer more, as if they cannot kill themselves

because an evil Providence were not finished with them. Such is Stahr's fortune in love. Love smiles on him, awakens dead feelings, so he might suffer more before death. The joke is that Providence neither knows nor cares what happens to Stahr.

Conclusion

1. Susan Henchard in *The Mayor of Casterbridge* opens the letter too soon, thus hastening Henchard's downfall; Tess in *Tess of the D'Urbervilles* accidentally slips the letter to Angel Clare under the rug; calamity ensues in *The Return of the Native* when a series of accidents keeps Eustacia Vye from getting her husband's letter of reconciliation until too late.

2. A.H. Steinberg, "Hardness, Light, and Psychiatry in *Tender Is the Night*," *Literature and Psychology*, 3 (February 1963), 6.

3. Lehan, *F. Scott Fitzgerald and the Craft of Fiction*, p. 74.

4. Doherty, "*Tender Is the Night* and the 'Ode to a Nightingale,'" 198.

5. Ibid.

6. Morris, *The Territory Ahead*, p. 167.

7. Guy Owen, "Imagery and Meaning in *The Great Gatsby*," in *Essays in Modern American Literature*, ed. Richard E. Langford (Deland, Fla.: Stetson University Press, 1963), p. 49.

8. See Fitzgerald's letters to his daughter, Scottie.

9. See *The Crack-Up*. Fitzgerald could describe the twenties in these glowingly romantic terms: "It all seems rosy and romantic to us who were young then, because we will never feel quite so intensely about our surroundings any more" (p. 20). Yet he can also say,

> By this time contemporaries of mine had begun to disappear into the dark maw of violence. A classmate killed his wife and himself on Long Island, another tumbled "accidentally" from a skyscraper in Philadelphia, another purposely from a skyscraper in New York. One was killed in a speak-easy in New York and crawled home to the Princeton Club to die; still another had his skull crushed by a maniac's ax in an insane asylum where he was confined. These are not catastrophes that I went out of my way to look for—these were my friends; moreover, these things happened not during the depression but during the boom (p. 20).

The moralist could also say, "but I was pretty sure living wasn't the reckless, careless business these people thought—this generation just younger than me."

10. Marius Brewley, "Scott Fitzgerald and the Collapse of the American Dream" in his *The Eccentric Design* (New York: Columbia University Press, 1959), p. 282.

11. See Cowley, "Third Act and Epilogue," 54. "Fitzgerald was among the wildest of romantics, but he was also among the few Americans who tried . . . to make romance real by showing its causes and consequences."

12. Brewley, "Scott Fitzgerald and the Collapse of the American Dream," p. 287.

13. Lehan, *F. Scott Fitzgerald and The Craft of Fiction*, p. 5.

14. John Berryman, "F. Scott Fitzgerald," *Kenyon Review*, 8 (Winter 1946), 107. Fitzgerald's "finest work is saturated with the desperate or ecstatic nostalgia, the firm hope and even firmer despair, of the superb conclusion of *The Great Gatsby*."

15. *The Crack-Up*, pp. 28–29.

16. Samuel Beckett, *Waiting for Godot* (New York: Grove Press, 1957), p. 57.

17. *The Crack-Up*, p. 87.

18. Robert L. Gale, *The Caught Image*, (Chapel Hill: University of North Carolina Press, 1964), p. 10.

19. Mizener, *The Far Side of Paradise*, p. 152.

20. William H. Hildebrand, "*The Great Gatsby* and the 'Utter Syntheses,'" *The Serif*, 2 (March 1965), 19.

21. Charles Samuels, "The Greatness of Gatsby," *Massachusetts Review*, 7 (Autumn 1966), 784.

Selected Bibliography

Primary Sources

Fitzgerald, F. Scott. *Afternoon of an Author.* Ed. Arthur Mizener. New York: Charles Scribner's Sons, 1957.
_____. "The Rich Boy." *Babylon Revisited and Other Stories.* New York: Charles Scribner's Sons, 1960.
_____. *The Beautiful and Damned.* 1922; rpt. New York: Charles Scribner's Sons, 1950.
_____. *Correspondence of F. Scott Fitzgerald.* Eds. Matthew J. Bruccoli and Margaret M. Duggan. New York: Random House, 1980.
_____. *The Crack-Up.* Edmund Wilson. New York: New Directions Paperbook, 1956.
_____. *The Great Gatsby.* 1925; rpt. New York: Charles Scribner's Sons, 1960.
_____. *The Last Tycoon.* 1941; rpt. New York: Charles Scribner's Sons, 1969.
_____. *The Letters of F. Scott Fitzgerald.* Ed. Andrew Turnbull. New York: Charles Scribner's Sons, 1962.
_____. *Tender Is the Night.* 1934; rpt. New York: Charles Scribner's Sons, 1960.
_____. *This Side of Paradise.* 1920; rpt. New York: Charles Scribner's Sons, 1970.

Secondary Sources

Armstrong, Edward A. *Shakespeare's Imagination: A Study of the Psychology of Association and Inspiration.* London: Lindsay Drummond, 1946.
Audhuy, Letha. "'The Waste Land': Myth and Symbol in 'The Great Gatsby.'" *Etudes Anglaises,* 33 (1980), 41–54.
Babb, Howard S. "*The Great Gatsby* and the Grotesque." *Criticism,* 5 (Fall 1963), 336–48.
Baer, William, and Steven McLean Folks. "Language and Character in *The Great Gatsby.*" *The Language of Poetry,* 6, (1975), 18–25.
Bawer, Bruce. "'I Could Still Hear the Music': Jay Gatsby and the Musical Metaphor." *Notes on Modern American Literature,* 5 (Fall 1981), Item 25.
Beckett, Samuel. *Waiting for Godot.* New York: Grove Press, 1957.
Bettina, Sister M., SSND. "The Artifact in Imagery: Fitzgerald's *The Great Gatsby.*" *Twentieth-Century Literature,* 9 (October 1963), 140–42.
Bewley, Marius. "Scott Fitzgerald and the Collapse of the American Dream." *The Eccentric Design.* New York: Columbia University Press, 1959.
Bird, Christine M., and Thomas L. McHaney. "*The Great Gatsby* and *The Golden Bough.*" *Arizona Quarterly,* 34 (1978), 125–31.
Booth, Wayne C. *The Rhetoric of Fiction.* Chicago: University of Chicago Press, 1961.
Bruccoli, Matthew J. "A Note on Jordan Baker." *Fitzgerald/Hemingway Annual* (1970), pp. 232–33.
_____. *The Composition of "Tender Is the Night": A Study of Manuscripts.* Pittsburgh: University of Pittsburgh Press, 1963.

_____. *Scott and Ernest: The Authority of Failure and the Authority of Success.* New York: Random House, 1978.

_____. *Some Sort of Epic Grandeur: The Life of F. Scott Fitzgerald.* New York: Harcourt Brace Jovanovich, 1981.

_____. *Supplement to F. Scott Fitzgerald: A Descriptive Bibliography.* Pittsburgh: University of Pittsburgh Press, 1980.

_____, ed. *"The Great Gatsby": A Facsimile of the Manuscript.* Washington: NCR Microcard Editions, 1973.

_____. *"The Last of the Novelists": F. Scott Fitzgerald and "The Last Tycoon."* Carbondale: Southern Illinois University Press, 1977.

Bryer, Jackson R., ed. *F. Scott Fitzgerald: The Critical Reception.* New York: Burt Franklin & Co., Inc., 1978.

_____. "Style as Meaning in *The Great Gatsby:* Notes Toward a New Approach." *Critical Essays on F. Scott Fitzgerald's "The Great Gatsby."* Ed. Scott Donaldson. Boston: G. K. Hall & Co., 1984, pp. 117–29.

_____. *The Critical Reputation of F. Scott Fitzgerald: A Bibliographical Study. Supplement One through 1981.* Hamden, Conn.: Archon, 1984.

Bufkin, E. C. "A Pattern of Parallel and Double: The Function of Myrtle in *The Great Gatsby.*" *Modern Fiction Studies,* 15 (Winter 1969-70), 517-24.

Buntain, Lucy M. "A Note on the Editions of *Tender Is the Night.*" *Studies in American Fiction,* 1 (Autumn 1973), 208-13.

Burhans, Clinton S., Jr. "Structure and Theme in *This Side of Paradise.*" *Journal of English and Germanic Philology,* 68 (October 1969), 605-24.

Carpenter, Richard C. "Fitzgerald's *The Great Gatsby.*" *Explicator,* 19 (October 1969), Item 63.

Clemen, Wolfgang A. *The Development of Shakespeare's Imagery.* Cambridge: Harvard University Press, 1951.

Conrad, Joseph. *Three Short Novels.* New York: Bantam Books, 1971.

Cowley, Malcolm. "The Romance of Money." *Three Novels of F. Scott Fitzgerald.* Ed. Malcolm Cowley. New York: Charles Scribner's Sons, 1953.

_____. "Third Act and Epilogue." *The New Yorker,* 21 (June 30, 1945), 53, 54, 57, 58.

Crosland, Andrew T. *A Concordance to F. Scott Fitzgerald's "The Great Gatsby."* Detroit: Bruccoli Clark, 1975.

Deegam, Thomas. "Dick Diver's Childishness in *Tender Is the Night.*" *Fitzgerald/Hemingway Annual* (1979), 129-33.

Dessner, Lawrence J. "Photography and *The Great Gatsby.*" *Essays in Literature,* 6 (1979), 79-89.

Ditsky, John. "F. Scott Fitzgerald and Jacob's Ladder." *Journal of Narrative Technique,* 7 (Fall 1977), 226-28.

Doherty, William E. "*Tender Is the Night* and the 'Ode to a Nightingale.'" *Tender Is the Night: Essays and Criticism.* Ed. Marvin LaHood. Bloomington: Indiana University Press, 1969, 190-206.

Donaldson, Scott, ed. *Critical Essays on F. Scott Fitzgerald's "The Great Gatsby."* Boston: G. K. Hall & Co., 1984.

Doyno, Victor A. "Patterns in *The Great Gatsby.*" *Modern Fiction Studies,* 12 (Winter 1966-67), 415-26.

Eble, Kenneth E. "The Craft of Revision: *The Great Gatsby.*" *American Literature,* 36 (November 1964), 315-26.

_____. *F. Scott Fitzgerald.* Boston: Twayne, 1963; rev. ed. 1977.

Ellis-Fermor, Una. *The Frontiers of Drama.* Suffolk: Methuen & Co., Ltd., 1964.

Elmore, A. E. "Color and Cosmos in *The Great Gatsby.*" *Sewanee Review,* 78 (Summer 1970), 427-43.

Emmitt, Robert J. "Love, Death, and Resurrection in *The Great Gatsby.*" *Aeolian Harps: Essays in Literature in Honor of Maurice Browning Cramer.* Eds. Donna G. Fricke and Douglas D. Fricke. Bowling Green: Bowling Green University Press, 1976, 273-89.

Ferguson, Robert A. "The Grotesque in the Novels of F. Scott Fitzgerald." *South Atlantic Quarterly,* 78 (1979), 460–77.

Finkelstein, Sidney. "Alienation as a Literary Style." *Existentialism and Alienation in American Literature.* New York: International Publishers, 1965.

Fraser, Keath. "Another Reading of *The Great Gatsby.*" *English Studies in Canada,* 5 (Autumn 1979), 330–43.

Fussell, Edwin. "Fitzgerald's Brave New World." *"The Great Gatsby":* A Study. Ed. Frederick J. Hoffman. New York: Charles Scribner's Sons, 1962.

Gale, Robert L. *The Caught Image: Figurative Language in the Fiction of Henry James.* Chapel Hill: University of North Carolina Press, 1964.

Gallo, Rose Adrienne. *F. Scott Fitzgerald.* New York: Frederick Ungar, 1978.

Gere, Anna R. "Color in Fitzgerald's Novels." *Fitzgerald/Hemingway Annual* (1971), 333–39.

Goheen, Robert F. *The Imagery of Sophocles' "Antigone."* Princeton: Princeton University Press, 1951.

Gombrich, E. H. *Meditations on a Hobby Horse.* London: Phaidon Press Ltd., 1963.

Greenberg, Hazel. "Cluster Imagery in the Novels of Edward Lewis Wallant." Ph.D. Diss., Southern Illinois University, 1972.

Gross, Barry Edward. "The Dark Side of Twenty-Five: Fitzgerald and *The Beautiful and Damned.*" *Bucknell Review,* 16 (December 1968), 40–52.

———. "Scott Fitzgerald's *The Last Tycoon:* The Great American Novel?" *Arizona Quarterly,* 26 (Autumn 1970), 197–216.

Gross, Dalton H. "The Death of Rosy Rosenthal: A Note on Fitzgerald's Use of Background in *The Great Gatsby.*" *Notes and Queries,* 23 (January-December 1976), 22–23.

Grube, John. *"Tender Is the Night:* Keats and Scott Fitzgerald:" *"Tender Is the Night":* Essays and Criticism. Ed. Marvin LaHood. Bloomington: Indiana University Press, 1969.

Harvey, W. J. "Theme and Texture in *The Great Gatsby.*" *English Studies,* 38 (February 1957), 12–20.

Heilman, Robert B. *This Great Stage: Image and Stucture in "King Lear."* Baton Rouge: Louisiana State University Press, 1948.

Hellman, Lillian. *An Unfinished Woman: A Memoir.* Boston: Little, Brown and Co., 1969.

Higgins, Brian, and Hershel Parker. "Sober Second Thoughts: The 'Author's Final Version' of Fitzgerald's *Tender Is the Night.*" *Proof,* 4 (1975), 111–34.

Hindus, Milton. *F. Scott Fitzgerald: An Introduction and Interpretation.* New York: Holt, Rinehart & Winston, 1968.

Hoffman, Frederick J. "The Modern Novel Between Wars." *The Modern Novel in America.* Chicago: Henry Regnery, 1963.

Howell, John M. "The Waste Land Tradition in the American Novel." Ph.D. Diss., Tulane University, 1963.

Keats, John. *The Letters of John Keats.* Ed. Maurice Buxton Forman. London: Oxford University Press, 1960.

Knight, G. Wilson. *The Wheel of Fire: Interpretation of Shakespearian Tragedy with Three New Essays.* London: Methuen & Co., Ltd., 1959.

Knodt, Kenneth S. "The Gathering Darkness: A Study of the Effects of Technology in *The Great Gatsby.*" *Fitzgerald/Hemingway Annual* (1976), 130–38.

Kohler, Vincent. "Somewhere West of Laramie, On the Road to West Egg: Automobiles, Fillies, and the West in *The Great Gatsby.*" *Journal of Popular Culture,* 7 (Summer 1973), 152–58.

Korenman, Joan S. "A View from the (Queensboro) Bridge." *Fitzgerald/Hemingway Annual* (1975), 93–96.

Langer, Susanne K. *Feeling and Form.* New York: Charles Scribner's Sons, 1953.

Langman, F. H. "Style and Shape in *The Great Gatsby.*" *Critical Essays on F. Scott Fitzgerald's "The Great Gatsby."* Ed. Scott Donaldson. Boston: G. K. Hall & Co., 1984, 31–53.

Latham, Aaron. *Crazy Sundays: F. Scott Fitzgerald in Hollywood.* New York: Viking Press, 1970.

Lehan, Richard D. *F. Scott Fitzgerald and the Craft of Fiction.* Carbondale: Southern Illinois University Press, 1966.

Le Vot, André. *F. Scott Fitzgerald: A Biography.* Tr. William Byron. New York: Doubleday, 1983.

Lewis, C. Day. *The Poetic Image.* London: Johnathan Cape, 1947.

Long, Robert Emmet. *The Achieving of "The Great Gatsby": F. Scott Fitzgerald, 1920–1925.* Lewisburg: Penn.: Bucknell University Press, 1979.

Lucas, John. "In Praise of Scott Fitzgerald." *Critical Quarterly,* 5 (Summer 1963), 132–47.

MacPhee, Laurence E. "*The Great Gatsby's* 'Romance of Motoring': Nick Carraway and Jordan Baker." *Modern Fiction Studies,* 18 (Summer 1972), 207–12.

Marx, Leo. *The Machine in the Garden.* New York: Oxford University Press, 1964.

Millard, G. C. "F. Scott Fitzgerald: *The Great Gatsby, Tender Is the Night, The Last Tycoon.*" *"Tender Is the Night":* Essays in Criticism. Ed. Marvin LaHood. Bloomington: Indiana University Press, 1969, 20–47.

Miller, James E., Jr. "Fitzgerald's *Gatsby:* The World as Ash Heap." *The Twenties: Fiction, Poetry, Drama.* Ed. Warren French. Deland, Fla.: Everet/Edwards, 1975, 181–202.

———. *The Fictional Technique of Scott Fitzgerald.* New York: New York University Press, 1964.

Minter, David L. "Dream, Design, and Interpretation in *The Great Gatsby.*" *Twentieth Century Interpretations of "The Great Gatsby."* Ed. Ernest Lockridge. Englewood Cliffs, N.J.: Prentice-Hall, 1968, 82–89.

Mizener, Arthur. *The Far Side of Paradise.* Boston: Houghton Mifflin, 1965.

Monk, Donald. "Fitzgerald: The Tissue of Style." *Journal of American Studies,* 17 (April 1983), 77–94.

Morris, Wright. *The Territory Ahead: Critical Interpretations in American Literature.* Forge Village, Mass.: Atheneum, 1961.

Moyer, Kermit W. "*The Great Gatsby:* Fitzgerald's Meditation on American History." *Critical Essays on F. Scott Fitzgerald's "The Great Gatsby."* Ed. Scott Donaldson. Boston: G. K. Hall & Co., 1984, pp. 215–28.

Nishimura, Sadao. "Symbols and Images in *The Great Gatsby.*" *Kyushu American Literature,* 24 (July 1983), 92–95.

Ornstein, Robert. "Scott Fitzgerald's Fable of East and West." *Twentieth Century Interpretations of "The Great Gatsby."* Ed. Ernest Lockridge. Englewood Cliffs, N.J.: Prentice-Hall, 1968, 54–60.

Perosa, Sergio. *The Art of F. Scott Fitzgerald.* Trans. Charles Matz and Perosa. Ann Arbor: University of Michigan Press, 1965.

Pinkster, Sanford. "Seeing *The Great Gatsby* Eye to Eye." *College Literature,* 3 (Winter 1976), 69–71.

Piper, Henry Dan. *Fitzgerald's "The Great Gatsby": The Novel, the Critics, the Background.* New York: Charles Scribner's Sons, 1970.

———. *F. Scott Fitzgerald: A Critical Portrait.* New York: Holt, Rinehart and Winston, 1965.

Podis, Leonard A. "The Unreality of Reality: Metaphor in *The Great Gatsby.*" *Style,* 11 (Winter 1977), 56–72.

Prior, Moody E. *The Language of Tragedy.* New York: Columbia University Press, 1947.

Randall, Dale B. J. "The 'Seer' and 'Seen' Theme in *Gatsby* and Some of Their Parallels in Eliot and Wright." *Twentieth-Century Literature,* 10 (July 1964), 51–63.

Ring, Frances Kroll. "Footnotes on Fitzgerald." *Esquire,* 52 (December 1959), 150.

Roulston, Robert. "Dick Diver's Plunge into the Roman Void: The Setting of *Tender Is the Night.*" *South Atlantic Quarterly,* 77 (Winter 1978), 85–97.

Samuels, Charles. "The Greatness of Gatsby." *Massachusetts Review,* 7 (Autumn 1966), 783–94.

Sanders, Barbara Gerber. "Structural Imagery in *The Great Gatsby:* Metaphor and Matrix." *Linguistics in America,* 1 (1975), 53–75.

Saposnik, Irving S. "The Passion and the Life: Technology as Pattern in *The Great Gatsby.*" *Fitzgerald/Hemingway Annual* (1979), 181–88.

Schneider, Daniel J. "Color Symbolism in *The Great Gatsby.*" *University Review,* 31 (Autumn 1964), 12–17.

Searles, George J. "The Symbolic Function of Food and Eating in F. Scott Fitzgerald's *The Beautiful and Damned.*" *Ball State University Forum,* 22 (Summer 1981), 14–19.

Sklar, Robert F. *F. Scott Fitzgerald: The Last Laocoön.* New York: Oxford University Press, 1967.

Speer, Roderick S. "*The Great Gatsby*'s 'Romance of Motoring' and 'The Cruise of the Rolling Junk,'" *Modern Fiction Studies,* 20 (Winter 1974–75), 540–43.

Spurgeon, Caroline F. E. *Leading Motives in the Imagery of Shakespeare's Tragedies.* New York: Haskell House, 1970.

———. *Shakespeare's Imagery and What It Tells Us.* Cambridge: Cambridge University Press, 1971.

Stanton, Robert. "'Daddy's Girl': Symbol and Theme in *Tender Is the Night.*" *Modern Fiction Studies,* 4 (Summer 1958), 136–42.

Steinberg, A. H. "Hardness, Light, and Psychiatry in *Tender Is the Night.*" *Literature and Psychology,* 3 (February 1963), 3–8.

Steinbrink, Jeffrey. "'Boats Against the Current': Mortality and the Myth of Renewal in *The Great Gatsby.*" *Twentieth-Century Literature,* 26 (Summer 1980), 157–70.

Taylor, Douglas. "*The Great Gatsby:* Style and Myth." *The Modern American Novel: Essays in Criticism.* Ed. Max Westbrook. New York: Random House, 1966.

Thrall, William Flint, and Addison Hibbard. *A Handbook to Literature.* Revised and enlarged by C. Hugh Holman. New York: The Odyssey Press, 1960.

Trilling, Lionel. *The Liberal Imagination.* Garden City, N.Y.: Anchor Books, 1953.

Turnbull, Andrew. *Scott Fitzgerald.* New York: Charles Scribner's Sons, 1962.

Weimar, David R. "Lost City: F. Scott Fitzgerald." *The City as Metaphor.* New York: Random House, 1966.

Weir, Charles, Jr. "An Invite with Gilded Edges." *F. Scott Fitzgerald: The Man and His Work.* Ed. Alfred Kazin. New York: Collier Books, 1962, 133–46.

West, James L., III. *The Making of "This Side of Paradise."* Philadelphia: University of Pennsylvania Press, 1983.

West, Suzanne. "Nicole's Gardens." *Fitzgerald/Hemingway Annual* (1978), 85–95.

Whitley, John S. *F. Scott Fitzgerald: "The Great Gatsby."* Southampton, England: The Camelot Press, 1976.

Index

Artificial light imagery: in *The Beautiful and the Damned*, 32–34, 70–71; in *The Great Gatsby*, 66, 67–70, 85; in *The Last Tycoon*, 123, 133; in *Tender Is the Night*, 97, 116; in *This Side of Paradise*, 25–27

Automobile, as characterization device: in *The Great Gatsby*, 58–59; in *The Last Tycoon*, 120; in *This Side of Paradise*, 16–18

Automobile imagery: in *The Beautiful and the Damned*, 20–21, 54; in *The Great Gatsby*, 12, 58–60, 84, 148n.10; in *The Last Tycoon*, 133; in *Tender Is the Night*, 89–92; in *This Side of Paradise*, 15–17, 18, 54

The Beautiful and the Damned (Fitzgerald): artificial light imagery in, 32–34, 70–71; automobile imagery in, 20–21, 54; communication imagery in, 22–25, 55; corruption theme in, 38; darkness imagery in, 124; dirt-disease-decay imagery in, 38–43, 51, 52, 55; image patterns in, 1, 139, 141–42; irony in, 38, 43–44, 50, 51–52, 53; light-dark imagery in, 29–34, 55, 136–37; moon imagery in, 29–30; natural light imagery in, 30–32; obstruction of light in, 34; snow imagery in, 49, 50, 52–53; telephone imagery in, 22–24; time imagery in, 40–43; cf. *This Side of Paradise*, 38; transportation imagery in, 18–21; water imagery in, 48–53, 55

Cleanliness imagery, 38–39. *See also* Dirt-Disease-Decay imagery

Color imagery, 58, 149n.20, 150n.27

Communication imagery: in *The Beautiful and the Damned*, 22–25, 55; and Fitzgerald's world view, 136; in *The Great Gatsby*, 60–64, 67–68, 84; ironic use of, 60–61; in *The Last Tycoon*, 120–23, 133; in *This Side of Paradise*, 21–22, 54, 64; in *Tender Is the Night*, 92–96, 115

Conrad, Joseph, 6, 140–41

Corruption theme: in *The Beautiful and the Damned*, 38; in *The Great Gatsby*, 76–78, 85–86; in *The Last Tycoon*, 128, 133–34; in *Tender Is the Night*, 103, 104, 106–9, 116

The Crack-Up (Fitzgerald), 83

Darkness imagery: in *The Beautiful and the Damned*, 31–32, 124; in *The Great Gatsby*, 65–66; in *The Last Tycoon*, 124; in *Tender Is the Night*, 97–99, 116; in *This Side of Paradise*, 26, 124

Death imagery: in *The Great Gatsby*, 59–60, 79, 80, 81–82, 83, 86; in *The Last Tycoon*, 10, 129–30; in *Tender Is the Night*, 102; in *This Side of Paradise*, 48

Dirt-Disease-Decay imagery: in *The Beautiful and the Damned*, 34, 36, 37–43, 51, 52, 55; and Fitzgerald's world view, 137; in *The Great Gatsby*, 73–78; in *The Last Tycoon*, 126–29, 133–34; in *Tender Is the Night*, 102–9, 116–17; in *This Side of Paradise*, 34–38, 54

Dramatic irony, 1

Eliot, T. S., 140

Fitzgerald, F. Scott, development of as an artist, 139–41

Flying imagery, 9–10, 119–20, 129, 133

The Great Gatsby (Fitzgerald): and the

American dream, 73; artificial light imagery in, 66, 67–70, 85; automobile as characterization device in, 58–59; automobile imagery in, 12, 58–60, 84, 148n.10; color imagery in, 58, 149n.20, 150n.27; communication imagery in, 60–64, 67–68, 84; corruption imagery in, 76–78, 85–86; darkness imagery in, 65–66; death imagery in, 59–60, 79, 80, 81–82, 83–84, 86–87; dirt-disease-decay imagery in, 73–78; Icarian imagery in, 68–69; image patterns in, 60, 78, 141–42; irony in, 1, 60–61, 68, 78–81, 82, 84–85, 119, 150n.30; letter imagery in, 62; light-dark imagery in, 64–73, 84, 137; moon imagery in, 66–67, 85; music imagery in, 57; natural light imagery in, 70–73, 85; newspaper imagery in, 62; photography imagery in, 57; Promethean imagery in, 68–69; season imagery in, 57; sport imagery in, 57; telephone imagery in, 61, 63–64; cf. *Tender Is the Night*, 8; time imagery in, 86–87; transportation imagery in, 58–60; water imagery in, 60, 78–84, 86, 129; the world of, 2

Icarian imagery: in *The Great Gatsby*, 68; in *The Last Tycoon*, 10–11, 119, 129, 133
Image, defined, 5–6
Image patterns: author's conscious use of, 6, 7; in *The Beautiful and the Damned*, 21, 139; development of in Fitzgerald's work, 5, 139–42; in *The Great Gatsby*, 60, 78; importance of, 6, 11–12; and irony, 119; in *The Last Tycoon*, 119; as manifestations of author's subconscious, 6; as networks within a novel, 7; in *This Side of Paradise*, 18, 21, 139; and verse tragedy, 5
Imagery: interdependency of in an artistic work, 7; and irony, 2, 3, 84–85, 130, 132, 134, 137–38; negative treatment of positive images, 1, 3, 44; thematic function of in the work of Fitzgerald, 5, 7, 24, 34, 38, 57, 141–42; theories of function of, 4–5
Ironic tension, 11
Irony: in *The Beautiful and the Damned*, 38, 43–44; development of in the work of Fitzgerald, 2; in *The Great Gatsby*, 60–61, 68, 78–81, 82, 84–85, 119, 150n.30; and imagery, 2, 3, 119; in *The Last Tycoon*,

119–20, 134; in *Tender Is the Night*, 114, 119; in *This Side of Paradise*, 44–45

James, Henry, 8, 140
Joyce, James, 140

Keats, John, 140
Knight, G. Wilson, 2

The Last Tycoon (Fitzgerald): and the American dream, 73; artificial light imagery in, 123, 133; automobile as characterization device in, 120; automobile imagery in, 133; communication imagery in, 120–23, 133; corruption imagery in, 128, 133–34; darkness imagery in, 124; death imagery in, 10, 129–30; dirt-disease-decay imagery in, 126–29, 133–34; dramatic irony in, 1; flying imagery in, 9–10, 119, 129, 133; Icarian imagery in, 10–11, 119, 129, 133; image patterns in, 119, 141–42; irony in, 119; letter imagery in, 133; light-dark imagery in, 123–26, 133; moon imagery in, 124–26, 133; natural light imagery in, 123, 133; newspaper imagery in, 122, 133; perversion imagery in, 126–27; Promethean imagery in, 129; telephone imagery in, 121–23, 133; train imagery in, 120, 133; transportation imagery in, 9–11, 119–20, 133; violent natural phenomena in, 129–30, 134, 154n.4; water imagery in, 129–33, 134
Letter imagery: in *The Great Gatsby*, 62; in *The Last Tycoon*, 133
Light-Dark imagery: in *The Beautiful and the Damned*, 29–34, 55, 136–37; and Fitzgerald's world view, 136–37; in *The Great Gatsby*, 64–73, 84–85, 137; in *The Last Tycoon*, 123–26, 133; in *Tender Is the Night*, 96–101, 115–16, 137; in *This Side of Paradise*, 25–29, 54

Madness, 91, 104–5
Moon imagery: in *The Beautiful and the Damned*, 29–30; in *The Great Gatsby*, 66–67, 85; in *The Last Tycoon*, 124–26, 133; in *Tender Is the Night*, 96–97; in *This Side of Paradise*, 27–29
Music imagery, 57

Natural light imagery: in *The Beautiful and the Damned*, 31; in *The Great Gatsby*, 70–73, 85; in *The Last Tycoon*, 123, 133; in *Tender Is the Night*, 96, 99–101, 116; in *This Side of Paradise*, 25–26
Newspaper imagery: in *The Great Gatsby*, 62; in *The Last Tycoon*, 122, 133; in *This Side of Paradise*, 21–22
Night imagery, 25

Perversion imagery: in *The Last Tycoon*, 126–27; in *Tender Is the Night*, 106–7, 108, 116
Photography imagery, 57
Portrait of the Artist as a Young Man (Joyce), 45–46
Promethean imagery: in *The Great Gatsby*, 68–69; in *The Last Tycoon*, 129
Protagonists, 3, 37–38

"The Romantic Egotist" (Fitzgerald), 15

Season imagery: Fitzgerald's ironic use of, 138; in *The Great Gatsby*, 57; in *Tender Is the Night*, 112–13, 115
Snow imagery: in *The Beautiful and the Damned*, 49, 50, 52–53; in *This Side of Paradise*, 44
Sport imagery, 57

Telephone imagery: in *The Beautiful and the Damned*, 22–24; in *The Great Gatsby*, 61, 63–64; in *The Last Tycoon*, 121–23, 133; in *Tender Is the Night*, 92–96, 115; in *This Side of Paradise*, 21–22
Tender Is the Night (Fitzgerald): and the American dream, 73; artificial light imagery in, 97, 116; automobile imagery in, 89–92; communication imagery in, 92–96, 115; corruption imagery in, 103, 104, 107–9, 116; darkness imagery in, 97–99, 116; death imagery in, 102; dirt-disease-decay imagery in, 102–9, 116–17; cf. *The Great Gatsby*, 8; image patterns in, 141–42; irony in, 1, 114, 119; light-dark imagery in, 96–101, 115–16, 136–37; madness in, 91, 104–5; moon imagery in, 96–97; natural light imagery in, 96, 99–101, 116; perversion theme in, 106–7, 108, 116; season imagery in, 112–13, 115; telephone imagery in, 93, 94–96, 115; time

imagery in, 103–4, 115; train imagery in, 18, 91; transportation imagery in, 89–92, 115; water imagery in, 109–15, 116–17, 129–30
Theme as function of imagery, 5, 7, 57–58, 141–42; in *The Beautiful and the Damned*, 24, 34, 37–38
This Side of Paradise (Fitzgerald): artificial light imagery in, 26–27; automobile imagery in, 15–17, 18, 53–54; cf. *The Beautiful and the Damned*, 38; characterization in, 16–18, 46; communication imagery in, 21–22, 54, 64; darkness imagery in, 26, 124; death imagery in, 48; dirt-disease-decay imagery in, 34–38, 54; image patterns in, 1, 18, 139; irony in, 44; light-dark imagery in, 25–29, 54; love theme in, 46–48; moon imagery in, 27–29; natural light imagery in, 25–26; newspaper imagery in, 21–22; night imagery in, 25; and *Portrait of the Artist as a Young Man*, 45–46; snow imagery in, 44; structural movement in, 15; telephone imagery in, 21; train imagery in, 18; transportation imagery in, 15, 21; water imagery in, 43–48, 54
Time imagery: in *The Beautiful and the Damned*, 40–43; in *The Great Gatsby*, 86–87; in *Tender Is the Night*, 103–4, 115
Train imagery: in *The Last Tycoon*, 119–20, 133; in *Tender Is the Night*, 18, 91; in *This Side of Paradise*, 18
Transportation imagery: in *The Beautiful and the Damned*, 18–21; and Fitzgerald's world view, 135–36; in *The Great Gatsby*, 58–60; in *The Last Tycoon*, 119–20, 133; in *Tender Is the Night*, 89–92, 115; in *This Side of Paradise*, 15, 21

Verse tragedy and image patterns, 5

Water imagery: in *The Beautiful and the Damned*, 48–53, 55; as death symbol, 60, 117, 129–130, 131, 132; and Fitzgerald's world view, 136–39; in *The Great Gatsby*, 60, 78–84, 86, 129; ironic treatment of, 44–45, 50, 51–52, 53, 130, 132, 134; in *The Last Tycoon*, 129–33, 134; as life symbol, 129, 130, 131–32; in *Tender Is the Night*, 109–15, 116–17, 129; in *This Side of Paradise*, 43–48, 54
World of the novel, definition of, 2

.